KIDS WHO CARRY OUR PAIN

KIDS WHO CARRY OUR PAIN

Dr. Robert Hemfelt
Dr. Paul Warren

THOMAS NELSON PUBLISHERS

NASHVILLE

❖ *A Janet Thoma Book* ❖

Published in Nashville, Tennessee, by Thomas Nelson,
Inc., and distributed in Canada by Lawson
Falle, Ltd., Cambridge, Ontario.

Scripture quotations are from the NEW KING JAMES
VERSION of the Bible. Copyright © 1979, 1980, 1982,
Thomas Nelson, Inc., Publishers.

Library of Congress Cataloging-in-Publication Data

Warren, Paul, 1949–
    Kids who carry our pain / Paul Warren, Robert
    Hemfelt.
        p.   cm.
    ISBN 0-8407-7476-1
    1. Co-dependence (Psychology)—Popular works.
2. Co-dependence (Psychology)—Prevention.   3. Parent
and child.   I. Hemfelt,
Robert.   II. Title.
RC569.5.C63W33   1990
616.89'156—dc20   90–39583
                                                                    CIP

Printed in the United States of America
1 2 3 4 5 6 7 — 95 94 93 92 91 90

ACKNOWLEDGMENTS

The authors wish to express loving appreciation to the friends, family members, and co-laborers who have made the publication of *Kids Who Carry Our Pain* possible. We especially want to thank Sandy Dengler for sharing her creativity and composition skills to create a complete, coherent product out of the authors' scribbles and thoughts. We are grateful, too, for the inspiration and support of Dr. Frank Minirth and Dr. Paul Meier, for their pioneering work in Christian psychiatry. Many thanks also to Janet Thoma for her faithfulness and editorial wisdom throughout the production of this book; Jennifer Farrar and the staff at Thomas Nelson Publishers for their editorial assistance; our gracious wives, Susan Hemfelt and Vicky Warren, for their ever-present love, support, and cooperation; and finally, our children—Katy, Kristin, and Robert Gray Hemfelt; and Matthew Warren—who are daily reminders of the joys of childhood and parenthood.

CONTENTS

PART 1

IDENTIFYING THE PROBLEM

CHAPTER 1

Li'l Troublemaker

Regina Kolbin was such a pretty child, seven years old, with a blue-eyed, rosy-cheeked innocence. Her father, James, claimed she was blonde. Today, sitting close to her mother in Dr. Paul Warren's office, she wore an unbecoming brown wig. Her eyebrows were singed off.

"She crunched these newspapers up in the back of the doghouse," James explained, "and then set fire to them. The doctors say we're extremely lucky the fire didn't scar her face."

"It would appear so." Dr. Warren looked from person to person. The Kolbin family looked so utterly healthy and typical, except for the little problem of their daughter being a firebug. Melanie Kolbin, the mother, appeared a bit overweight, but she wore clothes well. She sat quietly, with an air of placid acceptance. James, slight of build, countered her air of tranquility with a rushing exuberance. He seemed always to be moving, even when sitting still. Seven-year-old Regina's eyes darted about, missing nothing. Her four-year-old brother, Victor, crowded tightly against his mother's right side, gripping her light sweater firmly with both hands. The two year old, Gerald, perched in Melanie's lap.

"I didn't know this," James continued, "but setting a fire like that is illegal, even when a little kid does it. The fire marshal insisted we come in for counseling. He says she has problems." He shrugged. "Frankly, I figured she's just a mischievous kid, but the fire marshal insisted, so here we are."

"She's what you call an active child?"

"Not hyperactive, go-go-go. She just gets into things."

Melanie smiled wanly. "She sometimes does destructive things, like cut holes in the curtains or break things, but she never hurts anyone. I mean, she didn't try to burn the dog up. She'd never hurt anything or anyone."

"Does Victor ever get into trouble like that?"

"Oh my, no!" Melanie smiled down at her son. "Victor stays right in the house near me. If I'm out back hanging up clothes or something, he's there. He doesn't do anything destructive or, uh, what you'd call a prank. Of course, he's only four."

"And Gerald?" Dr. Warren asked.

"He stays close too."

"James, I understand you manage a garment factory."

From his seat in the easy chair across from Dr. Warren, James nodded. "My father, Joseph, owns it. It'll probably be mine someday. He started it when he came over from Bulgaria after the war. Family business. Not big. Ten on the payroll."

"You said 'probably.' There's some question?"

James grinned. "Grandpa changes his will a lot."

Throughout the interview, Gerald sat on his mother's lap, or stood on it. Victor stayed plastered tightly against her side. Regina began squirming, knocking her wig askew.

Dr. Warren closed the interview: "I strongly recommend the two of you seek counseling to explore your marriage."

"But we're here because of Regina," Melanie protested.

"That's true. I really believe, however, that marriage counseling will help her more than anything I can do."

"Does that mean you won't take her as a client?"

"No. I'll be glad to take her. But as I work with her, I'm asking the two of you to work on your marriage."

"I can't see why." Melanie frowned. The frown disappeared. "But then, you're the expert."

Within a few days, the Kolbin parents entered into counsel with Dr. Robert Hemfelt. Dr. Hemfelt soon learned that Melanie constantly fought severe depression. And James, usually even-tempered, occasionally flew into unpredictable rages.

Typical family, the Kolbins? Not in some ways. Few of us have daughters who set fire to doghouses. But the problems and disappointments threading through their family from generation to generation are very common. Throughout this book, for obvious reasons, we have changed names and situations in order to mask the identities of case examples such as the Kolbins. They are all real people, however, with parenting problems that might look very much like problems you yourself face.

Katzenjammer Kids

The Sunday comics of a generation ago featured the "Katzenjammer Kids," two bratty little guys with German accents. Every week they pulled nasty pranks and in the last panel always found themselves across someone's knee getting paddled. The spankings had no effect, obviously, or there would not have been a new prank, and thus a strip, the next Sunday. Do you have your own Katzenjammer kid?

Understand, though, we're talking about degree here. Every parent of a normal, active child has amassed a trove of war stories, for every child misbehaves, either deliberately or innocently. For example, three-year-old Taylor's parents kept their house and yard immaculate. One day when Daddy had washed the car, vacuumed the interior, and then went inside, Joseph quite naturally completed the job by washing what Daddy had missed. He ran the gushing hose up the tailpipe. When Daddy next turned on the ignition, all he got was a gentle squish.

The story ends happily; it was an indestructible old Volkswagen, so Daddy simply jacked up the front end and drained the engine block. Taylor drives it to school now and yearns for the day he can afford a zippy pick-up instead of this jalopy. Poetic justice.

Such episodes of creative destruction now and then, as well as contests of will, scenes in the cereal aisle of the grocery store, or a certain reluctance to take part in bedtime, sharing, and other family rituals, represent healthy steps to growing up.

The path to adulthood never lies smooth and easy. But when your child misbehaves constantly and excessively; when your child seems to be channeling normal aggression and frustration in dangerous or perverse ways . . . you worry.

In a nutshell, when you can't live with your child, yet you can't live without him or her, you face trouble. Even more so will trouble plague you in the future.

The Problem with the Problem

Even if you don't already have some familiarity with the nature of codependency, you will soon be able to pick out certain unhealthy patterns of behavior the Kolbins display, as well as unhealthy family roles. You will then be able to discern patterns and roles in your own life.

What is a codependent family?

In a codependent family, the members are either walking around with an emptiness inside them or are carrying the pain of this emptiness for someone else in the family.

Let's say that another way. In a codependent family one or both of the parents are walking around with an emptiness inside them and the kids are carrying the pain of that emptiness.

Regina Kolbin's overt destructive behavior indicated that she was bearing troubles—in this case someone else's. Victor would not leave his mother's side. Gerald clung even more closely. All children cling at times—we're talking about excess.

Melanie would admit instantly to an emptiness, diagnosed as chronic depression. But James—empty? "Hardly!" he laughed. "I'm too busy to feel empty. My yard is the best in the neighborhood. I even found out how to get rid of moles and gophers."

And herein lies a paradox of codependency: Emptiness may be disguised as a form of obsessive-compulsive behavior. In the case of James Kolbin, the disguises were workaholism, perfectionism regarding his yard and garden, and rageaholism. Emptiness is expressed also in the person who tries to run away from the emptiness.

We often call children like Regina, who are carrying the pain for someone else in the family, "codependent kids." In counseling we work to help these children recover from two basic symptoms of codependency in kids: a lack of definite boundaries and attention hunger.

A Lack of Definite Boundaries

The child may be too involved in another family member for his or her own good—boundaries are too loose, identities too close. Perhaps the child is engaged in constant conflict with another member, arguing, rebelling, resisting—boundaries are too rigid. Possibly the child is completely detached from any close relationships at all—boundaries are not even on this planet.

The boundaries between a codependent kid and his parents may be skewed because the parents are addictive or compulsive, codependent in their own right. His or her parents may be too restrictive or too permissive—bounds of discipline are too tight or too loose. Victor and Gerald Kolbin, for example, possessed almost no boundaries of their own: They were attached like mustard plasters to Mommy, physically and emotionally, with no clear individual identities.

In any case, children with dysfunctional family boundaries stand at immense risk of developing severe emotional problems, compulsions, and addictions as they grow up.

Attention Hunger

Every child needs love; we all know that. And most parents love their children dearly. But children also need attention—time spent with them, interaction with them, persons (especially adults) to simply talk to them and play with them. Children derive their identity from many sources, but most of the sources are other persons in their life. The underlying need for attention, then, is a need for identity—identity derived from relationships with others.

Melanie and James both loved their little Regina dearly. Love was not an issue. Attention was. Melanie's depressions and James's compulsive outdoor activity robbed Regina and her brothers of attention. Codependent traits, as both depression and compulsive behavior are, were moving down to the new generation.

15

The tragic fact about codependency is this: Unless dealt with, the problem transmits itself from generation to generation, causing misery from father to son to son, down the line.

The Multigenerational Chess Game

Remember the old Star Trek series and Mr. Spock playing chess against the Enterprise computer? In one first-season episode, in a plot too long to relate here, Spock saved the day by playing chess against the computer. Spock's chess board was a three-dimensional wonder of futuristic design—three clear, squared-off playing surfaces stacked one above the other. The pieces could move horizontally on any of the three surfaces, or vertically, from one level to another.

That exactly illustrates the family of the child who carries our pain. Codependency, as well as everything else in the family, is multigenerational. Let the top tier represent the grandparents. The middle playing surface is the parents, the children the bottom one. Any piece, any element of family life, in the upper two surfaces can be played to the child's surface. Anything on the child's surface can move about. The child, in short, is vulnerable.

The Kolbin family's problems had started forty-five years ago in Bulgaria when the small village of Svolen was destroyed by the German army. That day Josip Kolbinski, at the age of twenty-one a veteran of World War II, had gently led his sobbing bride to the train station to emigrate to the New World, for Bulgaria had been devastated.

Once in America Josip Kolbinski had discouraged any reference to the past. Bulgaria lay forever behind them. "Look ahead! Not back!" he had urged his wife. He Americanized the family's names. His wife Hdrecka was now Harriet. Kolbinski he shortened to Kolbin. And he himself became Joseph. He waged a lifelong war with the English language: *Why not say "smashed potatoes"? That's what they were.* His three girls, born in the United States, adapted comfortably to the New World and its ways. "Study!" Joseph had cried. "You have a golden opportunity. Do not waste it!"

Joseph himself quickly rose to foreman of a garment factory and, by working sixteen-hour days, eventually built his own company, the Kolbin Shirtwaist Factory. When shirtwaist dresses went out of style, Joseph nearly went broke. He might have given up except for the birth of his son James. To James would pass the reins of power in the Kolbin Shirtwaist Factory.

The family crown rested uneasy upon young James Kolbin. Born in 1954, James had missed military service in Vietnam. He was the only Kolbin male never honed in battle. At age twenty-four he still had neither married nor finished college. "Eh, James," moaned his mother, "I will be four years in my grave before I see my first grandchild from you." James had finally married in 1983 and five months later became the father of Regina. His mother had moaned some more, for different reasons.

Nothing else James did seemed to measure up in Joseph's eyes either. The cantankerous old Bulgarian was still trying to tell his son what to do, even though James now ran the shirtwaist factory.

Unfinished Business

Joseph's rage over the Germans destroying his village. His obsessive-compulsive workaholism to prove himself in the New World. James's rebellion against his father. His rage over his dad's continual interference, both at work and in the affairs of James's own family.

All this anger and pain and rebellion was being carried by Regina Kolbin, without her even realizing it. All this anger, bottled up in this small child, was bound to explode, and it did—into flames the day Regina set fire to that doghouse. To his horror, James was seeing his kids start to fall into the codependent line.

James talked to Dr. Hemfelt at Dr. Warren's request. "I've read all those books on codependency. The Hero role where the child tries to be the perfect one. The Mascot, always making people laugh and drawing their minds off the pain. The Scapegoat—I see Scapegoat in so much of what Regina does. And now here's Victor, picking up the Mascot thing."

"Those are good observations. Many people see these roles in others but can't make them out in their own families."

"I had such a rotten childhood. Now all I can think of is, good heavens, what am I doing to my kids?"

That's a statement Dr. Hemfelt hears quite frequently. Over and over in his practice, he sees this vignette: a codependent adult in counsel—perhaps, but not always, the adult child of an addicted parent—sees the damage done in his or her own childhood. Then comes the inevitable revelation: If these factors caused so much pain and problems in my life, what are my problems doing to my own children? The parents eat grapes and the children's teeth are set on edge. It's so, so true in the Kolbin's case.

Dr. Hemfelt assures these clients, "You can break the codependent chain, if you understand how your own relationship with your parents (and their relationship with their parents) influences your relationship with your kids. During the next sessions I will help you answer three questions: What happened in my childhood? Is the same thing happening to my children? And what opportunities do I have to change this behavior?"

"Change," Dr. Hemfelt says, "can only begin when parents understand the healthy boundaries that are necessary to the parent/child relationship. When a parent says, 'Because you are my child, you must think and act exactly the way I do,' the child's boundaries are violated. Or if a parent ignores or neglects the child, the child's boundaries are also violated. The child will then look for a substitute, counterfeit relationship by acting out or by depending on addictive substances or unhealthy relationships with his or her peers."

Is Your Family Codependent?

How do you know if codependency issues are snagging the fabric of your own family? Let's explore some questions to guide you in that assessment. As you consider each question, do not amend your response with "Yes, but . . ." or "No, but . . ." At this time you're looking only for broad patterns. We want to get you thinking objectively about what is really happening in your family. You need feel no pressure to excuse or defend an answer, and certainly never to pass judgment. Yes or no? Is it happening or isn't it? Keep it simple.

Assessing the Family Relationships

• *Do you find yourself doubting frequently that you really know your children?* Have they become strangers, inscrutable? An allied question: *Has your child become secretive, withdrawn?*

• *Do you and your spouse promise over and over to spend more time—better time—with each other and the kids? Are such promises frequently broken?*

• *Does the level of busyness* remain *high in your household?* Every home sees spates of frantic activity, such as Christmas time. The grade-schooler is preparing for a school program, the high-schooler plays basketball, Dad gets extra seasonal work, and Mom's on both the school bazaar committee and the church food bank committee. Mayhem. But it's temporary mayhem that will pass with the season. Rather, does the frenetic pace seem never to slow down in your home? Is it pre-Christmas every day?

• *Are there more than one or two evening meals per week at which the entire family is not gathered?* Dad may leave town on business for a few days. Your junior-high child has late cheerleading practice for the two weeks preceding the first game of the season. Your grade-schooler stays overnight at her friend's. Such glitches are normal. We're looking here for the constant glitch, the every-night-it's-something-else situation. This also includes episodes when one of the members leaves the dining area or is ejected for misbehavior.

• *Does anyone in your family (parent or child) regularly use alcohol or mood-altering drugs?* It makes no difference whether the drugs are prescribed or not. For purposes of this assessment, prescribed drugs weigh just as heavily as illicit ones, including cocaine and marijuana. We're assessing absence/presence, not legality. This is not a court, nor are you standing in judgment. We're looking for other things altogether. Now consider the question again. Yes or no?

• *Do one or more members of your household seem constantly to be at war with another member(s)?* Sibling rivalry is normal. This question refers to friction that goes beyond that. Also include constant altercations between a parent or parents and a particular child or children.

• *Does your child seem to avoid one parent and attach excessively to the other?* Similarly, while looking at attachments: *Has one parent come to depend heavily on a child?* While you're examining this facet of family relationships, consider whether a child is taking over jobs the parents are normally expected to do: prepare meals regularly, handle household tasks beyond the usual chores of childhood, act as confidante to either mother or father, supply frequent ego strokes to the parents.

• *Does work, homemaking, or community service consume your time and interest?* Examine your spouse's time priorities and ask the same question: *Is your spouse inordinately caught up in one or more of these activities?* We hate to use the word obsession, because hardly anybody will admit to an obsession. Rather, try these on for size: "terribly fond of," "intensely interested in," "just has to get such-and-so done," "spends every waking moment either doing it or thinking about it," or "driven to excel in."

• *Has the sexual dimension of your marriage diminished significantly?* An elderly Eskimo gentleman, dependent upon his children in his dotage, was quoted as saying he'd be glad when his son got older; then the man would think less about sex and more about finding food. We all expect ardor to abate as we age, and in some ways it does. But the affection, the attraction, the basic bond should, if anything, improve with age. "We aren't kids anymore" is no license to abandon the many facets of your marital union. A related question that must be answered: *Have you or your spouse taken your sexual expression outside the marriage?*

• *Is your marriage in trouble? Does either of you entertain the prospect of separation or divorce?*

Assessing the Children

But wait. It's the children we're talking about, the kids we want to help. Now ask yourself some questions that pertain strictly to the children themselves.

• *Has one or more of your children been diagnosed as hyperactive?* We're looking for a formal diagnosis by a professional, and not just your opinion as you cope with the kid at the end of a long, tiring day.

• *Has one or more of your children begun to display acting out patterns with babysitters, school officials, or other authorities?*

"Acting out" deserves some definition. Psychologists use the term to mean "acting out the unexpressed residual anger within the family," in the sense of acting out a fantasy or releasing pent-up emotions. But you have no idea at this point whether any covert anger exists in your family. So let's express "acting out" with these common, everyday phrases: "mouthing off" to the teacher, principal, bus driver, etc.; "acting up" disruptively in class or church, where the child knows quiet is expected; "bullying" or acting aggressively; using excessively foul language; "rebelling" by adopting music, clothes, hair styles, lifestyles known to irritate or shock adults, especially adults in authority. That's acting out.

• *Does your child struggle to be perfect?* At the other end of the spectrum from acting out, does your child feel a need to score a hundred on every test, earn those extra credit points, make the perfect impression, fulfill every task expected? Last summer a twelve year old named John, who had yearned for years for a big, tough mountain bike, finally saved enough to buy one. Not long after he bought one he lost his traction on a steep hillside trail and wrapped the bike around a granite rock. He and the bike came through the accident fine, with only a few scuffs and scrapes. John's parents finally realized the boy suffered serious problems and brought him in for counseling when they found his seven-hundred-dollar wheels in the trash. He threw the bike away because he couldn't stand the imperfection—those scuffs and scrapes on his new mountain bike.

• *Does your child suffer persistent or chronic physical health problems not explained by medical work-ups?* Headaches, fatigue, frequent recurring illness? We are talking about a form of hypochondria that surfaces in small children. Physical complaints or problems that have no real medical explanation.

• *Does your child seem to love to disrupt the family?* Regina Kolbin provided the classic example. Everywhere she went turmoil followed. Her behavior was mostly whining, argumentative, nitpicking, dissatisfied, bored, manipulative.

• *Does the child get along better and more easily with adults than with other children?*

• *Does one or more of your children have great difficulty separating from you?* Again, this is a matter of degree. The very young, in particular, go through a stage where any separation is agony. Normally, once a temporary separation is made, the child settles in to a relatively happy state and may even forget Momma or Daddy is gone. Note, rather, whether that stage persists, and also whether the child consistently refuses to be comforted after the separation is made. Two-year-old Gerald Kolbin screamed so hard for so long when he was separated from his mother, Melanie, that babysitters refused to sit for the Kolbins after that experience.

• *Have you been getting questions or negative feedback from persons outside your immediate family regarding the children's grades or conduct?* Sometimes it takes someone with a bit of distance to be able to see the forest instead of the trees.

Were your family to enter our counsel, we might not ask these specific questions in just this way. We would, however, generate conversation designed to raise the red flags these questions do. No one family will display all the above problems; we've illustrated here a whole spectrum of symptoms.

However, if you could honestly answer yes to more than one or two, quite probably trouble lies ahead for your family.

Codependent Families Are Not Rare

Not too long ago we were discussing codependency and our earlier book *Love Is a Choice* on "The Minirth-Meier Clinic" radio program, a daily, one-hour talk show. One listener called in with this distressing comment: "I'd always thought that our family was pretty normal. Now, as I listen to you, I realize that we are codependent—or as you sometimes call it, dysfunctional. What should I do?"

Dr. Frank Minirth, cofounder of the clinic, quickly answered this woman's question. "I know how you feel. We've forgotten to make a very important statement: All families are somewhat codependent or dysfunctional. That's natural, since none of us are perfect. All of our parents have made some mistakes and passed some of their pain on to us, and we'll pass some of that pain on to our own children."

You might not have a child like Regina, who set fire to the family's doghouse. Or a child like her brother, Gerald, who is overly attached to his mother. Yet your family is probably somewhat codependent.

Can the trouble be fixed by reading a book (or even two or three books)? Codependency is not an either/or situation like measles. With measles, either you have it or you don't. Rather, codependency presents a spectrum from very low to extreme. Is anyone free entirely? No. Neither does anyone suffer totally. Persons at the low end of the scale may exhibit interesting quirks and endearing eccentricities, or perhaps nothing extraordinary at all. Persons at the high end need help desperately if they are to become whole people with a fairly bright prospect for happiness. For the broad range of us that lie between, books will indeed provide helpful insight and useful answers.

Whether or not you already know anything about codependency, you can break its wicked, intergenerational chain by dealing with it in your own life and by freeing your children of its grip. Not all child-rearing problems, of course, are rooted in codependency issues. But a good many are, and some others can be ameliorated using the principles of healing we offer in this book.

Perhaps you are reading this book in order to better understand why your child or teenager is acting impossible so much of the time. Perhaps you're reading it, not because you fault yourself as a parent, but simply because every parent can use helpful tips and you want to improve your parenting role. Possibly you feel totally inadequate as a parent, whether your child is difficult or not, and feel a desperate need for help in shaping your child's life.

This book is meant to help persons serving as parent (either natural, step-, or surrogate parent) to a child eighteen or younger. However, we trust we will be of help also to any persons dealing with children—teachers, doctors, social workers—who must understand better what is happening in children's lives.

The Kolbins' lives, though tidy on the surface, suffered from severe undercurrents of codependency. Through counsel with Dr. Hemfelt, the parents found a measure of happiness they had previously not known was possible. We will show you how they did it, by exploring first the individuals, then the marriage.

Regina in her wig, Victor with his fears, and Gerald the mustard plaster, built solid identities; their emerging personalities promise happiness, not grief. We will explore the ways Dr. Warren works with children to help them, as he helped the Kolbins and others you will meet. You will find his methods both useful and effective in your own relationships with children.

What can you expect from this book? In this first part we will explore the nature of codependency and its causes, particularly as it pertains to a family with children. If you are a single parent, we also hope to help you. How much and in what ways do circumstances and pressures weigh? What specifically does your child need and are those needs being met?

Once you see the problems, we will walk the individual family members down the road to recovery in Part 2. Dr.

Paul Warren will show parents how to help their children answer the essential questions of growing up: Who am I inside me? Who am I in my family? Who am I in my community? And Dr. Hemfelt will help parents look at their own childhoods, their marriage, and their parental relationship with their children.

Then we will bring the family together to look at their family interactions in Part 3. We will help the parents and the children discover the excitement of an interdependent relationship, which gives each person the freedom to make decisions without fearing the loss of another person's love.

Who's Minding the Store?

When Dr. Paul Warren went into pediatrics, he realized that certain physical problems of childhood actually had their roots in behavioral and emotional problems. As a behavioral pediatrician he still deals primarily with children, but he addresses all their needs, not just physical ones. Dr. Robert Hemfelt specializes in the codependency problems faced by adults. So now let us together imagine that your family is entering into counsel with Drs. Hemfelt and Warren. All of us working in concert can improve the quality of your life markedly.

Far more importantly, we can break the chain of codependency that can rob your children of happiness and endanger the happiness of their children and grandchildren. When a child displays a significant behavior problem, that problem may be three generations old. In order to understand our children, we must understand ourselves. To understand ourselves, we must appreciate the emotional legacy of our own childhoods. The place to begin is here, while your children are still under your aegis.

The time to begin is now.

CHAPTER 2

The Many Kinds of Boundaries

Thirteen-year-old Joel "Joey" Trask was a conservative, church-going parent's ultimate nightmare. If his black Jack Daniels T-shirt, leather jacket, and worn jeans all said "punk," his hair screamed it. It tumbled down around his face and hung down his back, begging for less mousse and more cutting. Around his neck hung not one but three chains with huge links—sort of the Early Tire Chain look. He slouched in his chair, sullen, as his eyes flitted here and there examining the carpet on the floor.

Whalon and Elizabeth Trask were his conservative, church-going parents.

The Trasks sat in Dr. Paul Warren's office, Joey on one side in the easy chair, his parents on the sofa opposite. His parents appeared the perfect middle-class couple. Whalon, a paragon of physical fitness, coached church-league soccer and taught the junior boys' Sunday school class. Elizabeth Trask's short, layered hair style perfectly framed a face that could win a beauty contest. She permitted no spare pound on her graceful body. Dr. Warren learned she had organized not one but two Pioneer Clubs in nearby Plano, handled treasurer's duties for the school parent-teacher organization, and served as chairman of her church altar guild.

Whalon straightened his already-perfect tie. "Frankly, I did some research on you and the clinic, and I understand that in counseling you're supposed to pour out your faults. Is that correct?"

"That is correct. It is important to share your feelings," Dr. Warren answered as he settled back in his chair. Interviews often started out like this. "However, you may have a few misconceptions about what counseling is and is not. Faults? Let me clarify something: This isn't a judge's chamber. No one is going to be exposing fault here. We're not going to declare one person or another 'wrong.' "

Dr. Paul Warren knows that power struggles and control issues lie at the heart of most family problems. He knows, too, that those same struggles enter the counseling chamber as the family walks in the door. To be able to guide the healing of the parties on both sides of the struggles, he must remain separated but not aloof. He must not take sides. It isn't always easy because the family will use him as the rope in their bitter tug-of-war.

Dr. Warren could feel the tension, though he made no mention of it. He addressed Joey: "Why do you think we're here?"

Joey looked at the coffee table rather than the doctor. "I dunno."

"I'm sure your parents told you something about why you had to come here."

His shoulders heaved in an exaggerated shrug. "We can't get along. They don't like anything I do."

Whalon glared at his son. He spoke gruffly, impatiently, "We're a close family, doctor, the kind of family the books say we ought to be. We have family devotions every night to build up Joey spiritually. We spend time together; we do a lot together on weekends. And sports—sports build character as well as bodies. Joey refuses to participate in anything anymore—not soccer, not track. I want to see Joey back in sports."

"Must be frustrating for you, when the parenting techniques you're certain will work don't," Dr. Warren commented.

"It was the beer. The hair and his clothes bothered us. But the beer—that's why we came. Twice now we've caught him."

Dr. Warren nodded. "Do you yourself drink beer, Whalon?"

"Absolutely not! That's one reason we were shocked when

Beth found an empty can under his bed. Then last week he came home reeking of it!"

"Elizabeth, why do you want your family to enter counseling?" asked Dr. Warren.

"Like Whalon said, the beer." She looked near tears. "It's just . . . I don't know what happened to my son. He's not what he used to be. He used to make good grades—excellent grades—and he smiled all the time. He went to Sunday school, wanted to go to Sunday school. And he was so good at soccer. All-city in his league. Now he won't even go to practice."

"He's out of control." Whalon completed her thought. "Something has to be done."

Something Has to Be Done

Symptoms. Something had to be done about Joey Trask's maddening rebellion. And yet, every normal child disrupts and rebels as a natural part of growing up. Every normal child is naughty now and then (as is every normal adult, occasionally). What sets this case and others apart as abnormal codependency?

On the surface, normal expected misbehavior and codependent misbehavior look alike. Both are nerve-wracking, especially for the parents. Both can compromise a child's education, and therefore the future, if not checked or redirected. Both could place the child in danger—drug and sex experimentation and taking chances are a few of many ways. The difference lies beneath the surface.

As a part of growing up, all normal children test the limits. What can I get away with? How far can I go? Am I more trustworthy now than when I was small? By trial and experimentation, normal, healthy children find their places first in the family and then in the world. Eventually, after the tussling and testing, they emerge with a solid sense of personal identity, ready to seek happiness.

Codependent kids, however, are driven by forces outside themselves to do what they do. The most common statement

Dr. Warren hears in counsel with codependent kids is "I don't know why I do what I do." It is an honest admission. Very commonly, such children don't even *want* to do what they're doing. They think they are captains of their destinies. In reality they are pawns in an unwitting battle that may have been joined generations ago.

The Kolbins, whom we met in Chapter 1, illustrate this well. Little Regina's problems are not her own exclusively; she has no idea what drives her actions. James would like to be the perfect father, but his rages mar that perfection. James excuses the rages as inherited temperament: his father, Joseph, ranted and hollered around the house too. James pictures a lot of Bulgarian ragers doing what comes naturally. In truth, the rages are the results of the battle, a legacy to Joseph, in fact, from his father, Damyan, before him.

To understand this battle we need to examine the many kinds of boundaries that exist in our relationships with one another. At the clinic we often use a dollhouse metaphor to describe this relationship.

Your Child's Dollhouse

Such a charming dollhouse. It sits in the Minirth-Meier Clinic in a playroom which Dr. Warren uses when communicating with young children. Boys and girls alike enter the playroom wide-eyed and check out all the wonderful toys and games. Eventually most of them settle down at the dollhouse. Open and airy, with bright colors and minimal furniture, it becomes every child's house. An array of dolls approximating the child's race and personal relationships— a daddy, baby, a friend, whatever—awaits the child who would sit down and play with them.

Let us now visualize your child's house, the relationship between your child and those around him or her. This house is necessarily an imagined dollhouse, for we're going to do strange things to its walls and rooms to symbolize the family relationships.

Picture first the outer walls. They represent the invisible

boundary around your family. The family equals the inside; the rest of the world lies outside. Each child in the family has a room of his or her own, one of the upstairs rooms (if yours is a particularly large family, that's quite an upstairs!).

If yours is a two-parent family, Mom and Dad each have a room. They are, after all, individuals as well as marriage partners. There is also a master bedroom representing the marriage, for, we shall see, the marriage is an entity unto itself. This room, typically a very large room, houses the marriage bed. If you are separated, widowed, or divorced, that room will stand empty, although as a single parent you still have your own private room.

Downstairs in the living room, all the family members can join together in whatever ways your family normally interacts. You eat together in the dining room. Don't forget significant family pets, giving them whatever size room their prominence in the family suggests. For example, in addition to Mom, Dad, and three children, the Hemfelts' imagined dollhouse includes a room for a delightful little white mop of a Maltese named Timmy.

The interior walls symbolically represent the boundaries between family members, the exterior walls the boundaries between the family and the outside world. People enter and leave the family through the doors. Outsiders might come in for a visit or even a longer stay—a member of the extended family such as grandparents or an aunt or uncle, a foreign-exchange student, a foster child. Members leave as children go off to marry or as someone dies.

Let's treat the doors figuratively, the way our language does. The front door is the main entry/exit, the proper and bold way. Someone slipping out the back door is doing so on the sly. If Mom and Dad are involved in an extramarital affair, that's back-door stuff. To complete the metaphor, windows on the world let us both see out and be seen from outside while we are inside the family unit.

Set your imagined personal dollhouse firmly in mind. Got it? Good. Now we're going to use it throughout the book.

Your Child's Boundaries

Some years ago, a James Garner film titled *Support Your Local Sheriff* became something of a comic-western cult favorite. In one scene the sheriff arrested a member of the local gang of bumbling terrorists. The only hitch: The interior bars had not yet been installed in the brand new, brick jailhouse. The enterprising sheriff painted a line across the floor, splashed a bit of red paint about to indicate what happened to the last fellow who tried to cross the line, and successfully incarcerated the bad guy in an open cell. So effective was the ploy, the baddie's buddies worked six ways from Tuesday to break him out through a heavily barred window when he could have simply walked out the front door at any time.

Boundaries. The power of suggestion was boundary enough in the movie. Yellow "Do Not Cross" tapes work splendidly as physical barriers, despite the fact that they are so flimsy anyone age three or older can simply rip them aside. Boundaries come in many forms. Some we already use in common speech. We talk about putting boundaries on a relationship or on our passions and anger. "Whoa, pal! You're way out of bounds!" And, too, persons from the tiniest baby on up possess—or fail to possess—psychological boundaries, boundaries of spirit and personality.

The Perfect Boundary

Healthy boundaries, as for example interpersonal boundaries between you and me, consist of two parts: the part I erect and the part you put up. Associates of former President Richard Nixon considered it impossible to really know the man well. He had erected an impenetrable boundary around himself. Contrast such an intensely private person with the candor and boundaries of a small child, who lets it all hang out, as the saying goes; a three year old strips to the buff, walks into a living room full of guests, and announces to Mommy that she wants to take a bath. No problem.

Most of us construct boundaries somewhere between the extremes.

Partial autonomy describes the perfect interpersonal boundary between parent and child, and indeed between parent and parent as well.

Autonomy with attachment is another way to view it. Total autonomy would be "I answer to neither man nor God." Children may yearn for such independence (can you imagine the Calvin of the *Calvin and Hobbes* cartoon strip exercising complete autonomy? The world quakes at the thought!), but what they need is a limited measure of autonomy in order to forge an individual identity. Total dependence, the other extreme, is appropriate only for a newborn babe. Partial autonomy permits the child to be himself even as attachment satisfies his need to be cared about.

Such autonomy does not come easily for either parent or child. The process of growth is something like a teeter-totter. One end is dependence, the other independence. A healthy child learns how to stand approximately in the middle and balance the seesaw flat across, one foot on either side of the line. The codependent child never quite gets the balance right and ends up running from one end to the other, from clinging dependence to desperate independence, as life wildly bounces up and down. He or she will inevitably fall.

One for the Seesaw

A perfect example is Joey Trask. Dr. Warren asked Joey to leave the room for a few minutes while the doctor chatted with the parents.

The moment the door closed, Whalon exploded. "Can you believe that kid? The hair is disgusting. Somebody looks at him now, they'll think he's a street punk. And the way he won't look at you when you're talking to him! Believe me, when he was in sports he wasn't like this at all. He was a decent kid."

"When did the change really start becoming noticeable?"

Whalon looked at his wife. "A year ago?"

She nodded.

He grimaced. "About a year ago. Joe Janes, the little league coach, said, 'Don't worry about it. All kids rebel a little.' But this is too much."

"What did you do about the change prior to coming here?"

Whalon's fist hit his knee. "I put my foot down! I made devotions a nightly thing instead of a couple times a week. We did more things together as a family, sporting events, church activities, things like that. Dr. Warren, we're good parents. I'm giving Joey the things I never had. I'm giving him family."

Beth Trask added her perspective to her husband's. "Joey and I used to talk a lot, and read together," Beth offered. "In fact we used to tell stories to each other. Friends, you know? Pals, Joey and me. Now he'll argue just for the sake of argument. He says all the time that he wants his freedom, but every time we've let him do something—loosen up, you might say—he gets into trouble. We don't dare give him any freedom. He's best, actually, when he's grounded, but we can't ground him forever."

Dr. Warren nodded. "What did you do, Whalon, when he dropped out of soccer?"

"What could I do? He didn't drop out. Hank Sprague, the coach, kicked him off the team. He was always late to practice, or he wouldn't show up at all. When he mouthed off at Hank, Hank sacked him. Told him to come back when he changed his attitude and got his hair cut."

"Do you fault the coach for ejecting your son?"

"Of course not. You can't have an effective team when the players are goofing up like that. I would have done the same thing. No, it's not Hank's fault. He did what he had to. It's the kid's."

"Dr. Warren," Beth's voice sounded plaintive, ready to break, "I want Joey to be good again, like he used to be. I want my boy back."

Dr. Warren completed the hour by talking to Joey alone as his parents waited outside. "Joey, your father says he holds family devotions every evening. I assume you participate?"

"Yeah."

"Because you have to?"

"Yeah."

"What do you think of them, honestly?"

Joey shrugged and glanced at Dr. Warren. After a moment's hesitation he said, "I dunno. It's not like we're really learning the Bible or something. It's a daily lecture. Dad reads something out of the Bible, and then tells me how I'm not doing that and I should shape up."

"Every night."

"Yeah."

"Must get a little old after a while."

"Yeah." And for the first time the boy showed a spark of interest.

Dr. Warren could begin to see in Joey's whole demeanor the progression that such youngsters follow during counseling: hostility, then suspicion, curiosity, and finally enough trust to open up a little.

"Like the hair business." Joey waved a hand. "He reads this place in the Bible where a man's supposed to have short hair. But that same place says a woman's supposed to have long hair. He never comes down on Mom for having short hair and her hair's shorter than mine."

"I see what you mean. Tell me what else your parents do that frustrates you."

"Um . . . well, for my twelfth birthday, Mom had one of those parties like always, with the hats and stuff. You know."

"Oh." Dr. Warren settled back farther in his chair and laced his hands across his belt buckle. "Now, as I recall my own twelfth birthday, it was a pretty important time. I wasn't just a little kid anymore. It was special to me in some ways."

Joey thought about that a moment, no doubt weighing whether to spill his real feelings. "I dunno. I got to thinking then, and I just got sick and tired of trying to please everybody else, you know? I got a life too, you know? No matter what I do, Dad doesn't think it's enough. Practice. Run. Go out for cross-country in the fall. Then try out for basketball. That season's over, so now try out for track. And soccer all summer. Man, I could run clear to the moon and he wouldn't be satisfied. So I figured to heck with it, y'know?"

"Yes, I believe I understand how you feel. I get those feelings, too, sometimes. Does your mother encourage your participation in sports also?"

"Mom changed, too, this last year. I don't think she knows it, but she did. One minute she'd be all sugary and tell me to go along with Dad, and the next minute she'd be yelling and screaming at me, whether I did anything or not." Joey wagged his head. "And she says I'm weird."

Out of Balance

Around the age of twelve, give or take some, children start getting the urge to try their wings. For most there's a little tussling, a little friction, a little trial and error, and their boundaries readjust successfully. Life goes on. Not for Joey.

Listen to the unspoken desires in that first interview. Joey the child was Mommy's little pal and Daddy-coach's little team member. As puberty approached, those little-kid roles didn't fit anymore, but the parents were loathe to say goodbye to the child and hello to the emerging adolescent. Mom and Dad both wanted things returned to the way they'd always been, when Joey was the any-parent's-dream-kid who looked good to the outside world.

Biologically and emotionally Joey was ready for increased independence. But at that age, as does every other child, he still needed the dependence also, especially guidance through the next few years. Besides, it's hard to say goodbye to familiar childhood just when you've about got it figured out.

Joey had never learned how to keep the seesaw level between dependence and independence. He would run to one end—demanding and sometimes getting privileges of greater freedom. Frightened by the prospect of leaving the comfort of childhood, he would unconsciously run back to the other end by messing up. The parents then removed the privilege, bearing down on Joey all the harder.

Human beings are so exceedingly complex; many other dynamics were working simultaneously in the case of the Trasks, and we will explore them as we continue. The aspect to look at here is boundaries.

The Trask Dollhouse

In an imaginary, symbolic dollhouse, the rooms representing family members ideally ought to be each about the size of the person in question. Mom's room and Dad's are biggest because adults have the most responsibilities, duties, privileges, wisdom, and experience. A new baby's room is smallest, reflecting the baby's limited duties, such as burping when patted.

Notice from the conversation that in the Trasks' house, Dad's room was by far the biggest because he was the controller. Dad's boundaries burgeoned way out. It was he who decided to engage in more family activities. It was he who increased the frequency of devotions. Joey mentioned that Mom tried to cajole the boy into going along with Dad's wishes. At no time did anyone mention Mom taking any initiative. Her room was small, perhaps much smaller than it ought to be.

Developmentally, Joey was ready for a bigger room. He was at an age when it was appropriate to push the walls out a little farther—to extend his boundaries. He could not. Not only was he afraid to, his parents unconsciously did not want him to. As he struggled to grow, they were struggling just as hard to keep him in the old mold. They wanted to hang on to the little boy with his little-boy boundaries.

Lida Armstrong presented another problem. Lida, a child of alcoholics, married a handsome, smooth-talking man named Randy. Wedded bliss lasted two weeks. Then Randy came home drunk and stinking of marijuana and the war began. The unwitting victims were their two children, Pete and Sarah. Lida gave up the battle on Pete's fifth birthday. She filed for divorce.

Today she sat in Dr. Hemfelt's office listening to the dollhouse allusion. She snorted. "All right, so the marriage room in my dollhouse is empty. The kids didn't cause it. Randy did. He's using coke regularly—snorting and smoking—and he makes his living selling drugs. The state thinks his unemployment check is all he makes, so of course I don't get a cent of child support, except for child welfare payments. Certainly nothing from Randy. But, Doctor, I know he's pulling down a thousand a week at least with the methamphetamines."

"Legal proof? Evidence?"

"No. He's smart enough not to cook at home. That's another thing. He lives in this ratty little apartment with a woman he's not married to. When the kids visit every other weekend, they sleep on the living room floor. While he and that woman are sleeping in . . . ." She stopped and bit her lip. "What kind of dollhouse are my kids living in? And what kind of dollhouse is Randy providing them when they're with him?"

Not all dollhouses are pretty.

Egomass

A similar way to illustrate the family is to draw a circle. That's the family as a unit. Within that circle draw a circle representing each family member. Each individual member has a separate ego. Each is his or her own person.

A word of explanation may be needed here. "Ego" is not just an overweening absorption in oneself, the popularized negative meaning. Ego also is the sense of self. Personal identity. A state of balance between dependence and independence. Every healthy person has a solid ego. "I am me."

In that broader sense, the nuclear family shares a corporate ego, a common identity, a communal sense of balance between dependence and independence. We can thus refer to the shared family entity as a collective ego, an egomass. "We are us." Even the smallest member intuitively takes part in this shared identity from the moment of birth.

What we are doing, in essence, is illustrating boundaries. We are most comfortable if we have a little breathing space, even in a very close-knit group such as a nuclear family. Thus the circles ideally have spaces between them. Infants and toddlers are touching Mom or nearly so, but even they have clearly defined personhood.

Figure 1 shows a healthy family with normal relationships. The circles are fairly equidistant; no one's crowding

Figure 1. Healthy Family Boundaries

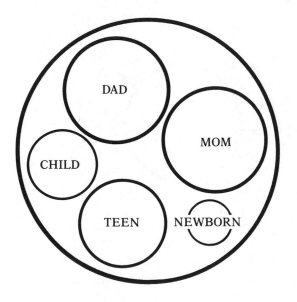

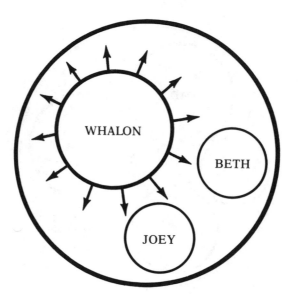

Figure 2. The Trask Family

the others. The boundaries are firm, as indicated by good solid lines; each person has a sense of self, appropriate to his or her age. Figure 2 symbolizes the Trask family. Whalon's circle is bigger because of his powerful need to control and direct. As he insists on calling all the shots, he encroaches on the others' space. At an age when Joey should be getting a little more room to maneuver, he's being crowded more tightly into a corner. His developmental schedule says, "Expand." His situation replies, "I can't!"

Mom's circle is about the same size as Joey's. She, too, is dominated, powerless. If Mom feels uncomfortable in this situation, she has so far made no indication of it.

We can get more picturesque with this circles-within-a-circle representation of the family if we wish. Let's say the father in a hypothetical family is rageaholic. He's blustering, sometimes violent, often and unpredictably flying off the handle. We might draw daggers radiating out of the much-enlarged father circle, indicating not only that Dad is crowding everyone else and pressing on their boundaries, but he's explosive about it. The other circles are shoved away toward the edges, cringing from the onslaught, trying to mollify him, trying to minimize his excesses.

If, for another example, Mom is addicted to alcohol or drugs, her circle shrinks down as she turns inward on herself. She becomes more distant from the other members, more detached, harder to reach.

The circles of Lida Armstrong (Fig. 3), the divorced mother, might look like two circles crashing into each other. Though no longer part of the family, the errant father, Randy, remains an overwhelming presence. He is applying pressure from the outside with his drug addiction and immoral behavior. The children must hop from circle to circle as per the court order allowing Randy visitation rights. How very easy it will be for Lida, herself the child of an alcoholic, to become codependently enmeshed with her children! But that is only the beginning of her concerns.

"How much damage is Randy inflicting on the children?" she asks. "And is there any way I can minimize it?" Her goal:

41

Figure 3. Lida Armstrong's Family

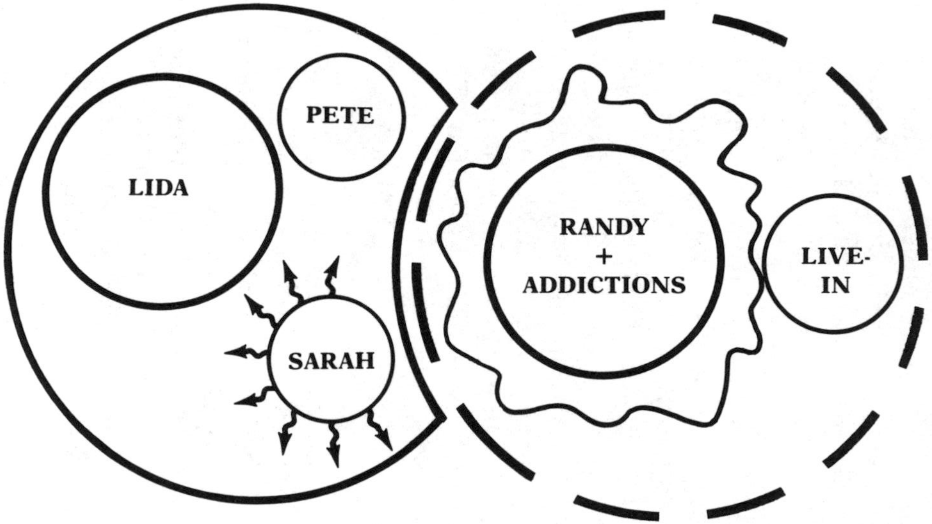

to make her family circle as firm and round as possible, and to keep a healthy distance between their circles.

Using this circles-within-a-circle motif, try drawing your family as you see it today. How does that simplistic diagram compare with your imagined dollhouse? Now draw your family of origin—that is, your own parents and siblings. Let both memory and gut-level feelings guide you. What do you see? Do the children in that diagram occupy the same sort of position your own child does in your current family diagram? If so, it's no coincidence.

But then, almost nothing in the relationships between parents and their children is coincidental, as we shall learn. "Nothing happens by chance," Drs. Hemfelt and Warren claim.

As a necessary background to healing, let us explore the needs your child shares with every other child, and how those needs must be met.

CHAPTER 3

Attention Hunger: The Natural Cry
for Identity and Love

"Mom? I'm hungry. I wanna eat now."

Alice Newport sighed. "Stop whining, Jenny-Jo. It won't be long." She glanced out the living room window for the four hundredth time.

"But I don't wanna wait any longer. Why can't we eat at five like Sarah's family does? She gets to eat any time she wants."

"Jennifer, stop it! Now go find something to do."

"I don't wanna go do something."

Brian called from the living room archway, "Come on, Jen, I'll play you a Zelda Two."

"I don't feel like Nintendo. I wanna . . ."

"Jennifer, for heaven's sake, get out of here! Now!" Alice wheeled and gave a shove in the general direction but Jennifer ducked away. Whining something about the video game, she followed Brian through the hallway to the game room.

Alice sank onto the sofa. You would expect that kind of behavior from a two year old, but Jennifer was nine now, almost ten. If it weren't for Brian, solid, dependable Brian, Alice probably would have done something desperate by now. And the school business—her father was going to be livid.

Alice's headache was returning. Why hadn't she taken a pill when she felt that usual, dull ache?

Well, finally. Here came Rob Newport up the walk, and the scowl on his face told her his work wasn't going well. Of course, she'd hear about it. She always heard about it.

He burst in through the door, filling the foyer with his six-feet-four bulk. "Jennifer left her bike on the lawn again. Can't you make that kid remember anything?"

"I'll have her put it away after supper. You're late. You said you'd be home on time."

He hung his jacket in the closet. "Yeah, Mark called just as I was leaving. Those door sashes were still out at the warehouse. I had to pick them up and take them over to the site. I don't know when Mark is going to figure out that if Sam promises something, it's not going to happen. Bunch of incompetent bonzos. Where's Brian?"

"In the game room, I think. Please come to the table. Dinner's been ready for over an hour."

"Brian sign up for driver's ed. yet?"

Alice followed Rob out to the dining room. "He talked to his counselor. If he waits until he's eighteen, the insurance premiums will be over four hundred dollars a year less. He wants to wait."

Rob snorted. "Every kid I ever heard of can't wait to get his license. That kid can't wait to wait." He wedged into his chair. Since that brief, futile attempt at dieting, he had gained another twenty pounds at least, Alice was certain.

Alice called down the hall to the kids and seated herself at the foot of the table. "Jenny-Jo's teacher phoned today after school."

"Now what?"

Alice bit her lip. She hated these scenes. She hated them! "She's having Jenny-Jo evaluated by a school psychologist. They're putting her in a special ed. class."

Rob's eyes went wide. "Like blazes they are!" he exploded. "That kid's staying in the regular class and she'll shape up!"

"It's out of our hands. Apparently Jenny-Jo did all right for a few days after they sent us that second written warning, but now she's back to the old stuff: disruptive, unable to concentrate, not completing her work."

"There's not a thing wrong with that kid that a little discipline won't cure. You were supposed to take care of this months ago, when they started sending notes home."

"I had a big talk with Jenny-Jo and went in for a conference with her teacher. I don't know what else I can do." Alice noticed for the first time that the children had silently seated themselves. Brian looked embarrassed. Jennifer looked bored.

Rob scowled. "No rinky-dink school psychologist is going to mess with my kid's head. That's that. Brian, say grace."

Brian mumbled the familiar words, but Alice's headache pounded too hard for her to hear them. Brian leaped to his feet. "You relax, Mom. I'll serve it."

Alice listened to him clank around in the kitchen. Brian was good in the kitchen, just as he was good at everything else. He'd be a good bachelor cook—he might have to be someday, since he had just turned sixteen and had not yet found a real girlfriend. She yearned for her medicine. "Jenny-Jo, you left your bike out," Alice reminded her.

"Yeah, I know. I was going to ride it after supper, but now there isn't gonna be any 'after supper.' It's getting dark." Jenny-Jo looked at Brian dishing out the vegetables. "Aw, Mom, you know I hate green beans! Why do you always hafta serve green beans?"

Rob snapped, "We don't *always* have green beans. Every night's a circus with your complaining. Just cut it out right now."

"Well, why do we always hafta eat stuff I don't like? I don't want any scalloped potatoes, either. They have onions in them."

"Here, Jen." Brian served her plate. "I'll just give you a few beans, and I'll try to give you potatoes without any onions, all right?"

Alice closed her eyes. Immediately after supper she'd take some of that medicine Dr. Bower prescribed. She didn't like to; it made her so drowsy. But she had to have something to ease this headache.

"Mom, there's mushrooms in the gravy! I hate mushrooms!"

"Jennifer, I said cut it out and I mean it!" Rob's face glowered darker than ever. He took a huge mouthful of the potatoes with gravy. Alice had tried saffron in the potato dish tonight and liked the effect. She had added the merest dash of tabasco to enhance the gravy. Would he notice?

Pouting under her own little black cloud, Jennifer picked up her knife and sawed at her pork chop. Suddenly it scooted off her plate onto the rug.

"I've had enough," Rob roared. "Go wash it off and eat it anyway!"

"Oh, Rob, please don't be that way," Alice wailed. "You're not going to make her eat it now. She didn't mean to."

"If you didn't let her constantly whine and make trouble, we'd have a peaceful family here," Rob shot back. "I'm sick of it. She's a kid. You're her mother. Why can't you control her?"

"I want another pork chop. I don't want this one." Jennifer squirmed to her knees on the chair and stabbed her fork at the chops on the serving dish.

"Sit down right!" Rob was yelling now.

"I can't reach the pork chops. I want a different pork chop." She lurched. Her milk went splashing across the table.

"Get out!" Rob's face flushed. "Go eat in your room! And I mean *eat*. You hide the beans under your bed again and I'll blister your hide."

The tears boiled up and over her eyelids and down her cheeks. "I don't know why you always yell at me. All I wanted was another pork chop." She dragged her plate off the table and headed for her room.

Brian continued to eat in painful silence. So did Rob. Alice waited. She had done the pork chops with four seasonings and her own special breading. If he noticed at all he made no mention of it . . . or of the green beans mornay with shallots.

Alice Newport didn't just take her nerve pill that night or Dr. Bower's prescription. In addition she dug out the Seconal Dr. Grant had prescribed, prepared a large dose, and went to bed at eight-thirty.

Opposites Attract

"Opposites attract," claims the adage. If so, the Newports certainly were an attractive family. Rob, the father, was as commanding as Alice, the mother, was reticent. Dr. Warren observed the parents as they introduced themselves and their two children to him. Alice, already physically slight, sagged down in her seat on the sofa, making herself appear smaller still. Rob absolutely loomed, massive in personality as well as build. He filled the easy chair opposite Dr. Warren and then some.

The children, too, differed completely. Sixteen-year-old Brian sat beside his mother, calm and composed. In the chair opposite them nine-year-old Jennifer fidgeted, untied her shoes and retied them, picked her nose and was up-braided for it, took the barrette out of her hair and bumped the telephone on the table at her elbow, all within the first minute.

"I'm a contractor," said Rob, "so I know what the term *lowest bidder* can mean. The school was going to turn one of their shrinks loose on Jennifer, and those school psycholo-gists are all lowest-bidder material, you know what I mean? Underpaid kids who want to get some practice in before they go out *robbing* people with their own offices. So I decided, if it has to be, I'm gonna be the one to choose which doctor, not the school. That's why we came here."

During the next twenty minutes, Dr. Warren chatted with first one person then another. Every member, even Jennifer herself, agreed that Jennifer was the problem in this family.

"If only she would listen better, I wouldn't yell at her so much," Alice offered.

"If only someone would make her settle down and get a better attitude, she'd do all right in school," Rob insisted.

"Jennifer," Dr. Warren asked, "let's not talk about how you think you might change. Let's talk about what your par-ents just said. How do they think you should change?"

Jennifer looked from face to face. "If I had a different teacher, I'd do OK."

"You mean someone who would settle you down?"

"No, just someone who doesn't pick on me. My teacher picks on me all the time."

"Is that what your parents think?"

She nodded. "Then they think I'd get good grades like Brian. But Brian's got it easier. He's in high school and he has lots of different teachers and he gets to take courses and choose what he learns. I can't choose. I have to learn it all."

"You see?" Rob fumed. "That's why she does so lousy in school."

"She just doesn't listen." Alice sighed. "If she would only listen . . . !'"

The Gnawingest Hunger

A three year old repeats, "Mommy, look!" twenty-seven times consecutively, whether or not Mommy actually looks. A nine year old, allowed for the first time to bake cookies without direct supervision, brings the bowl into the dining room to show Mommy every time an ingredient is added, "Is this right? Is this right?"

Every child hungers for attention. Jennifer Newport was no exception. And yet, in a curious way she was not a part of her family. At least on the verbal level she didn't communicate well at all, being unable to hear well or be heard well. Brian fit comfortably. Jennifer was odd man out. In the Trask family, Joey tried consciously to make himself odd man out. Surely this seemingly deliberate alienation is no way to serve attention needs, is it?

Attention hunger is more than just the need for undivided attention. It is, in effect, a need for identity.

The Real Needs

During the first two decades of life, every child has certain personal needs that must be met. The child intuitively knows (not just thinks, *knows*, in the most profound sense) when those needs are met or unmet. The child almost never articulates that knowledge. Rarely does the child realize whether his or her needs have been satisfied. But the knowledge is there, and the effects will out.

The most basic needs can be categorized as "attention hunger." They are time, attention, and affection. Those three primary needs must be served by adults, not by other children. When parents and caregivers meet these three aspects of attention hunger, they are well on the way to satisfying a fourth childhood need also—affirmation.

Attention hunger underlies the other aspects of a child's growth and development. This hunger can be filled by a relationship or attachment to parents. Counselors are seeing more clearly that attachment needs are met only by personal attention; objects and gifts won't do it. Technology won't do it. Daddy can greet the kids on videotape as he flies around the country on his business trips, but that won't cut the mustard as a substitute.

A corollary: Material things never reward. Social situations do.

Unfortunately, one of the better ways to grasp what attention hunger is, and how parents can satisfy it, is to see how it is choked off in dysfunctional families. As we examine the ways parents inadvertently fail to fulfill their children's emotional needs, ask yourself two continuing questions: "Did this happen in my own childhood?" and "Is this happening to my children now?"

The Many Faces of Abuse

If we frame the concept of attention hunger in the context of a child's tasks and boundaries, an encompassing definition for abuse emerges.

When a child's boundaries are violated, or the child is prevented from completing a developmental task, abuse has occurred. When abuse occurs, attention hunger goes unsatisfied.

Jake was disciplined with a razor strap when he was a lad, and see what a stalwart man he has become. He shaves with an electric shaver today, but he keeps a razor strap for disciplining his own sons. How can he shape his boys into men now, though? Ever since a teacher saw the raw marks on his youngest son's back, police and social workers have been harassing him.

Abuse. Such an ugly word. It deserves all the nasty things you can say about it and more. Some forms of abuse are recognized as such by our legal system. Most are not.

Conduct a man-on-the-street interview, asking, "What are some forms of child abuse?" and you'll hear some obvious responses:

"Sexual."

"Beating."

"Just yelling at the kid can be abusive, I think."

"Locking the kid out, or making him go hungry. You know, that kind of thing."

Yes, that kind of thing. But abuse takes other forms as well, some of them unexpected and unrecognized, such as verbal abuse and emotional incest. Counselors also believe that "passive" sexual and physical abuse can be as destructive to children as overt physical and sexual mistreatment.

Passive Sexual Abuse

Sexual abuse encompasses any inappropriate sexual expression, not just touching or other physical contact. For example, Jean at age twelve can't take a shower without her father inadvertently popping in, and it's been happening for years. "Oops; didn't hear the water running," he says. Or "Only be a moment; need a box of tissues out of the closet." Many and varied are his excuses. The fact is, his intrusion into her privacy is sexual abuse. He is violating her boundaries. And yes, it does make her very uncomfortable, although her range of life experience is too narrow yet for her to know why.

Children develop awareness of self, of sexual roles, of sex itself in stages separated by what might be called long dry spells. Once one plateau of awareness is achieved, the child enjoys a hiatus as that awareness sinks in, becoming incorporated into the child's very being. Then the child moves to the next stage of awareness, perhaps by experimentation, by reading, by formal education, by accident. . . .

If a developmental task that would occur naturally at, say, thirteen is thrust upon the child at age seven or eight, that child is abused. The child is simply not ready for the experience or awareness that has been forced upon him or her. In short, any sexual contact or discussion that is not appropriate to the child's age and maturity is abusive.

Understand we're not talking about legal parameters in this section at all. No court in the world would convict Jean's father of sexual abuse for getting a box of tissues when his daughter's in the shower. Rather, we are talking about patterns of behavior and attitudes that harm a child psychologically.

No one claims occasional lapses scar a child forever. Children, young ones especially, are quite resilient. By our definition, "abuse" is recurring behavior on the part of others, unattended to and uncorrected, which stunts the child's growth or damages the child's sense of identity.

Any experience or absence of experience that delays, neglects, or reverses completion of those identity-building tasks is abuse.

In almost every case we see in counsel, abuse both violates the child's boundaries and changes them, by either breaking them down or forcing the child to thicken them.

By extension, then, passive sexual abuse is harmful as well. This is the absence of education or appropriate discussion of sexual matters by parents. The child's boundaries are not being violated; they're not even being set. From the time the preschooler becomes aware of his sexual identity until the new adult walks out the front door, the child needs gentle guidance.

"I was twenty-two years old before I found out girls weren't just soft boys," claims Whalon Trask, only half facetiously. He cannot remember either his father or mother so much as breathing a word about anything even remotely sexual. He had to set any boundaries in that area himself. He had no help with the tasks of discovering himself and his sexuality. Everything he learned came from "the wrong kind of movies, the wrong kind of girls, and books with plenty of steamy parts." Abuse.

Passive Physical Abuse

When does discipline cross the line into physical abuse? Some parents eschew any physical punishment and others laud the occasional well-placed swat on the backside. Taken to the extreme, both of these approaches become abusive.

53

Both? Consider a case in Dr. Hemfelt's counsel. Anne Vickery struggled through an intensely dysfunctional childhood. As a young adult she succumbed to multiple addictions—drugs, alcohol, a spending compulsion, overeating. Through therapy she managed to clean up the drug, booze, and food abuses. The spending still plagues her. Against the advice of many, she married a man who, like her, cannot say no. He, too, spends as if there were no tomorrow.

Neither of them can say no to their only child, Aaron, either. For years the little boy has been groping for boundaries the only way a small child can, by testing the limits. Aaron never hears the word *no*. He never receives a swat on the behind. There are no boundaries for Aaron.

Aaron developed a taste for cola and now he refuses to drink milk. So his mother gives him cola at breakfast and at bedtime. He refused to give up his bottle of cola, so he still gets it. He never bothers with tantrums anymore, because a simple display of righteous indignation nets him whatever he wants. Even as his parents are undergoing intensive therapy, he is being seen by a play therapist, a child psychologist, and a speech specialist. Aaron will be five next June. His problem? Passive physical abuse. This lack of any punishment has been as destructive to Aaron as constant beating would have been.

Now let's look at those other forms of unrecognized abuse: verbal abuse and emotional incest.

Verbal Abuse

Picture this: Your only contacts with adults other than Mom and Dad have been polite and casual. Mom and Dad and your brothers and sisters are the only people in the world you've ever had to really deal with or get to know. To you, they are All People. Home is your refuge because it has to be; living here is the only choice you have. Mom and Dad, along with most of the rest of the world, are bigger than you. Moreover, they are perfect. Mom and Dad are the gods of the everyday.

Mom (big and scary) and Dad (even bigger and scarier) yell

at you—really yell. Whether you deserve it or not doesn't matter; "God" is upset with you. And you have nowhere to hide.

Parents grossly underestimate the effects of screaming at their children. Rebellious though the child may be, the parent is still an authority figure tantamount to God. The child has no way of escape and no way to process the messages he gets. Mom is out of sorts with a headache, but the child doesn't perceive that this might be why she's yelling. The child is not capable of ascertaining, "Dad is really mad at his boss; no wonder he came home and yelled at me. Clearly this is displaced anger." Whew! Few adults can always reason that way. Children absolutely cannot. The child swallows everything whole and then internalizes it.

Such active, primary verbal abuse is bad enough by itself, but it generates an even more insidious source of problems: negative messages. Long years after Mom in her frustration screamed, "You're no good! You can't do anything right" (and perhaps she didn't even really mean it; she was simply having a bad day), that message whispers in the grown child's ear, *You're no good. You can't do anything right. You can't do anything right.*

If you work much with a computer, you have probably lost at least one file. The file, perhaps a letter or memo, is on a disk somewhere, but unless you can call up the pathway of directories and subdirectories by which you retrieve it, it's essentially gone forever, buried in electronic limbo, still taking up disk space. Our memories work that way. Some researchers think your memory may well be nearly photographic. Everything that happened to you, all you've ever read, every minute of TV you've watched—it's all there somewhere among your memories. The trick is retrieving it. The brain has selectively erased certain pathways and perhaps accidentally removed others, severing conscious access to the memories. But they are still there, their echoes still haunting you: *You're no good! You can't do anything right.*

Just as absence of sexual guidance is passive sexual

abuse, parents can generate verbal abuse without a word. Children can feel messages just as clearly as if they were shouted.

Patrice Cooper's mom bore two boys by a previous marriage and her father brought a daughter into the stepfamily. Patrice was the only "ours" of the "his, hers, and ours" union, an unwanted intrusion. No one once ever mentioned out loud that Patrice was a mistake. Yet, Patrice unconsciously felt it. The truth did not come out until thirty years later, when Mom took part in Patrice's hospital therapy for her prescription drug abuse.

Rachel grew up the quintessential PK—preacher's kid. Hers looked for all the world like a Norman Rockwell family. No one suffered severe problems or sneaked out the back door of the dollhouse. Dad, a compulsive workaholic, tended his flock faithfully. Mom kept a spotless house as befits a pastor's wife and held the four kids (Rachel was youngest) to the straight and narrow. The bottom line: Rachel essentially grew up in a single-parent household. Dad's responsibilities consumed most of his waking hours and Mom—poor, harried Mom—had scant time for one-on-one conversations. Keeping a household with four kids picture-perfect is draining. A responsible adult, Rachel still felt totally unimportant years later. "I feel like I don't exist," she explained. "I have always felt ignored, even in my job and marriage. It colors everything I do."

Negative messages are also powerfully conveyed by what a child witnesses every day (let's be fair; so do positive messages). Consider the case of Wade Ames, a recent client at the clinic. Wade's parents treated him well. He was obviously and clearly loved. On the surface, nothing appeared wrong. The way Dad treated Mom, though, created lasting scars on Wade. Constantly caustic and sarcastic, Dad made gallows humor out of her appearance (not all that bad, as Wade recalls in retrospect) and cooking. Every meal generated a barrage of put-down jokes.

Dad himself may have thought he was joking, but his scorn came across to Wade in no uncertain way. By disparaging Mom, Dad damaged Wade's bond with her, a needed factor of growing up, and damaged Wade's vision of marriage itself—Wade's bond with his parents' marriage. To this day—and Wade is entering his thirties—he experiences immense difficulty opening up to a woman, any woman, whether she be a marriage prospect, a supervisor, or even a medical doctor. The negative message that women are objects of scorn persists, whispering in the untapped corners of Wade's mind.

There is one other source of negative messages, no less damaging but extremely subtle and difficult to discern: projection. The parent in hidden ways projects the parent's own feelings about himself or herself onto the child, as Marie Armand's mother did.

As an adult, Marie couldn't understand why she kept sabotaging herself. She'd start doing well at a complex job, or in the night courses she took, and bingo! She'd mess up. When she sought counsel her mother's messages gradually revealed themselves. Mom was always unsure of her own academic skills. When Marie came along—and Marie is one of the truly gifted—Mom constantly warned her to scale back her expectations. "That may be too hard for you." "Don't take too much risk; you'll only be disappointed." The messages, actually Mom's but projected as Marie's, sounded benevolent on the surface; a loving mother protecting her daughter from pain and disappointment. In truth they were malevolent and most damaging. Speaking in terms of boundaries, the mother had subtly transposed boundaries with her child.

You cannot count on your own children rejecting negative messages; it rarely happens because it is so exceedingly difficult to do. It's time right now to pause and examine the real messages you are sending your children.

Look first at surface words. Are they positive? Encouraging? Will they promote a strong sense of self? How about your attitudes—we mean the true attitudes, not the things you mouth aloud to the world. Your child is soaking up those unspoken attitudes. Are they positive, something you want incorporated into your child's being forever? This very moment you are shaping the rest of your child's life, for better or worse.

Emotional Incest

Judy, thirty-five, threw herself across the bed of her daughter, Amy, fourteen. They often talked like this, not so much mother-daughter as friend-friend. Amy, quite mature for her age, folded laundry.

"It's so hard." Judy sighed. "Your father used to be very affectionate. You remember when you were little how he brought me flowers sometimes? He never does that now."

"I remember the roses that one time, especially. Yellow ones."

"The Groundhog Day surprise! That's right. It was so silly. We laughed for days. Celebrating Groundhog Day. I wish he still thought about me that way. You know . . . silly."

"He gets silly sometimes. Just not as often."

"True. And frankly, Amy, our sex life is going the same way. Not as often, not as much fun." She flopped on her back and stared at the ceiling. "I'm telling you this for your own good, you know. I don't want you to think marriage is all a bed of roses."

Judy, for all her good intentions on the surface, is committing emotional incest, not to mention sexual abuse. Despite her disclaimer "for your own good," her revelations are doing Amy great harm. Why?

For one thing, she is pressing marital sexual matters upon a fourteen-year-old girl who is not mature enough to be properly concerned with them. One of the most devastating revelations children grasp around this age is that parents aren't the perfect demi-gods the children once thought them to be. Judy isn't helping ease the blow at all by commenting on basic failures in the marriage.

Even more damaging, though, is a situation where the nurturing role has been reversed. The child is called upon to act as confessor and confidante to the parent. Any time the child takes over an adult parenting role, emotional incest occurs.

The Anatomy of Emotional Incest

Healthy Family

1. Nurturance flows from parent to child.
2. Both parents have strong boundaries and identities, and are capable of self-love and other-love.
3. Parents' marital bond is sound.
4. Boundaries around family show the three S's:

   • *Structure:* Each person fills an appropriate role regarding marital fidelity, control and degree of authority.

   • *Stability:* Life is positive and comfortably predictable from day to day.

   • *Safety:* The family offers the child safety, protection, and, if needed, support when dealing with the outside world.

Emotionally Incestuous Family

1. Nurturance is reversed, flowing from child to parent.
2. Parents lack good personal identity or solid boundaries.
3. The marital bond is weakened or ruptured—"shaky marriage."
4. Children provide some or all of the three S's:

   • *Structure:* Authority roles are inappropriate. Control either lacking or overused. Kids fill adult roles (for instance, Christian child of unbelieving parents may assume religious leadership).

   • *Stability:* Parents emotionally unstable, so child stabilizes the family egomass (such as, parents throw the tantrums, normally the child's prerogative).

   • *Security:* Child must act as mediator between the family and the outside world, or within the family between members. The child seeks safety from sources outside family.

It is never the child's job to be there for the parent. It is the parent's job to be there for the child.

Consider the episode that opened this chapter, an evening with the Newport family. Brian drew Jenny away from Mom, entertaining the little girl to ease the friction between two persons, neither of them himself. He served dinner for Mom, again pouring oil on troubled waters. He struggled to mollify Jenny-Jo. These were not the usual chores that might be assigned a child in order to teach responsibility. Brian was assuming the role of a surrogate parent. He could not just be a kid.

Other inappropriate roles lead to emotional incest. For example, when parents expect a child to act as mediator to either each other or the outside world, they have reversed the parent-child role. Lida Armstrong found herself committing just that error, when she expected the children to bring news of her ex-husband back from their visits with him. Similarly, Randy pumped the kids about Lida's private affairs. Another case in our care involved a mother, a fearful, insecure woman, who just couldn't face bill collectors. When trouble in that form came knocking, she sent her daughter to the door to make up some story.

Where is the line between the chores usually assigned during childhood and emotional incest? It varies from house to house and situation to situation—not a very helpful answer. Consider some instances by way of illustration:

On the traditional family farm, the kids are up and about at dawn along with Mom and Dad, feeding animals, perhaps doing the milking, tending the million and one routine jobs the farm demands. On today's farm as much as yesterday's, chores are normal and acceptable. The kids are not pressed beyond their level of maturity. After all, a five year old can feed the chickens; a ten year old can flake hay for the steers.

Suburban kids who think milk comes from the grocery store might handle a paper route or get into recycling in a big way. Somebody has to take the garbage out, and he or she doesn't need a Ph.D. for the job. Teenagers may find themselves up to their elbows in dishwater. Chores appropriate to the age level indeed foster responsibility.

Picking up the slack because Mom is whacked out on drugs, or Dad never gets home til nine, or the baby needs changing and no one else is bothering to do it—that goes beyond chores. Acting as confessor steps way over the line. Children, even relatively mature children, have no experience or background to act as counselor or sympathetic ear.

Emotional incest, regardless of its form, drains identity away from the child and two things happen. For one, the child, forced too early to become a nurturer, develops a sense of responsibility for the parents' happiness and welfare. There is no way the child can fix the parents' unhappiness; therefore, the child falls prey to outrageous false guilt. Mommy and Daddy are unhappy and I'm not doing anything about it.

The other negative result will last much longer. When Mom and Dad's emotional needs have not been met, the child intuitively tries to redress the lack. But the child's normal source of identity is the parents, so he or she must tap into other sources: success in sports, a dogmatic approach to religion, the trappings of a school clique or community group—the list is endless. Such children are extremely open to peer pressure that adults would consider negative— gangs, for example, or the boozing crowd. It's a counterfeit identity, but even a phony ID is better than no ID at all. The underlying unspoken message becomes, "If I can seize a strong identity, I'll have identity for all of us."

We must consider one more form of abuse we so frequently deal with in counseling. Our society refuses to recognize a common form of it as being destructive to children.

Abandonment

During a counseling session, Dr. Warren asked Joey Trask, "What's the worst thing in the world you can imagine that might happen?"

"To lose Mom or Dad." And this reply came from a boy who was bitterly angry with his parents.

When he asked the same question of Sarah Armstrong, she replied, "It already happened. Mom kicked Dad out."

The most devastating thing that can happen in a kid's life,

bar none, is to lose either a parent or the parents' marriage union. The loss, and the rupture of that union, whether avoidable or not, constitute abandonment.

A child's innate need of family emerges in many ways. Most of the steps in growing up require Mom and Dad and a healthy union. The child needs to bond with Mom, with Dad, and with the marriage itself. When those bonds fail, trouble fills the voids. Regardless of how liberal the visitation rights and how amicable the two parents are, divorce inflicts a great loss upon the child, not just of a parent but of the union itself. A divorced parent must recognize that and be prepared to help the child cope. Throughout this book we will offer help for these special problems.

There are other ways a child might lose a parent, even when the parent is sitting right there at the kitchen table.

Alice Newport breast-fed infant Jennifer because she'd read that was best. Also, breast-feeding lent itself to doing other things at the same time. Alice got very good at snuggling Jennifer on her arm to plug her in while, with her free hand, she would start the potatoes for dinner, call the carpet cleaners, or set up a baby shower luncheon for her neighbor. As her youngest child grew and made more and more demands on her time, Alice occasionally took a "pepper-upper" pill for energy.

Then Alice suffered a painful ankle fracture within two days of her own mother's unexpected death. By the time little Jennifer reached four, Alice was solidly hooked on prescription drugs. She knew a dozen subtle ways to keep her stash well stocked. Alice was a stay-at-home mommy because she'd read that was best too. But Alice wasn't home. She sat at the table all morning. She spent whole afternoons dozing on the sofa. She fixed meals and waited a lot for her workaholic husband. Little Jennifer entered school without ever once having had a real conversation with her mommy. Mommy would look Jennifer right in the eye and smile and say, "That's nice, dear," without really hearing a word. Jennifer, for all practical purposes, was abandoned, twice. First she was abandoned by Mom's busyness. Later she was abandoned by Mom's drug-induced stupors.

The Beginning of Improvement

The Newports were completing their first visit with Dr. Warren. As usual, he spoke with each family member individually as well as in a group interview. The children waited outside, their part completed.

Dr. Warren addressed Alice, "I was hoping you would feel a bit more comfortable as the hour proceeded, Alice. You seem a lot more nervous now than when you first arrived."

She smiled wanly. "I feel fine."

Rob waved a hand. "She's like that. Nerves. They come and go. I think she takes something for it."

"Ah. Who is your doctor?"

"Bower," she replied, even as Rob said, "Grant."

They looked at each other. "Wait a minute." Rob frowned. "What about that Dr. Hoffman? I thought you were going to him now."

Dr. Warren nodded. "What prescriptions are you taking, exactly?"

"Well, uh, it depends." Alice's hands fidgeted worse than Jenny ever squirmed. "It depends on how bad it is. You see, I don't ever want to overmedicate. So, uh, it depends."

Dr. Warren left that for the moment and skated off to the other side of the pond. "Who keeps the financial records in your family?"

Rob smiled, "Alice does. She's a whiz, doctor. Really good with figures. She uses Lotus, I think, to keep my business records in order. All I have to do is give her the invoices, receipts, and checks, and she keeps it all straight. I have a business accountant handle taxes and Social Security—that kind of thing—but she keeps the day-to-day stuff."

"And all the household expenses."

"Certainly. I don't even look at the checkbook. She does all that." He frowned. "She's so efficient at the financial stuff. That's why I can't understand why she doesn't keep Jenny in line better. The kid's nine, for Pete's sake; it's not like she's a teenager who'd be a handful or something. And Alice is home all day. She has all the time in the world."

Dr. Warren saw a pattern here that he sees all too often.

The family breadwinner felt that since Mommy wasn't out in the work force, Mommy had time on her hands. The big problem, though, was those three different doctors for what appeared on the surface to be a simple headache problem. That Mrs. Newport floated between several different doctors for one disorder suggested the possibility of prescription drug addiction.

Dr. Warren drew a deep breath. "Rob, this first interview, as you know, is basically an evaluation. In that regard your visit here has been most fruitful. I would like to work with Brian and Jennifer. I believe we can achieve excellent results. But, in most cases the children make real progress only when the whole family enters into . . ."

"Wait a minute!" Rob scowled. "You're talking about Brian too? There's nothing wrong with Brian. It's Jenny."

"Before you assume that's true, let me ask this: When did you get your learner's permit?"

"The minute I could. But that's not . . ."

"Then why is Brian postponing it? That's a red flag. There are other red flags that I'll be pleased to discuss with you if you wish. Yes, Brian as well as Jenny. I further recommend in the strongest terms that you and Alice enter counsel independently with a specialist in marriage issues."

"Now that's too much! Our marriage is as good as anybody's."

Dr. Warren kept his tone of voice quiet, measured. "You came to me for an evaluation because you sensed something was wrong. Well, so do I. Serious problems. When you subcontract plumbing on a job, you don't hire a roofer. You hire a plumber. A good one. I'll refer you to an excellent psychologist if you wish, or you can choose your own. But do get the opinion of one who understands codependent marriage dynamics."

Huge, hulking, overpowering Rob Newport stared at Dr. Warren. He stared at his wife. He seemed to shrink a bit. "Sense something wrong. Yeah, that's true. OK. Give me the referral."

CHAPTER 4

Unfinished Business:
The Wrong Kind of Legacy

Jennifer Jo Newport sat in front of the dollhouse in the clinic playroom, totally absorbed. While she manipulated the dolls, bounding them from room to room and supplying dialogue as her plotless drama unfolded, Dr. Warren relaxed quietly in a chair nearby.

Little Girl Doll bounced up the stairs to the marriage room. She wiggled about in front of a printed, inflatable plastic chest of drawers. Mommy Doll came zipping up without benefit of stairs and pushed Little Girl Doll down.

"No, no, no! You never get into Mommy's chest of drawers! Never, never mess around with Mommy's medicine! Now go play. Go!"

Little Girl Doll bumped down the stairs. Mommy Doll waggled back and forth in front of her chest of drawers. "Ah. Now I feel better."

Eventually Dr. Warren sat forward. "I'm sorry, Jennifer, but our time is up. We have to make the room available for another little girl now."

"Aw, can we stay just a little longer? Five minutes. Please?"

"Sorry. Here we go." He crossed to the door and opened it for her.

Still bargaining for time, Jennifer shuffled out into the hall and walked beside Dr. Warren to his office.

"Jennifer, I'd like to talk to your dad and mom a while. You wait here, please."

Dr. Warren's suspicions had been pretty well confirmed by Jennifer's innocent play with the dollhouse. Jennifer had picked up her mother's secret without fully realizing either the nature or the gravity of it.

Doing the Splits

A trick of the human mind that we see again and again in counsel is the phenomenon called "splitting off." When a person either large or small dismisses, denies, or ignores some part of himself or herself—that is, fails to deal with it—that part, whatever it is, floats free in the family system. Some other family member will be bound to pick it up without even knowing what is happening.

Think for a moment about the old clunker you used to drive. Talk about a love-hate relationship! Let's imagine a bit of steel shearing off one of the flying parts in the engine— not too hard to imagine with that old beater. The piece literally splits off. Now it churns about in the oil bath, a disaster in the making. It might get stuck harmlessly somewhere, but don't count on it. It will almost certainly lodge someplace critical and kill the engine. As you're waiting for the tow truck you can reflect on the dangers of splitting off.

The first step toward recovery for Jennifer and her family was to ferret out Alice Newport's hidden problem so that Jennifer could be relieved of carrying this pain.

Dr. Warren invited Rob Newport into his office. The burly gentleman settled into the overstuffed arm chair. "It's a little unnerving, you know, letting some stranger talk to my kid. You wonder what she's going to say that's not really true."

Dr. Warren smiled. "I understand your fears, but you can rest easy. We don't actually talk, as such. We play. My definition of play is, 'joining the child at her level.' At Jennifer's age, facts, as you call them, are almost always colored by the child's perceptions. Realities, though, reveal themselves as the child plays."

"So what realities did you reveal today?"

"Understand, Rob," Dr. Warren sobered, "psychologists and psychiatrists must of necessity work from observation. We watch, then we ask ourselves, 'What seems to be going on down inside?' We're just beginning to grasp the intricacies of the human mind below the conscious level. And that's where children operate, for the most part. Tell me what you know about your wife's medications. Have you been monitoring them at all?"

Rob frowned. "Why should I? She's a grown-up. I figure she can take care of her health. You think something's wrong?"

"I'm certain of it. I just mentioned observation. Whether or not we can figure out what's going on underneath, we see very clear surface patterns of behavior. Repeated patterns so distinct we can identify what's happening."

Rob looked just plain worried now. He sat back to listen.

"The verb *to own* takes on a special meaning in psychology. It means to accept something as a part of you. When I own my anger, that means I accept that I'm angry, whether it's a logical anger or not. I agree to myself that it's part of me. I own my sexuality when I admit I'm a sexual person and that sex is as basic a need for me as for any other person."

"All right. . . ." Still that careful, guarded frown.

"The family is a closed unit. The opposite of 'owning' is 'splitting off.' When something we'll call X goes on with one member, and that member fails to own it, X splits off. Once split off, X is up for grabs and any member of the family unit might unconsciously pick it up."

"Sounds weird. Really left-field stuff."

"I agree. But our repeated observations indicate that's what goes on. Most frequently the children pick up what was split off. They carry the unowned anger or pain and don't even know it."

"So how does this concern Jenny-Jo?"

"Whatever else she's carrying—pain, anger, whatever—she's bearing a secret. From several different observations I believe your wife is misusing her prescription medications. I doubt Jenny understands the scope of what she knows, and I emphasize that she has not articulated it as such. But she knows."

"That's ridiculous. You're calling Alice a drug addict."

"*Addict* is a serious word. I said 'misusing.' To what extent, I don't know yet."

Rob studied him a few long moments. "You're very careful with your words, aren't you?"

"I have to be."

"That's true. What do you suggest?"

"Have her evaluated by someone other than myself—an independent determination. Then, hospitalization if necessary."

"Do you realize what you're saying?"

"Every word, Mr. Newport. Every word!"

The Power of the Family Egomass

From Dr. Warren's conversation with Rob Newport, you might think that Jennifer had no control over what she knew or how she behaved. To a very large extent, that is true. A child intuitively absorbs what is going on in the family and rarely understands the full implications. If that is so, how could Dr. Warren, or anyone else, change Jenny-Jo's attitudes and behavior unless the whole family was altered in significant ways?

Therein lies the secret. That is exactly why, when a child evidences problems, the whole family is urged into counseling. Families often believe falsely that it's merely a good way for the psychologists or psychiatrists to fatten their wallets and pay for their kids' braces. Not so. Unless the whole family identifies the problem and works together to solve it, the child stands little chance of complete wholeness. Remember, a behavior problem displayed by a child is at least three generations in the making. That is why both parents and children must enter into recovery.

The cover article of a recent *People* magazine featured Drew Barrymore, the young actress. Her grandparents were alcoholics, her mother just as troubled. Drew herself became a full-blown alcoholic by the age of nine. The best minds and all the money in the world could not help her until her mother also entered therapy. Once her mother began recovery, Drew made solid progress toward health and wholeness.

But let's say the parents do not seek recovery. Let's say that you the reader see no problems in your own world; you want only to help your child feel better about himself. Maybe you and your child's other parent have separated, and there's no way you can get that person to work on a communal problem now that the family is broken. Or perhaps you are reading this book to gain insight into the life of a child outside your immediate family, a child whose closest kin you cannot directly influence. There is still much you can do, and we shall examine that in Chapters 7 through 10. First, though, it's important to see some of the dynamics that make the family work the way it does on the inside. We'll use the Holtz family as an illustration.

Why Lilyponds Are That Way

Eric Holtz worked for an aerospace firm near Houston. His wife, Marcia, volunteered at a local hospital by managing the gift shop during school hours. She made certain she got home when their three children did, and life was good.

Government research contracts being what they are, Eric found himself suddenly jobless. Marcia managed to move from her volunteer job to paid employment as a file clerk, earning minimum wage. The sudden financial strictures threatened the very roof over their heads.

They chose not to tell the children. Marcia put on a happy face when the kids came home from school, and Eric refused to accept that he was virtually unemployable in that town. Within months the first-grader's teacher was recommending him for special ed., the fifth-grader had developed an insatiable hunger for rock music, and the seventh-grader had been caught with booze at school.

"There's no way they could guess we're having money problems," Eric moaned. "They eat three square meals a day. We manage to buy things they ask for just like the old days, even if it means getting behind on the phone bill. No hints."

"Why didn't you mention anything to them?" we asked.

"They're too young to be bothered with that stuff. I mean, what does a first-grader know about defense contracts? Besides, it's all cyclic. It'll come around again, I'll be back on a payroll, and they won't be any the wiser."

"You're seriously underestimating kids' intuitive knowledge," we told the Holtzes. "They know. They may not know they know, but they know."

Still Eric refused to acknowledge the situation to the children. To him the writing on the wall said, "Any day now!" when actually it declared, "Change your line of work or move!" Marcia knew the seriousness of the situation, but she refused to accept it. Surely some "miracle" would save them. The thirteen-year-old child could not articulate the resulting breakdown of trust and integrity, and certainly the little ones could not. But their intuition understood. This family was severely out of joint and someone was covering up.

Use our model of a family as circles inside a larger circle. Picture the outside circle as a round pond with lilypads representing each family member. Every time the pond ripples, the lilypads move. Anything at all that stirs the water (counselors call these pressure points) makes the lilypads bob and wave, even if that stirring agent lies on the far side of the pond. So it is with the family.

Everything occurring in a family, regardless of how carefully it may be hidden, impacts the children. Everything.

Another case in our care involved the child of a man undergoing severe legal difficulties with the IRS. The child was admitted to the hospital with a spastic colon, a condition generated by nervous tension—stress. There was no way that child could properly perceive the extent of his father's problems. The child was five years old!

Don't fool yourself. Kids know.

The Solid Unit

In a John Candy movie, the film's title character, the bachelor Uncle Buck, is portrayed as crass and hopelessly out of

whack, both as a relative and as a baby-sitter. But his boor-
ishness is excused with "What the heck; he's family!"

Family. What a powerful, rewarding, dynamic, frustrating
Godzilla in our lives is our family! For a few years there, as
the age of divorce swept over us in a destructive wave, we
lost track of the pervasive force family exerts upon us. Break
one up, shuffle the players, and rebuild another. Nothing to
it. We're beginning now to realize it just isn't that easy. The
family, including aunts and uncles, cousins and in-laws,
stepfolk and grandfolk, works its effects even when shattered. Look at it something like all those brooms gone berserk in *The Sorcerer's Apprentice.*

Already Lida Armstrong finds herself in a complex tangle
of family, some of whom blame her for the divorce and some
of whom do not. She lives in one side of her elderly mother's duplex, and Gramma Robbins lives in the other side.
Gramma is, frankly, quite demanding. The Armstrong
grandparents, her ex-in-laws, similarly complain about a
lack of attention. "After all," they claim, "you may have divorced Randy, but we are still the children's grandparents.
You can't separate us. You must bring the children to see us
more often." Think about the three-ring circus Lida will endure if ever she remarries and introduces yet another set of
in-laws to the mix. Family.

If you are from the Judeo-Christian tradition, you know
that the family is the foundational human agency. Hebrew
Scripture and the New Testament both go into great detail
about how a smoothly running family should function. To
parents—not to a youth organization, camp, school, or Sunday school—is given responsibility for training children in
the way they should go. To parents is given the task of
religious education, of passing on the faith, all within the
structure of the family. Foremost, we are born to love.
Family.

Anthropologists also attest to the strength of the family in
every culture worldwide, especially those very much unlike
our own. Indeed, we modern folk minimize family ties, com-
pared to most societies. But even we can't ignore them. Ex-

tended family is almost always the key source of children's nurturance and learning regardless of the culture.

As a shaping influence on the child, the family must be thought of as a solid unit, even when it is damaged by death or divorce. Family members have so much influence over one another that parents and grandparents can often inflict their own "unfinished business" upon the children.

Unfinished Business

"Avenge me." "Reward my friends." "Hate whom I hate and love whom I love." "Complete the tasks I left undone." These are all the messages of unfinished business. They may be passed blatantly from generation to generation, or they may be transferred in oh-so-subtle ways. Most frequently the silent, intuitive messages wreak havoc unnoticed.

Unfinished business is just as abusive as any other abuse mentioned in Chapter 3. Like sexual abuse, physical abuse,

---

Sources of Family Dysfunction

1. Active and Passive Abuses

2. Emotional Incest

3. Negative Messages

4. Unfinished business

5. Split-off feelings and needs

---

and the others, it damages the child's boundaries in many ways and scars the child's ability to get on in life. It short-circuits the developmental tasks a child must complete in order to cope well as an adult.

To look at the matter in terms of boundaries, we can say that unfinished business is the tearing down of proper boundaries. The parents' boundaries become the kids', but neither parents nor kids realize that.

Life as Goodbye

An extraterrestrial, observing the surface of our culture, would wag its head in amusement at the instant fluctuations of our emotions (assuming, of course, the alien is not a headless blob). We cry at weddings and then pop the cork in joyous celebration immediately thereafter. Momma carefully prepares her child to start school (O gladsome day! Five blessed hours of peace!), then weeps as the little one first boards the bus.

The alien probably cannot grasp the depth and scope of the human condition. Funerals are obviously goodbyes; "last respects" are exactly that. But every step forward, every passage of growth, also calls for a goodbye just as surely. The bride and groom say goodbye to the independence of their singleness as they enter a new interdependent relationship with each other and take on the formidable responsibility of melding two houses into one. The parents of the happy couple say a poignant goodbye to the close parent-child relationship at the same time that they celebrate the new partnership. The mother sending her child off to school says goodbye to her special relationship with the child, which will never again be quite the same. Her child's boundaries are spreading far beyond her. Others will share the honor of being the sun in her little one's sky.

Children similarly must say goodbye constantly as they grow, for saying goodbye is a part of growth, and it can be a very frightening thing. The process begins, literally, at birth. Goodbye to the womb and hello to the world. Goodbye to the

security of Mommy's arms and hello to the exciting, sometimes terrifying, growth step of exploration and discovery.
Goodbye to the home, and hello to the universe beyond the
dollhouse. Goodbye to youth, hello to wisdom.

As you can see, there is a duality to this goodbye process,
involving both grief and joy. Parents heading healthy families encourage goodbyes and grieve the pain those goodbyes
require. Right along with the goodbyes, healthy families celebrate the happy aspects of children growing in strength
and independence. John Bradshaw claims families are designed to systematically self-destruct, and so they are, as
children leave the nest by degrees, eventually to challenge
the world. The destruction calls for ample tears and plente-
ous joy.

Goodbye as Unfinished Business

Some people, it seems, get zapped with a lot more difficult
goodbyes than do others. Death, illness, and accident plague
one family and leave the next-door neighbor unscathed. But
even in the most traumatic life, major setbacks need not
damage the children so long as the parents deal with grief
issues—yes, and celebration also—in a proper and timely
way.

This poses a dilemma at times: What griefs does one share
with children and which ones do the parents keep to themselves? How does one avoid the abuse of emotional incest—
dumping everything onto the confessor/child—without
chilling the child's trust?

The case of Eric and Marcia Holtz illustrates the problem.
The Holtzes chose not to tell their children when Eric was
fired from his job as an aerospace engineer. Yet within
months, the children had picked up their pain.

Eric and Marcia must come to grips with their economic
problems and work them out, grieving the loss of Eric's job
and celebrating the new job appropriately. Until they do, the
children will pick up on the dysfunction, and yet never be
able to deal with the problem because they do not understand it. Eric and Marcia are passing their difficulties on to
the children as unfinished business.

On the other hand, let's say Eric and Marcia's difficulties were of a sexual nature. Then, revealing the problem to the children in all its lascivious detail would be totally inappropriate. In that case the parents must resolve their problem. If resolution is not on the immediate horizon, they might acknowledge a problem and assure the children they are not to blame for it, without specifying its nature.

Also, as you talk about problems and their possible resolution with your children, remember that kids don't always see things the way you do. For example, you identify a problem in your marriage: You and your spouse argue and fight all the time. To you this indicates terrible mismating. To the child it is just another form of attachment—attachment by conflict. Attachment by conflict isn't much fun. It's certainly not desirable. But it's better than no attachment at all. Conflict is no reason to dissolve a union, when seen from the child's point of view.

Children must learn that some things are to be worked out, to be either celebrated or grieved publicly, and others are to be handled privately. Just as importantly, they learn by the parents' model how to handle life's setbacks and griefs. This knowledge constitutes an important means of growth in children.

What they are learning, in essence, is coping skills. If the parents did not master those skills, however, their problems and their dysfunctions will be passed on to the children as unfinished business. The appropriate goodbyes have not been made. The problems, like the goo of an oil spill in our lilypond, will contaminate all the lilypads to a greater or lesser extent.

Sorting Out Unfinished Business

Often unfinished business occurs because we are disappointed with what has occurred in any of a number of areas: major losses, our gender, our outward appearance, our goals, our intelligence, our attempt to be perfect, and our susceptibility to addictions and compulsions.

As we examine these sources of unfinished business, evaluate your own situation. Because children's problems are almost always multigenerational, think about what you know of your parents' choices. Did they deal with these issues or ignore these issues? How do you yourself handle them? Finally, pause a moment to think how each of these issues could conceivably affect your child (this last part requires considerable mental digging; answers don't come easily).

Major Losses

Along the Yukon River, where death can come suddenly and without warning, certain Athapascan Indians perform a rite for the dead in addition to funerals. Along with other observances, living persons don symbolic garments of the deceased, and also don their spirits, then go from house to house among the deceased's friends, offering them the chance to say goodbye. Disregarding what the custom does for the dead, if anything, this rite is for the living. Saying goodbye is immensely important to those who endure the loss.

Death is not the only loss. Frustrations and disappointments are also losses. So are serious illnesses, crippling handicaps or diseases, loss of jobs or mobility—all must be appropriately worked through and grieved. List the major losses in your life and your parents' lives. What are the losses your children have experienced? How have these been handled?

Our Gender

Gender problems are of three different types, which can be identified by asking three questions.

Are the parents (both yourself and your own parents) *comfortable in their gender roles?* This has little to do with homosexuality. Rather, we sometimes find parents who secretly wish they were the other gender. Must some sort of peace be made there?

Are you and your parents at peace with the opposite sex, or does "the battle of the sexes" mean just that?

Are the children the genders they "ought" to be? Distressingly, we rather frequently find parents who wish their children had been born the other gender.

"Of course they're what they ought to be!" you may protest. "God wanted them to be as they are." Too glib. What did *you* want them to be? It is you who must make peace with what they are, not God. He's satisfied already. If you or your parents secretly wanted something other than what arrived, that must be dealt with.

Grace, already mother to a son, yearned for a girl, but she bore another boy. He was such a cutie, so bright and winsome, that she cast her disappointment aside. What a delight he was! Ten years later when she entered counsel for codependency, Grace realized she had never dealt with that bitter, though temporary, disappointment. She took her ten year old for ice cream one day and announced, "Jeff, I must ask your forgiveness."

"Yeah, I know," he said. "You always wanted a girl." Ten years old. Grace had never so much as breathed a word to that effect, but ten years after Jeff's birth, he knew.

Outward Appearance

Are you and your parents content with your physical appearance, athletic abilities, economic status, and other aspects of your outward appearance (or as our culture calls it "your image")? No one has it perfect; only a few make the A-team. Not everyone is gorgeous enough to grace the cover of *Cosmopolitan*. But some people feel a persistent, subtle, intense dissatisfaction, a restless yearning to be something or someone else. Most importantly ask yourself, "Do I deeply wish my child(ren) looked or acted differently?" Discontent in this area quickly and subtly passes to the children in the form of unfinished business.

Goals

Which yearnings of your youth have been fulfilled in your life and which ones remain empty dreams? How about your parents? Nearly every little girl wants to own a horse farm when she grows up, and nearly every boy wants to be a doctor at some point. Rather, what about serious, determined, unfulfilled wishes?

We were in counsel with a man, an adult child of alcoholics, whose son was in open rebellion. The man, John, played pro-quality baseball in high school and hoped to get into the majors. He ended up supporting his feckless parents. The dream died. Not surprisingly, his son had been attending batting practice four days a week, worked with a batting tutor, played in two city leagues, and attended baseball camps in the summer, with Dad serving as coach and mentor. Until six months before.

"The kid flat out quit trying," John told us. "I can't understand it. The chance of a lifetime—the kind of chance I dreamed of and never got."

"The batting tutor suggested you back off somewhat, is that correct?" Dr. Hemfelt asked John.

"Yeah, but that's dumb. Any boy would want this, and he's walking away from it."

"Have you asked your son what he wants?"

"He says he doesn't know. I expected that. Kids don't know what they want. You have to see the dream for them."

John had become so enmeshed in his son, completing the unfinished business of his own dream, the boy felt smothered. His father's boundaries were overlapping the boy's in the most oppressive way. He lashed back the only way he knew how—by stopping. The lad may well be a nascent major leaguer, bright with talent, but he is so muddled he no longer knows what he wants. Now both of them understand. Time will tell if understanding will lead to resolution of their unfinished business.

Intelligence

Jaime Escalante, the East L.A. math teacher who gained fame for showing his advanced math students the way out of the ghetto, discussed one of them in an interview. The young girl faced three cultural barriers: her Hispanic race, her nonacademic background, and her sex. Girls simply do not achieve intellectually; everyone "knows" that. Her own parents expected nothing from her, not even high school graduation. She surmounted all barriers, and today as a university postgraduate earns more per annum than does Jaime Escalante himself.

In many families, in many cultures, powerful pressure exists for girls to back away from intellectual pursuit. Indeed, in many cases even boys are silently shunted away from academic excellence, for braininess is considered somehow less than manliness. This is unfinished business at its worst—the parents' expectations never spoken, never recognized, assigned instead to faceless custom.

What are your expectations, intellectually speaking, for your children? What were your parents' expectations for you?

Perfection

Have you heard these quips before?

"Nobody's perfect except you and me, and I'm not so sure about you."

"I was only wrong once in my life; I thought I was wrong, but I was mistaken."

We joke about our search for perfection despite our obvious imperfection, but have we actually dealt with our own fallibility? If you have not literally said goodbye to the childish notion that you and your children will be perfect, and accepted the fact that your parents weren't perfect either, your kids will pick it up as unfinished business. They, too, will wage the impossible war against imperfection and, frustrated, wonder why they cannot win.

Sachiko, in the first grade, was so afraid of making a mistake that she had stopped trying to print altogether. Is it a surprise that her father, a tailor, is so extremely perfectionistic he sells less than half the number of custom suits one would expect?

An addendum to this unwholesome search for perfection is: Have you made peace with the fact that there is no Santa Claus? By this, we mean do you accept that no other human being can play the perfect God for you? Seeking the perfect mentor, the perfect parent, the perfect mate, the fairy godmother with all the answers is unfinished business.

Another addendum might be termed *completion of personhood*. The parents perceive either a real or imagined deficit in themselves, an inadequacy in their own personhood. This issue, whether actual or not, sits festering, unresolved, and the parents try to complete the deficit not in themselves but in their children.

A recent case in our counsel provides both an excellent example of this and a delightful feel-good story (we love happy endings as much as anyone else does). Mom completed eighth grade and Dad used night school to eventually earn his high school diploma. What they lacked in formal education, they more than made up for in business savvy. They built a highly successful dry-cleaning firm, with the main plant downtown and branches in six shopping malls spread across two counties.

This couple pushed their two children to go to college. It wasn't a merciless pressure but rather a constant, subtle expectation. At no time did it occur to the children that they would not excel in school. Neither child perceived that their degrees were intended to fill in Mom and Dad's imagined missing piece.

The son thrived on it. He obtained his master's and earned a doctorate. The daughter didn't want an academic career. She wanted to take over the family business. The parents objected, certain that advanced education was the key to life. With the parents' unfinished business guiding the daughter's course through life, it didn't look much like a happy ending. One day, in our offices, Mom and Dad and the daughter sat in joint counseling. For the first time the daughter was able to tell her parents how proud of them she was.

There wasn't a dry eye in the room.

It had never occurred to these parents, blinded as they were by their false imperfection, that their children might find cause for pride. They had always imagined that the children were ashamed of their parents' supposed ignorance because, you see, they had never made peace with it themselves.

At last coming to grips with their own unfinished business, the parents verbally and consciously gave the daughter permission not to pursue a college education. Walking the paths of her own desires at last, the daughter is now happily working shoulder to shoulder with Mom and Dad, who, incidentally, took their first vacation in thirty-two years last summer. They plan to open two more outlets next year.

Susceptibility to Addictions and Compulsions

If compulsive and addictive behaviors have not been dealt with, they represent unfinished business. The parent who is an addict has not said goodbye to them. Will the children pick them up? Every time. Just as Jennifer Newport did. As adults, the children may not take on the parent's specific addiction or compulsion, but they'll drift into something else addictive or compulsive: alcohol, drugs, work, cleanliness, rock music, perfectionism, rage, fitness, food and related eating disorders such as anorexia/bulimia, and sex. Some of these things, in their proper perspective, are very good of themselves; taken to excess they will ruin your life and your children's.

Relationship with God

On his deathbed a famous man was asked by his attendant priest, "Have you made peace with God?"

"I was not aware we were at war," he replied.

Consider this final issue: Have you made peace with God?

"I don't believe in God," you reply.

That may be, but His existence does not depend upon your faith. Whether or not you believe in Him, He exists, He is, and He must be dealt with. Most human beings sense this, even if they outwardly deny it.

We find that, at times, people who believe in God haven't necessarily made peace with Him. The Minirth-Meier Clinic serves many who profess to be Christians. As a result we frequently find persons who know God well and serve Him faithfully, yet they have never made peace with Him.

A situation in which our clinic was not involved: Newspapers and at least one talk show picked up the story of a schoolboy who quite volubly spent his day preaching in the schoolyard. Among other things, he accused his young girl classmates of whoredom and warned them about their ways. When pressed, he could not define the word *whore*. He had no idea what he was actually saying. Film actor Marjoe

81

Gortner began his career as a child evangelist and later rejected that role. Such precociousness almost always reflects someone else's unfinished business.

Making peace with God means, essentially, coming to terms with who He is and is not. Think about your relationship to your God, looking not so much at the number of times you pray or how many hours you devote to His work, but rather what your innermost attitudes are. Compare them with some of these cases in our recent counsel.

Jack W. prided himself on his intense Christian lay service. He literally could not do enough for his Lord. Yet, when he explored his deeper motivation, he came to see that he was working desperately to earn the love of a distant and demanding God. He serves as much now as ever, but these days he serves with joy, having made peace with the fact that God already loves him fully. Jack could not buy that love, but he can indeed bask in it and serve out of gratitude.

Marilyn R. lost a daughter to leukemia. She went through the motions of worship and praised God with her lips. Deep inside she had not forgiven God for taking away her child. There was no peace.

"Marilyn," we asked, "why do you suppose God made you suffer loss when none of His other followers ever had to suffer?"

"What do you mean?" she protested. "Think of all the saints martyred in the early church! And people today who die or go to prison because . . ." and she stopped. She whispered, "I'm not alone."

"Faith is trusting God to know what He's doing. He alone sees the big picture. You see only one tiny bit of the whole: your own life. It's a very important bit to God, but only a bit."

Peace came when she realized the scope of God's omniscience and love. She forgave Him as He forgave her. She admitted to Him that forgiving Him was solely for her benefit; He didn't need her forgiveness.

Have you grasped the depth and breadth of God sufficiently to accept Him for what He is—the only perfect parent who loves you without reservation?

No Power of Choice

The child bound to complete Mom or Dad's unfinished business has just lost the power of choice. Compelled to fulfill the dream, to right the wrong, to meet the unspoken expectation, that child is not able to live out his or her own dreams and personal expectations. Most tragically, that child cannot follow God's will in his or her life. These inabilities, hardly understood, cause constant frustrations, usually surfacing as chronic depression, anger, or even physical illness.

Maggie, a twenty-four-year-old woman, illustrates the insidious damage of unfinished business. She came to our hospital to work through her debilitating depression, for in her personal introspection she could find no reason for it. As the hospital regimen corrected her physical problems, some of them caused by plain old neglect—she didn't eat well—we sat down with her and worked through the facts of her life. It took days and days of intensive exploration to root out the underlying messages of unfinished business.

In summary, Maggie was the baby of a family that spread through three decades. Her eldest brother was forty-nine, with the other three siblings scattered between. All five grew up happy and well loved. All five attended college. Her eldest brother was a dentist, the eldest sister a periodontist, the middle sister a university professor, and the other brother a computer expert. All but Maggie had married. She lived at home with her parents and was just embarking on a rewarding career as a special ed. teacher.

All that was surface. Lying below the surface and influencing it were the messages. As the baby, her designated role in the family was to stay behind and take care of Mom and Pop. All the others had tacit permission to go out and make families. Maggie had permission to go to college, as did all the others. But then she "had to" move back with their parents and remain single.

Every bit of those expectations was implicit. At no time did anyone speak the plan aloud. Probably no one even consciously thought it out, even though the tapes playing inside

Maggie's older brothers and sisters' heads went something like this: "With my family, I can't handle taking care of Mom and Pop too. Maggie hasn't married yet; it's easiest for her."

These edicts were just as strong as if they'd been codified into law. This, you see, was the family egomass at work. Maggie had become the resolution to an unspoken problem, shoehorned into fulfilling a role in which she'd had no choice. She was not free to marry, to leave town, to pursue a life apart from her parents.

She told us about several young men she had fully intended to marry, but didn't. She thought of a postgraduate position offered to her in another city, an opportunity that would have greatly enhanced her professional standing. Now in counsel the reasons she had turned it down looked facetious. An intense sadness flooded over her, a vivid sense of loss.

Maggie, who thought she was free, was operating in a prison of unspoken unfinished business. Such chickens always come home to roost. Her crippling, chronic depression became the release for her predicament. Depression is anger turned inward, and you can be intensely angry without knowing why.

Maggie needed to change the tapes that played within her own mind. She needed to think, "My life is valuable. It is mine. Yours is yours. I cannot live yours and you must not live mine."

The Next Steps

Little Jenny-Jo is still wrecking the Newport family's tranquility. Joey Trask isn't doing a thing for the Trask family's egomass. The Kolbins don't enjoy their children; they endure them. Lida Armstrong still doesn't know how to cope with the problems she is facing across three generations.

Learning to listen and *hear* each other across the generational gap is the way to begin the healing.

CHAPTER 5

Getting to Know You

Dr. Warren sat with his hands folded in his lap and watched Joey Trask fidget in his chair. "You seem a little nervous. Ever do this before?"

"Yeah, the school counselor talks to me sometimes." Joey changed his voice to a nasal singsong, mimicking the woman. " 'You're too nice a boy to act like this. Why are you doing it?' "

"What was your answer?"

"I'm old enough. I can act any way I want to."

"Good answer. It's true. But I've also learned that there's a reason for everything a person does. Sometimes you have to dig for it, but the reason's there."

Joey shrugged.

Dr. Warren continued. "I have three rules in this office. One: You have permission to talk—anything you want to say. Also, you have permission not to talk; you don't have to talk about anything that you'd rather not discuss. Two: When we explore ideas there won't be any right or wrong. You can be honest without being zapped for it. We're exploring ideas, not judging them. Three: I won't abandon you. I'll stay with you and walk with you."

Joey raised his head, the first time the boy had actually looked Dr. Warren in the eye. "What does that mean?"

"I'll be with you during this whole process. I won't solve your problems for you. I won't rescue you. But neither will I abandon you. You'll understand better as we get into it. Oh. One more thing. I will not squeal. I won't spill anything to your parents, with one very important exception. If you tell me about something that is potentially harmful to you— something that can really hurt you—I'm going to tell them about it because I care about you and your safety. But. *Important but:* I'll tell you in advance that I intend to, and you'll be present when I do it. It will never be behind your back. Are we understood?"

That hopeless shrug shifted Joey's puny shoulders again. "Guess so."

"Good. Let's get started. Tell me about your family."

Your First Part: Listening

When Dr. Hemfelt deals with adults or Dr. Warren works with children, they both start out exactly the same way. They listen. Just listen. Now therapists have a big edge over parents when it comes to listening. Therapists are carefully trained to read body language as well as words, to hear subtle nuances and vocal pitches that either add to or contrast with the words. Too, therapists have emotional detachment and therefore can listen more objectively.

Still, parents can find value in exploring some of the methods professional therapists use. At the very least, parents can gain a little better insight into the way their children see the world. Dr. Warren's rules, with modification, should work well. You have permission to talk about anything or not to talk. We won't be judgmental. You won't be abandoned in your quest.

Speaking very generally (there are many noble exceptions), parents make excellent tellers and lousy listeners. When you've been around the block, and the callow kid is just starting out, it's so very easy to give him the advantage of your ample experience (P.S. As a form of convenience, throughout this section we'll refer to the child as "he", although "she" is quite as appropriate). He's naïve, even wrong, in so many areas. Is it not the parent's responsibility to redirect him and set him straight?

Usually. Not always. *Children don't think like adults.* Their mental skills and priorities are not inferior; they are different. It is absolutely amazing how much you will learn about your child by listening without imposing your adult mindset upon him. Let's concentrate on polishing listening skills.

Dr. Warren defines play as joining the child at the child's level. It's a loose definition and works as well for a thirteen year old as for a nine year old. Play is the single most effective way to communicate with children less than nine years old. Discussion, particularly about abstracts or about details of the past, simply does not yield much fruit. Two good ways to listen through play are with certain kinds of games and with imagination toys.

Imagination toys are things like a deck of newsprint tablets, crayons, and felt-tip markers on a rainy afternoon. They are dollhouses or little play schoolhouses, where a child can set up a scenario and play out what happens there. These need not be elaborate; in fact, they're better play tools if they aren't. If you don't have a dollhouse, draw some squares on a big piece of cardboard on the floor. *This square is the kitchen. Let's draw a stove here; see the burners? This square is the bedroom. Where shall we put the bed?* If you need dolls to approximate your family, use the time-honored method by which farm children of our grandparents' generation obtained paper dolls: cut out appropriate pictures from a magazine or catalog. All that's left now is to sit down and play—and listen.

What your child says in the course of imaginative play may well shock the socks off you! When a five year old talks about cutting the baby into many pieces, you sit stunned, wondering who slipped the child a Rambo video. Even in an extreme case such as this, there are certain things Dr. Warren will never, *ever* say to a child, and you'll not want to either.

Don't deny or disallow what the child is feeling

For example: "Oh, you don't really believe that, do you?" "How can you say such a thing!" "That's terrible!" "Surely you can't mean that!" Judgmental statements can chill the air instantly. Besides, you promised not to, remember?

"That's nonsense!" is another no-no

It's nonsense to you. It might well be nonsense to the child as well. But nonsense to children is different from nonsense to us. To them it's credible. When you're small, there's not a thing to doubt about Peter Pan's flying. Take care to avoid approaching play from an adult perspective.

Avoid taking over or asking leading questions

Let the child call the shots and direct the play. Don't say things like, "Oh, look. We haven't touched the daddy doll for ten minutes. What is Daddy doing?" Maybe in the child's mind he isn't doing anything, and that in itself will tell you something.

"Let's do it this way" is also leading the child. You want to see where he goes.

Dr. Warren often enters the play world of a child in counsel. He sits down beside (not behind, not in front of) the child and picks up a doll which will represent himself. He walks the doll up to the scene. "Hi, I'm Paul. What are you doing?" or something of the sort. With the doll, he is entering into the magic, but it's not magic to the child. It's just as much a form of reality as is any event outside the playroom.

Your Next Part: Thinking

Fine. You've decided to listen as the child unfolds some drama. Now think about what you hear.

How does your child view the family? For example, little Elaine kept laying the daddy doll aside.

Dr. Warren picked up a doll and entered the play world. "Hi, I'm Paul. I thought I'd stop by. Where is Daddy?"

"Oh, he went on a trip."

In another session, "He's away." And, "He's at work." "He's asleep." "He went somewhere."

In actuality, Elaine's father rarely went on business trips and spent much time at home. Alerted by the inconsistency, Dr. Warren was able to explore why Elaine wasn't dealing with her daddy. It turned out that Daddy was indeed distant. A literary agent, he spent time in the family's presence, but his mind was always elsewhere. He'd be jotting down notes, making phone calls (even during Elaine's birthday party), reading manuscripts, bringing home clients. Never did his wife or children receive his full attention, and neither he nor his wife realized that. Six-year-old Elaine knew.

Be alert most of all to relationships

How do the characters interact? Who gets the biggest parts and the most time? Why? Who gets shunted aside? Who does violent things? Who plays peacemaker? Who is the brunt of jealousy or anger? Does the child's view of family approximate what you think your family is? Your child's play is a mirror of the child's perception of reality.

A child's world is almost exclusively a world of relationships. Objects or possessions play a relatively small part, unlike the worlds we adults often construct for ourselves. So you may wish to pay special attention not just to your child's view of relationships, but to your child's view of himself. Is it denigrating? Exalting? Absent? Look on the characters in his play as mirrors. Are they uncertain of themselves? Noble? Sneaky? Angry?

Another good way to listen is to draw pictures together. Bridle your own formidable artist's skills and draw stick figures or scenes. After all, you're playing *with* the child now. Occasionally ask questions about the child's efforts:

- "What is happening in your picture? What will happen next, do you know?"
- "Explain that to me."
- "That's a beautiful fish." (Make certain it *is* a fish before commenting!) "Why do you like to draw that fish?"

What does the child say, both in words and pictures? Are the pictures bright or dark?

Older children also like to draw as a means of self-expression, though they might balk at doing it as a parent-child activity. Joey Trask brought a sketchpad of drawings to a session with Dr. Warren. Shyly he commented on each page. "This isn't very good; I can do better. This one's really messy. This one's really bad. I just brought them in because we were talking about drawing the other day."

"I appreciate it. Drawing interests me. Thank you."

When Joey consistently bad-mouthed his own work (work he had obviously spent a lot of time on), that said things about his estimation of himself: He didn't think much of the artist.

The progression through the wirebound pad went from bears, deer, eagles, and such to monsters and skeletons. Having come directly from school, Joey had brought his books. He doodled on his notebooks, as do all students. In addition to the obligatory moustaches on the cheerleaders, spears pierced the football and basketball players. Knives and skulls filled empty spaces. Elements of the occult were showing up in the artwork of this Christian lad.

(An aside here: Counselors have found that children may embrace the occult in a casual way, not because of any particular interest in it, but because it symbolizes rebellion. Dangling the occult in front of pious parents is certain to antagonize them; it is the antagonism the kids seek, at least at first. Seeking power in the occult comes later, if at all. Nevertheless, pay attention to everything the child shares.)

Finally, in all your listening, watch for incongruence. What is the child's body language saying? The child who says, "Naw, it's all right," while on the verge of tears is displaying incongruence. Children are very good at dismissing their own feelings in favor of saying what they want you to hear or what they think you want to hear.

One example of a child's denying his own feelings was Martin. Martin, at almost-nine, had been a parent's dream—mature, happy, good in school. When Mom went through her divorce, he was highly supportive. "I don't know what I would have done without him," she said, "especially because his little brother completely fell apart. Raul was an absolute basket case. Angry. It took him a year to straighten up. But Martin came through it so very well. He was my strength."

"Martin was recently evaluated by his school."

"Yes. Poor attention span, learning problems. That's not Martin. It's like they're talking about someone else's kid. When he was arrested for shoplifting they told me to get help for him. So here I am. Shoplifting! Doctor, that's not Martin, either."

From the mother, Dr. Warren was learning much about what Martin was not. In his interviews with Martin, he explored what Martin was. A routine get-acquainted question is, "Tell me about your family." Martin talked about his step-dad, with whom he had little interaction. He talked about his little brother, who was now doing better in school than was Martin himself. He talked about his mom. And as he spoke he grew sadder and sadder.

"I understand your mom and dad divorced several years ago. What was that like for you?"

"I did OK with it." And there the incongruence leaped out. His head hung, not the least OK. His eyes glistened.

Silence.

Dr. Warren gave him a moment. He finds that pauses are frequently productive. "Looks like this is a pretty sad thing to talk about."

"Naw, I got something in my eye."

"I thought maybe you were sad, because it's very sad for me to hear about a twelve year old whose mom and dad are divorced. I think all twelve year olds want their mom and dad to be together."

Another long pause hung on the air. And Martin, who took the divorce so well, started wailing.

Very frequently Dr. Warren comes across a case of this sort, where the little hero puts his feelings aside, then falls apart because he never dealt with them. But we present the episode because it provides an example of another technique Dr. Warren and others use. Rather than just *talk to* children, they *work to forge an alliance* with them.

When Martin tells his story Dr. Warren feels sad, and it's not phony. The child's loss is indeed sad, and Dr. Warren does indeed care. That sort of thing cannot be faked. But when care and empathy are honestly expressed, your child gains an ally in his search through his emotions.

The Tasks of Healing

In Part 2 we will explore three steps both the children and the parents can take toward completeness, toward a healthy life and promising future. The three questions that help clients move through these steps are:

1. *Who am I inside me?* Healthy children, with a strong

and growing sense of identity, are in touch with their feelings. The wounded child does not understand his or her feelings, and that is disastrous. Your child must come to know everything that is in his or her room of our imagined dollhouse.

We urge the adults meanwhile to carefully examine their families of origin—that is, their parents and grandparents—to gain insight into themselves. You can't tell where you're going until you know where you've been and where you are now.

Think of a friend calling from a phone booth. "Hello? Tell me how to get to your house."

"Certainly. Where are you now?"

"That doesn't matter. I want to go to your house."

"Yes, but I can't give you directions until I know where to start from."

"That's immaterial. I want to go to your house, not be here."

Silly? You'd be surprised how many people want to change their families and themselves without a starting reference point.

2. *Who am I in the family?* The child must know where everyone else's room is, where the child is positioned, what is likely to change, and how sturdy the walls are. Parents must examine their marriage bond and strengthen it wherever weaknesses appear. If that bond has been dissolved, the parent must examine whether the separation has been resolved in a healthy way.

3. *Who am I in the community?* Very small children feel no sense of community. Mommy and Daddy and the family are their whole world. But sooner or later, the child must take his place outside the cloister. Feeling comfortable outside the dollhouse (this includes fitting into God's family) is the whole purpose of growing up. At the same time parents are assessing their roles in the community and the pressures generated there.

These specific elements of the healing process will help both child and parent achieve the ultimate goal of recovery:

- I need permission to explore who I am inside me. (If I am a child, this permission must come from authority figures and also from myself.)
- I need a partner in this exploration, a journeymate, for it will be very frightening at times. Some parts of me that I've refused to acknowledge, or don't yet know exist, are absolutely scary. I need beside me someone who's been there (in the child's case either a parent or both parent and counselor; in the adult's, a counselor, spouse, or friend).
- I must own what's inside me. That is, I must accept it, both the good and the bad, as being part of what I am. This is all of what it feels like to be. This is what life is. In all my complexity, I am!
- I need help grieving the sad parts of what I found. Grief includes anxiety, anger, and sadness. I must not wall off what I don't like about me (that is, splitting it off, denying its presence). I must not hide unpleasant parts, lest they slip in from behind to hurt me later in life.
- I must come to realize that I have importance just being me. Further I must know that I, not others, ultimately determine what I do in life. I must accept responsibility for myself.

The Pitfalls . . .

You love your child. You would be proud to serve as his journeymate on his explorations. But face it: This kid isn't always a picnic in the park, particularly if he has problems. What if you lack the fortitude to see it through? But there's an even bigger stumbling block: it could possibly be your own rebellion, unfinished business, anger, or other needs that are contributing to his problems. "Physician, heal thyself."

And yet, your child's healing will not happen unless your child receives help finding the way—knowledgeable help. Like a small child lost in formless woodland, your child has no idea which way to turn or what to do.

. . . And the Promise

You have already noticed that your children possess selective memory. The kids who remember your promise, made three summers ago, to take them on the roller coaster cannot remember your order, made seventeen seconds ago, to clean their rooms. Your son can recite all the names and nicknames of the major rock groups performing in America today, but he can't remember a phone message left for you. Your daughter knows which designer clothes are in and which are out, but she doesn't recall which of her friends borrowed your hundred-dollar binoculars last month.

Also, you are aware that lecturing dents neither a child's armor nor ears. Talking until you're blue does nothing but change your face to an unbecoming color.

Take heart! Your child needs neither a lecturer nor a memory prompter for this. He needs a journeymate, a person to travel beside him down a terrifying and unknown path. You can take the trip with him; leading gently at times—after all, your life experience far exceeds his—but mostly listening, mostly sharing, mostly simply undertaking it with him. We can provide a generalized map for both you and your child to follow, if you will provide the comradeship.

PART TWO

THE INDIVIDUAL'S ROAD TO RECOVERY

CHAPTER 6

The Child:
Who Am I Inside Me?

The man puts on a big yellow coat, big black boots, and big baggy yellow pants, all with reflector strips on them. They make him seem a lot bigger than he is. He puts on a big helmet, making him look scary. Four-year-old Jessica cringes. He drops a visor down over his face. Now you can't see his eyes and it's scarier still. He puts on a backpack with a tank and a strange, ugly breathing mask. He hides his hands inside big gloves. Jessica hops up from her seat on the floor to press close to her teacher, Mrs. Cooney. Mrs. Cooney smiles and holds her hand.

Huffing and snorting in a weird, hollow way, the masked man begins to walk among the children, patting heads, hugging the brave ones. He's so scary! Eventually he manages to hug everyone, even Jessica. Then he takes off the breathing mask and backpack, raises the visor, and puts the helmet on LeRoy, who is the oldest and boldest of Jessica's nursery class. He takes off his coat and hugs Jessica again.

The man is an off-duty firefighter visiting this nursery school class to teach the children not to fear firemen. He is also Jessica's daddy.

At four, Jessica knew perfectly well with her head that this was her daddy. But at four, her eyes ruled her heart and determined her fears; her head had very little to say about it. She also knew he was a firefighter, but her experience was too limited to give her any idea what a firefighter looked like or did.

The most tragic situation a firefighter can encounter is to enter a burning home to rescue the children and realize the terrified tots are hiding from him. Fire departments go to great lengths teaching children to come in emergency situations to persons dressed in protective gear. Yet, the frightening appearance is nearly impossible to put aside when you're small because adult logic ("this professional fire-fighter is here to help me") simply does not function.

Adult styles of thinking do not operate in children.

What's more, *children's styles of thinking are age specific and change as they grow.*

The child you know today is not the child you will meet tomorrow. As horizons burgeon, attitudes shift and sexual maturity proceeds at its own pace. Reality changes from whatever-you-wish-it-to-be to what-is. Perceptions of time alter, a point we adults often forget. Most importantly, the child's ability to express feelings changes radically. The very small one cannot communicate feelings verbally. Even an eighteen year old may not be able to do a good job of it. At least the eighteen year old can develop a better sense of self and realize his or her emotions.

Jennifer Newport, at nine, was not a little kid anymore. But she was not a big kid yet, either. It's a confusing turning point for any child. With her father so deeply involved in his work and her mom affected by drug abuse, she had no travelmate to accompany her on the journey from little to big. She sat in Dr. Warren's office, perched on the edge of her chair, kicking her feet, eager to get to the playroom.

"How's it going at home?" Dr. Warren asked.

"OK, I guess." Jennifer shrugged. "Mrs. Bomberg from the church comes over and helps out with laundry and stuff. And she cooks terrible. She baby sits us 'til Dad gets home. She's a witch. Really strict. I want Mom to get home from the hospital. When is she coming home?"

"Her doctor didn't tell me. He did say she's coming along well. It's very difficult to break old habits, especially when they involve taking medicines, but she's doing it."

"I want her home now!" Jennifer paused a moment. "What does 'being a kid' mean?"

"Depends which kid. Kids are different at different ages and boys are different from girls. Where did you hear it? Can you explain what you're thinking about?"

"Dad says you told him Brian isn't supposed to get stuck with baby-sitting me all the time because he's supposed to have time to be a kid. That's why Mrs. Bomberg's there. I don't know why Brian needs time to be a kid. All he does is hole up in his room and read stupid magazines." She ripped at the wrapper of a purse-pack of cookies.

"Sometimes people think goofing off is a waste of time. It's not, especially if you're a kid. Kids need goofing off time to just do what they want and relax and learn about themselves."

"I wouldn't wanna know about myself like Brian does. His magazines are yucky. I saw one of them once until he caught me. Boy, did he get mad!" She offered the doctor a cookie.

Dr. Warren weighed the pleasure of having a snack against the price of the calories, but only briefly. The calories lost. He accepted. "Would you get mad if he messed with your things?"

"He doesn't want to. He says girls are stupid."

"Is he right? This is a nice treat before lunch. Thank you."

"I dunno." She frowned. "Are girls stupid?"

"I haven't met a stupid one yet. Sometimes a girl does something that looks stupid, but so do boys. It seems to me girls do some really neat things. I booked the playroom for us for this hour. Would you like to go there?"

"Yeah!" Jenny-Jo bounced to her feet and headed out the door. She paused, waiting for her play partner. "I hate Mom being gone. When is she coming home?"

Permission to Explore

Previously we suggested your children need permission to explore inside themselves and they also need a journeymate—presumably you, the reader. They need help understanding and accepting their feelings, grieving the bitter and tough aspects, and finally, accepting responsibility for themselves.

In his talk with Jennifer, Dr. Warren touched on one of the ways you as a parent can give your children permission to explore "who I am inside me." Give them time. Another way is creatively playing together. As we look at these avenues, let's also note the factors that can rob you and your child of the necessary time.

Time

Jason Collander is healthy, well adjusted, carrying nobody else's pain. On Monday he takes piano lessons following marching band practice. Tuesday is Library Day, when, after school, kids go to the city library for reading and games. Wednesday is junior choir practice. Thursday is Awana. Friday is soccer practice. Saturdays are always booked with something, and quite usually two or three things. Sometimes during the summer, the family goes somewhere, such as the zoo or an amusement park. Sunday is Sunday school, church, and kids' evening church. Monday morning he's off to school again for another week of scheduled existence. And that's not even considering watching his favorite television shows.

There is not a thing wrong with any of the endeavors into which Jason is booked, and he enjoys them all. Well, most of them. Piano lessons he could do without, he says. He is learning about soccer, the Bible, Jesus, the piano, and the trumpet, but when is he learning about Jason? Certainly not while he's watching television. In short, he has next to no time to simply look inside himself.

The fault is not Jason's. Blame the prevailing myth of modern society: Unscheduled time is wasted time. Wasted time is garbage.

Jason does indeed learn valuable things about himself in the course of his scheduled activities. Soccer, band—yes, and piano too—test his skills and reveal improvement when it occurs. He learns what he can do and how well he can do it—important lessons. Through the mirror of his accomplishments he can see himself grow.

If everything were peachy in Jason's life, those would be the only lessons he needs. Unfortunately, Jason is human. He messes up in a piano recital. He fails to block a key goal in soccer and the other team wins. He gets out of step and out of tune in band. During a parade. His best friend gets mad at him and tells false and embarrassing stories about him at school.

He must learn how to handle these things, and for that he needs a journeymate. Most of all he needs a strong concept of who Jason is.

Play

Play. The work of children. Play is not their recreation. It is not merely time spent in idle amusement. Through play and fantasy, children effectively process the world around them, perhaps in ways adults think are foolish, empty, or even damaging.

The play of children is their gateway to understanding both themselves and the outside world.

This is true not just of the very young, but of all children, and it is especially important to troubled children. When we counsel youngsters, we counsel at least in part through play, and the younger the child, the more important this play is. We suggest that as you help your own children in this "who am I?" quest that you encourage the play that will lead them best.

Consider Jennifer Newport, on the cusp between all-play and talk-and-play (Joey Trask is another step up, on the line between talk-and-play and talk). Jennifer knelt in the playroom ricebox running a pick-up truck. Dr. Warren perched on the edge.

Jennifer made the appropriate noises as her truck whipped around a sharp corner, its tires squealing. The rice flew.

Dr. Warren "drove" a police car out into the rice, its siren howling. "Roowwwrrrr! Hey, lady! What are you doing driving around city streets like that?"

"This isn't city streets. It's out in the country with the snakes and jackrabbits."

"Oh. That's OK then. Why are you out in the country?"

"I have to get away."

"Oh. What are you getting away from?"

"Brian." Suddenly, mischievously, that truck made another tight turn and smacked into the police car. Cackling and revving her engine, Jennifer drove over the top of the police car and roared away. Only in a play world can you do that.

We call toys that help children reveal themselves "revelators" or revelatory toys. It's just a fancy way of saying hands-on toys, which encourage imagination and fantasizing and thereby help children understand themselves and the world.

Revelatory Toys

When advising parents, Dr. Warren prefers not to list "acceptable" toys. Rather he suggests classifications of toys that seem to stimulate children to figure out the world around them.

Building toys are a good choice—blocks, Lincoln Logs, Legos, Tinkertoys, a sandbox, each offered according to age needs and capabilities. With his blocks, four-year-old Victor Kolbin can build. He can destroy. Certain limits cannot be violated and Victor must learn to work within them. He can, for example, stack blocks only so high.

Unlike Victor, Regina Kolbin, almost eight, can verbalize some of the inviolable rules; "You can't stack them that high, Vic; they'll collapse;" and she can handle more elaborate toys such as Legos and Tinkertoys without becoming frustrated. Joey Trask, at twelve, builds some amazing plastic car models. He's getting away from funny cars, though; now he's into tanks and military hardware.

Toys that do not walk, talk or act for the child will activate his or her imagination. Action toys are all right so long as the child can manipulate them and make them express the child's nonverbal feelings and plots. Plain old dolls are great. Dolls with batteries are not.

Simple, basic toys are effective. Elaborate toys can rob play value, leaving too little to the imagination. Children receive great value from manipulating reality until it comes out right. Too often parents unconsciously feel that if the toys are elaborate enough, the parents need not spend time with the kids, that the toys will suffice. Not so.

In essence, play has become a lost art. Television-viewing is the antithesis of play. We have raised a generation of children who have missed the crucial hands-on play experience that forms so important a part of their developmental tasks. Because of that lack, they are becoming addicted to play objects later in life because, you see, they never completed those necessary early tasks; they never got to play.

Keep in mind as you encourage your child in play (and sit down with him at play), that parents find it exceedingly difficult to play. It takes practice to get down to a child's level and truly engage in real play. Real play casts off the bonds of reality. Things can fly. Things can grow or shrink. Things can talk, giving voice to unspeakable thoughts.

Then there are adult distractions. You sit on the living room carpet. Where the child sees a rugged playscape you see vacuuming that ought to be done. Other matters call. You must close your ears to them.

Dr. Hemfelt counseled a young man, Sam, whose father was a workaholic. "I hated it on those rare times when Dad took me fishing or played catch or something. I never felt comfortable. There was always this feeling that I was keeping him from some more important task. We couldn't relax." Kids pick up that sort of unspoken message clearly.

Also, it seems parents have trouble talking about children's feelings, and that is part of both play and conversation. Said sixteen-year-old Brian Newport, "All my parents ever talk about is what I'm doing. They never ask me how I feel about things. I wish sometimes they'd talk about me instead of my grades or all the things I'm doing."

Joey Trask said, "I was a busy kid in grade school. All those years I was doing stuff. But it was always somebody else's stuff. I wanted to just be alone sometimes, you know? Be a lump. Pretend inside my head without moving my body."

"Did you ever talk to your folks about it?" Dr. Warren asked.

"Once, when Dad was taking me to soccer practice. He just laughed it off. Said daydreaming doesn't get anybody anywhere. So I quit talking about it. Why bother? They didn't care how I felt."

Conversation, play, and free time are natural avenues by

which children learn more about themselves. Parents can also provide other modes of self-exploration for their children.

Other Modes of Exploration

These ideas to help the troubled child are age-specific, so we will treat them by age groups.

Most Ages

Some methods work across several age divisions. Pets for example are a bigger boon to self-understanding than adults might suspect.

Dr. Warren talked to Jennifer. "Who's your best friend?"

"Wookie."

"Who's Wookie?"

"Brian's dog. Only Brian doesn't pay much attention to him anymore. You ever see *Star Wars?* And Chewie? Chewbacca, Han Solo's big furry friend? Well, Wookie looks like that."

"Why do you like him? Is it him or her?"

"Him. I dunno. I guess because he's him, you know? And he doesn't mind if I'm me."

"He accepts you for who you are, not what you do."

"Yeah! When I tried to fix the VCR and we had to buy a new one, Mom and Dad were mad at me like you wouldn't believe. But Wookie still liked me. And I can talk to him and tell him things and he never blabs it around. Marcy talks about me all the time. Marcy, at school; she says she's my friend, but if I tell her something, she tells the whole school. Not Wookie."

Children with healthy school relationships talk to their pets just as Jennifer does. But when the pet rates as best friend, perhaps as only friend, it may be a sign that the child, like Jennifer, has trouble making human friends. It's something to look for.

At home you'll find, as we do in the clinic, that drawing and sculpture are always good. Puppets are fun. You can make very modest little finger puppets or elaborate, talking works of art. Keep in mind as you interact with a child's drawing or sculpture (modeling clay, Play-dough) that the goal is not great art; it's great expression. Never criticize artwork meant to express feelings.

In fact, before you go into something like this, carefully assess your own attitudes. How do you stand regarding perfectionism and neatness? You'd get a A+. Then forget the grade and put your perfectionism aside. The child's doing this, not you, and the child has his or her own standards.

The Very Young (Infants to age two)

Melanie Kolbin laughed. "Gerald? He doesn't play. He just messes around. I mean, the kid's only two."

"Very well," Dr. Warren agreed. "Then instead of play, let's say exploration. Everything a child this age does is exploration. He's starting from scratch, remember; he knows nothing of the world yet. We adults are too old to remember how naïve a child of two still is. His play, or exploration, is all sensory-motor."

"Touchy-feely."

"Exactly. In a year or so, his play will take on important new dimensions. Now think back to when Victor and Regina were about three."

"Don't remind me. James brought home a Three Stooges video, and Victor pasted Regina with a hammer."

"You've got it. Imitative."

"Yes, but *that* imitative?"

"Gerald will imitate in two ways. He'll imitate what he sees around him . . ."

"Like Regina did. She'd see me ironing and she'd iron with a block. We bought her a cute little iron and ironing board but she still used the block."

"Sounds about right." Dr. Warren grinned. "A three or four year old's play is symbolic. A realistic iron or a block are the same—both a symbol of an iron. As Gerald gets older, then, like Regina and Victor he'll begin imitating the real issues of life. Violence, feelings, expressions, relationships."

"With Regina and Victor I don't need any more violence! What should I do?"

"Besides encouraging them and limiting exposure to violence, such as on television, not much. I suggest you simply observe closely what Gerald, Victor, and Regina say and do as they play. That's basically what we do here in the clinic. Look for insights into what they're thinking, particularly in areas where they might be hurting. And join them as much as you can at their level."

"So forget about toys that look real?"

"Don't worry about it. Just remember as you play and watch their play how very small children look at life and toys. It all stands for something else. That will be true right up through preschool."

Preschool (Ages three to five)

Victor Kolbin, at four, doesn't need anything elaborate or specialized because everything at his age is brand new, including self-awareness. All he needs is time to play and a variety of playmates—perhaps a few children of similar age and Mommy and Daddy. Because his sense of self is still shaky—in fact, Victor's in particular is especially so—his play reflects what's happening with Mom and Dad. If all is well upstairs in Mom and Dad's dollhouse rooms, Victor doesn't just accept permission to be a kid and grow; he seizes it.

Victor's room in the Kolbin dollhouse is larger than two-year-old Gerald's, but it's still small and rather sparsely furnished at first. It grows daily. To help Victor grow, we counseled Melanie and James to encourage the boy to explore with blocks and felt-tip markers and that sort of thing. We also suggested they let Victor do what a preschooler does so well: express feelings by acting them out. Rage is rage, happiness is uncontrolled delight, sadness elicits wails. We asked that they not suppress these outbursts unless the social situation absolutely demanded it (i.e., sorrow in the middle of church service).

"But he already explodes whenever I leave the room," Melanie protested. "I simply get too tired of the fussiness to tolerate it anymore."

"I hear you. It's nerve-wracking. Excessive explosions indicate a major problem, and almost always that major problem will be fixed only by correcting the situation at Mom and Dad's level. You'll recall we were talking about the intergenerational aspect of behavior. Preschoolers are superb reflectors of unfinished business. If you and James have some issue stewing that hasn't been resolved, Victor will pick it up. Bet on it. What we encourage, though, is *appropriate* emotional expression—rage when I hit my thumb with the hammer, for example. As your child explodes, he learns something personal about the inside."

Melanie sniffed. "Wish there were some nice, quiet way."

Grade School (Ages six to ten)

There is no quiet way for Jennifer Newport. Everything she says and does is followed by exclamation points. Somewhere around age seven or eight she left behind the world in which six-year-old Regina Kolbin now plays. Regina is into Matchbox cars. Jennifer lost interest in Brian's Matchbox vehicles in favor of her own wheels—her bike and skateboard. *Porsche* is now a working word in her vocabulary.

Grade-schoolers shift from symbolic toys to realistic toys, from miniatures to bigger things, as with Jennifer and her shift from tiny cars to a skateboard.

Melanie Kolbin complains to Dr. Warren. "I realize I should be playing with Regina, but it's not working."

"Tell me about it."

"Well, we get out the Matchbox cars and lay a 4'x4' plywood board out on the living room floor and drew roads on it with blackboard chalk."

"Excellent."

"Then we build some houses and factories with blocks and make ramps and bridges. It's fun."

"Wonderful."

"But Regina talks. And talks. And talks. She sends me right through the wall."

"You're seeing Dr. Hemfelt about your chronic depression, right?"

"Yes. I suppose if I were feeling better I could let her constant babble slide off my back better."

"You don't want to tune her out. That's not listening. It's certainly not interacting. May I suggest this: When she hesitates, repeats, stammers, loses her train of thought . . ."

"That's exactly what she does! It's maddening."

"I agree. I listen to children all day. So listen as we do here in the clinic. As you take note of the words themselves, observe her gestures and actions. Listen to the tone of voice. It's not so singsong as you think after you've listened a bit. Note what thoughts give her the most trouble with stammering and repeating, and which thoughts flow smoothly. In other words, what is she comfortable talking about, and what takes effort?"

"Listen to the meaning behind the words, you mean."

"That's it."

"Doctor?" Melanie sighed. "Isn't there something we can do besides Matchbox?"

A child Regina's age will respond well to any or all of the play devices we've mentioned so far. She's not yet so sophisticated that methods aimed at smaller kids aren't welcomed.

When Jennifer cruised through the playroom with Dr. Warren she nodded toward the Playskool people, those little blocks and round knobs that represent people. "I used to play with those all the time," she said. "I don't anymore. I don't know why."

Grade-schoolers can rarely articulate their needs or the feelings changing inside them. That's why listening beyond the words is so important if you want to understand your child.

But wait. . . .

Lida Armstrong is not only raising her kids alone, she's holding down an outside job. She simply does not have time to play with eleven-year-old Pete. "There's nothing I'd love better," she says wistfully, "than to be a housewife and be able to just kick back and spend an afternoon playing Monopoly with Pete."

Here's a compromise that's not ideal, but it's workable: Lida might spend half an hour a day just talking to Pete while he snacks on cookies and she does the mindless household chores—folding laundry, doing dishes, ironing, and the like. Talk about what?

Children Pete's age are getting into music. Lida might get Pete drawing or coloring to music. "When you hear 'The Star-Spangled Banner,' draw what you think of." Pete can draw what he's feeling while Lida runs the vacuum cleaner. They can talk about the picture afterward.

Grade-schoolers enjoy fooling around with music too. A keyboard, an inexpensive guitar, or joining the school band could all lead to bigger things, but their importance is not what they offer for the future. Cash in on what they do for your child's expression right now. Again, "garbage" time is not garbage. Pecking around is as valuable for exploration today as for proficiency in music tomorrow.

Fantasy is a big part of a grade-schooler's life. If Lida can remember that this is child-think and not adult-think she can join in Pete's fantasy talk. For example:

Pete says, "I'm going to be the world's greatest basketball player when I'm big."

What is Lida's response? Not "Not if you don't practice hard, you won't." That's adult thinking and not fantastic. "What will it feel like?" serves the occasion much better.

As children fantasize about careers and situations, they're doing far more than wool-gathering. They're processing how they think, what the world looks like, where their interests lie. This isn't conscious reflection, but it doesn't have to be. All the changes are happening down inside and need no verbalization.

Going through a toy catalogue, to a child Jennifer's age, is not the frustration of "I can't have it" that an adult might experience. Instead it's fun. Pick up the catalogue or flyer of local toy stores and discount houses. With your child, read it like a picture book for dreamers. "Here's a picture of one of those Playskool gas stations. The text says it's for little kids, but what might we do with it? Look at this picture of a backyard swing set. What is that little girl doing that's against the rules at school? Yeah, I wasn't allowed to stand up in the swing when I was a kid, either."

This fantasizing about using the toys does a couple of things for the child: Imagination gets some exercise (imagination can always use exercise). The child can play without risk. Nothing will break; nothing will go wrong or frustrate; no one will laugh. The child is also processing—*internalizing* is a word psychologists like to use—personal attitudes, preferences, and fears. This is exactly the goal we're seeking.

All that is part of figuring out precisely what is stored in these grade-school children's dollhouse rooms, and celebrating things therein that are fun.

We find that six- to ten-year-old children are perhaps at the most amenable age for effecting a healthy redirection of energy and outlook. Jennifer, when she was six or seven, was just beginning to reach out, with the bare beginnings of some background experience. She started then to think in abstract. Now Jennifer is getting good at it and by eleven will be routinely thinking in the abstract. She will be able to grasp then, even better than she can grasp now, the puzzling way she thinks. In addition, children in Jennifer's age group aren't case-hardened yet; they can change for the better much more quickly than their parents can.

Junior High (Ages eleven to fourteen)

The most difficult age your child will ever have to plow through is this one. If you remember that, patience might come a bit easier.

Joey Trask at thirteen, Sarah Armstrong at fifteen, and Brian Newport at sixteen are all pretty good at drawing by now. And they are well coordinated when it comes to detailed play, such as making elaborate models.

Dr. Warren asked Joey to draw a picture of a person. Any person. Joey drew an adult. He did a pretty good job too.

"Tell me what this man does, Joey."

"Drives around in his four-wheel-drive pickup. Goes where he wants to. You know: does his thing, makes big money."

Dr. Warren nodded. Children feeling confident in themselves usually draw a person about their own age. On another occasion Joey drew a child younger than himself. The message: older and free is OK and being a kid is OK, but it's not OK to be thirteen.

Lida Armstrong found that modeling clay could be good stuff. After a particularly bitter argument with Sarah one evening, she went down to the drugstore and bought a package of that old-fashioned, oil-base modeling clay in four colors, the kind that stays pliable forever and leaves spots on the living room carpet. She divided it with a kitchen knife into two equal portions, each portion with four colors. "Sarah, come out here to the dining-room table."

"Now what?" Sarah loomed in the doorway scowling. "Mom, that's stupid."

"OK, so I'm stupid. Sit down." She scowled just as hard as Sarah and raised her voice. "Sit down here!"

"Mom, I'm not gonna do this. It's . . . it's embarrassing."

"For me too. We can't say two words to each other without getting into a fight. Talking is out. But I'm not going to lose you, Sarah. I refuse to lose you. I love you. So we'll try talking this way." She kneaded her yellow lump. "Yellow is cheery. When I'm feeling good, I feel like this." For several minutes she worked almost painfully until she had fashioned a five-petaled flower of sorts.

Sarah watched skeptically.

"Please try, Sarah. We've got to do something."

Sarah wrinkled her nose and twisted off a wad of red. It took a while for her to get into it. An hour later, though, each of them had made and destroyed four or five models. Among Sarah's: a blue puppy with a droopy tail that she called "sadness"; a cavernous mouth, complete with a few white teeth, built in red to signify "anger"; a green kite, "hope."

At her bedroom door, Sarah asked. "Mom, can we do that again tomorrow night?"

For her own part, Lida learned even more than Sarah. Until that evening Lida had read in her sullen child's constant smoldering anger that Sarah simply did not love or care. She saw now how sensitive her child actually was and Sarah's instinctive use of symbolic color and form absolutely amazed her.

111

Young Sarah Armstrong could not put her feelings into words. She could, however, express herself visually and with her hands. And her mom, she learned, cared more than she had ever guessed. Sarah had taken the first step in letting her mother be a trustworthy journeymate.

Be advised not all stories end happily, particularly stories about the first attempt. We urge you to try anything you can think of. Don't give up trying to help your child find what's inside himself, particularly if your child finds verbal expression frustrating.

Joseph Morrison, a divorced father, couldn't get through to his fourteen-year-old son, John. The boy wasn't stupid; he did all right in school. He just never talked about anything. The trip was a year or two overdue, but Joseph finally made time to take John on a three-day fishing trip as a sort of rite of passage. Joseph would use the time alone with John to explain the facts of life and talk about anything the boy wanted to discuss. Surely John would be eager for the chance to clear up all the mysteries of growing up. The kid didn't discuss anything. He sat through the birds-and-bees lecture with, at best, disinterest.

Frustrated, Joseph asked him, "How do you feel when you're around girls?"

"Uh, you know; OK."

"Well, how do you feel when you score a goal in soccer?"

"Good, I guess."

"How do you feel right now?"

"OK."

The morning of the third day they decided to drown the last of the worms for a few hours before heading back. John hooked into a catfish that fought like a swordfish. It took him twenty minutes to bring that fish ashore and the fish, while nowhere near a record, measured a good eighteen inches long.

"Eeeyah-hoo!" John jumped up and down in delight.

"John! So that's what happy looks like. What does angry look like? Let's say you tried real hard but your big catfish got away. Show me what angry feels like to you."

John stopped and stared at his dad. The light came on as

he realized what was happening. He thought for only a moment before his face twisted. Anyone hearing his anguished yell would know a murder was in progress. He grabbed a stick and beat on the trunk of the oak beside him. The stick shattered.

"Show me sad."

That stumped John at first, and Joseph realized that not only had his son been blocking out sadness, so had Joseph himself.

Two years later young John finally was able to articulate that moment. "It wasn't just that I couldn't tell how I felt. I didn't even *know* I felt anything. All these guys would talk about how it felt to kiss a girl for the first time, or how they felt when they did something great. I thought I was just numb; I didn't feel anything. After that weekend with Dad I found out I have the feelings, all right; I just can't talk about them much."

But John can throw a world-class fit.

And he's gradually admitting sadness.

Junior-high children are old enough to enjoy and employ drama. They can distinguish clearly between fantasy and reality, at last, but fantasy still looms large in life.

A splendid method for kids from ten on is journaling, or keeping a diary. That, like play, is becoming a lost art. Since no one but themselves will ever see it, they can really dump. There are two approaches to journaling: The posterity method and the fireplace method. A journaler writing for posterity puts thoughts—sometimes brief entries and sometimes page upon page—into a ring notebook or bound notebook and saves them. The advantage is that years from now the writer can look back and see how far the road has wound since then.

The fireplace method is good for nervous kids terrified that someone else will read their thoughts. The child writes his or her deepest thoughts and weightiest secrets in the diary. Then he or she tosses it in the fire. What good could that possibly serve? Journalers will be quick to tell you that as you begin writing, as the words start to come, things tumble out of your mind that you never dreamed existed there. Curiously, the child still may not be able to verbalize feelings; writing down free thought is not the same as casting a spoken sentence. But the understanding will happen. As the light comes on the child begins to know what's happening in the dark closets of that dollhouse room, and that is the whole idea. *Internalizing*—there's that word again.

In the newspaper cartoon strip "Luann," junior-high-schooler Luann keeps a taped diary, dictating into a recorder. The method ranks in the high nines for expression, the low sixes if the child wants to retrieve recorded thoughts later. Wading through all that is a pain. However, any method the child feels comfortable with as a means of self-expression is a good method.

Teens' or even pre-teens' rooms in the dollhouse are rapidly approaching Mom and Dad's in size and elaborateness. Sometimes, as in the case of the Trasks, Mom and Dad have trouble accepting that gracefully.

Parents come to learn what we at the clinic have long known—preaching just doesn't work, particularly on small children. How do we get kids to accept new ways of dealing with life? Through play. You can do it too.

Using Play

You now already know that play is critically important for children exploring who they are inside, by far the most important thing kids do. As they come across their brand-new feelings—aggression, fear, and all—they resolve them through play. Also, you are aware that they do it in predictable fashion, from sensory-motor to symbolic-imitative expression into both fantasy and realism, all loosely age related. Therefore, you now know what is likely to appeal to a child of a particular age.

We appeal to children and reach their unspoken thought processes through the magic of play because *play communicates when lectures and explanations fail to get through, particularly for children who cannot think yet in abstracts.*

We use several methods, depending on the child. You

might wish to experiment with several. Such play, incidentally, is not so much to correct behavior as to provide different ways of thinking about things. We want to reach the child whose reaction to every situation is anger, for example. This is an unconscious process, not rote behavior.

In the course of play with toys, we model simpler ways for the child to process thoughts and feelings. When four-year-old Victor rams into things with a truck, we might run our truck up to the same object, yell and bounce the truck up and down, then drive the truck around it. We might drive toward the object rapidly and, with squealing tire sounds, hang a fast right to avoid it, spraying rice all over it.

We might ask a child to tell a story using toys, puppets, drawing materials, or a similar medium. Then we tell one. We pattern our story much like the child's but we change the ending. The unarticulated, nonverbal insight helps the child make different decisions about inner feelings, which were the source of the child's story in the first place. This technique works only if we first get the child to talk about his or her feelings.

A specific example was our own fidgety little Jennifer Newport, nine. We started her telling a story, drawing pictures of it as she went.

In Jennifer's story a little girl got very, very angry. She went out into a forest and chopped all the trees down. Her mom and dad and the rangers got extremely mad and spanked her. She had to eat pine needles for a whole year as punishment.

Dr. Warren nodded, pleased. "That's a good story! Now it's my turn." He picked up a pencil and drew crude sketches. "Once upon a time there was a little girl named Jane. All sorts of things went wrong with Jane. Her mom got sick. Her dad went away. Her brother yelled at her and slammed a door and got her fingers caught in it. Boy, did she get mad! So she took an axe and walked and walked and walked until she came to the forest."

To this point Dr. Warren's story almost exactly paralleled Jennifer's. But then he veered away from Jennifer's scenario.

"She decided she was so mad she was going to cut down all the trees with her axe. She picked up the axe, and she started to swing it, and she heard someone yell, 'Hey!'

"She said, 'Huh?' and put her axe down. 'Who said that?'

"What do you think came? Here came an owl, a really big owl. It sat down on a tree right by her and said, 'Hoo? Me.'

He paused a few moments to draw an owl of sorts. (Dr. Warren has never felt comfortable as a graphic artist.)

"The owl asked, 'Why are you doing that?'

" ''Cause I'm mad,' Jane replied.

"The owl hooted, 'Hooo!' Then he said, 'Why are you mad at the trees? What did they do to you?' "

"Here." In all seriousness Jennifer handed him a brown crayon. "Make the owl brown. Right now he looks like a piece of broccoli."

Dr. Warren colored the owl. "I'll make the eyes bigger too. Is that better? . . . Anyway, the owl said, 'Don't chop the trees down. We birds and animals live here. Talk to me about it instead, OK?'

"So Jane told him all about all the things that were going wrong and why she was angry. Then she didn't feel like she had to chop down trees anymore. So she didn't get into trouble after all. And every time things went wrong, Jane would go tell the owl. So they lived happily ever after."

Happily ever after? Not everything is happy even in the best of families. Now that you can see how children change with maturity, let's consider how to help them when life is less than happy.

CHAPTER 7

Helping Your Child
Through the Trouble Spots

Two-year-old Gerald Kolbin won't let Mommy out of his sight. She is his very existence. If she leaves, he's somehow gone.

Four-year-old Victor Kolbin won't leave Mommy, either, for other reasons: The world is just too frightening to deal with without her close at hand.

Seven-year-old Regina Kolbin isn't afraid to leave Mommy. She steals matches and feels compelled to set fire to things. She neither knows why nor cares why. It is, pun intended, a burning and mysterious desire.

As we help children explore themselves inside, some things are going to taste sweet and others quite bitter. In their dollhouse room they'll find things to celebrate, things uplifting and fun. But along with the strengths and talents come fears and terrors hiding in the dark corners, and dreams gone horribly awry. With the heady joy of "I am!" comes the realization that life can go terribly, terribly wrong.

It is exactly here that your children need the steadying company of an adult. When they come upon fear, pain, and sadness, the kids must recognize those ugly bits of life for what they are, and not split them off. For that matter, so must we as adults. How can you help your children learn to cope with the rough spots? Let's look at fear first.

Fears and Terrors

Kids face fears every day as part of their lives. Fear of the dark. Of monsters. Of angry parents. Of other kids, especially those larger, older, and tougher. Because none of us has complete control over our surroundings or the things that happen to us, we are naturally afraid of possible consequences, of the unknown. In children, that fear is magnified by the fact that they have neither experience nor knowledge for dealing with it.

A client, Marie Grolier, reported this exchange with her eight-year-old son.

"Mitchell, get up. You'll be late for school."

"I'm not going."

"Mitchell . . ." Marie paused. Was he sick? Being a wise guy? "Why not?"

"Please, Mom, don't make me go today, OK?"

"Of course you're going. You don't have a fever; your color's good. You don't have any reason not to go."

"I'm scared of something."

"That's ridiculous! Get up and get ready."

At two the school called Marie at work. They thought Mitchell was absent, but they found he was hiding in the boys' restroom all day. "He won't say why. So disregard that message on your answering machine, when we called at nine this morning about his supposed absence."

We asked Marie to think a minute. "If you expressed vague, unformed misgivings to your spouse—about taking certain suspect tax deductions, for instance—and your spouse brushed them away with a cavalier 'That's ridiculous!' how would you respond?"

She shrugged. "I suppose my first thought would be, 'Maybe it is ridiculous.'"

"But it wasn't."

"Then I'd get mad. 'It is *not* ridiculous, and you'll hear me out on this! I have a valid point!'"

"Very good. But Mitchell doesn't think that way. By dismissing his fear with a brusque 'That's ridiculous,' you just slammed the door of communication. Remember the elevated status parents have with their grade-school-aged kids, right up there next to God. Even when the kids misbehave, parents are perfect, in theory."

"That's scary."

"For the child too. Demi-god just declared the fear ridiculous. To the child it is not. Will the child express it to someone who just scorned it?"

"Not likely. I see."

We delved into Mitchell's feelings in part through play. "Here's a little boy going to school, Mitchell. Let's draw him like this, with a schoolbag. What color should the bag be?"

"Red."

Mitchell's backpack is red.

We colored the backpack and cut out the crude figure of a little boy. We walked it through a make-believe schoolroom. For rooms, a cardboard carton on its side does nicely.

We told a story about how there was a tough guy out back who took Mitchell's lunch money, so he told the teacher what happened. Then Mitchell, in his turn, told a story. It took several such exchanges of tales for the truth to emerge: His problem was an irrational fear of having an embarrassing accident at school.

Irrational fears are not irrational to the children who suffer them. Children's thought patterns cannot deal with them in adult ways.

Adults' masterful logic means nothing to kids. How then can you combat fear in persons who cannot listen to reason? Facts plus a trusting relationship is a formula we've found that works. How else might his mom, Marie, have handled the episode?

"Mitchell, get up. You'll be late for school."

"I'm not going."

"Why not?"

"Please, Mom, don't make me go today, OK?"

Here's where the red flag goes up—a mysterious request. Marie can dismiss it or deal with it. She might ask, "Can't you tell me why?"

"I'm scared of something."

"Mm. Being scared is serious business. You have to get rolling and I have to go to work, so we don't have time to talk about it this morning. Tell you what. I'll write myself a note here to keep extra time this afternoon, just for you. We'll see what we can do to help you out."

119

"But I don't have to go to school now, right?"

"Wrong. You have to go because the law requires you to. It's not my choice. I'll give you my number. Keep it in your pocket. If things go down too crooked, call me."

The above scenario may or may not help Mitchell reach the bathroom in time throughout the day, but it's a start. What did Marie do differently? She did exactly the same things we do when talking to children in counsel.

1. *Empathize.* "I know how you feel. I understand. It's not foolish." This is the opposite of "That's a stupid fear. Don't ever worry about that; that's not going to happen."

2. *Balance fear with facts.* "School is a legal requirement" is a good fact for starters. Later in the day, as Marie talked about Mitchell's fear with him, she could bring in facts without suggesting "that's dumb."

"There's a bathroom down the hall if you need it. If you have to get up and run out the teacher might get mad at you, but that's better than the alternative."

Another fact: "It's never happened before."

"It happened to Suzy last Friday. Right in class," Mitchell objected.

"Did it happen to you? Ever come close?"

"Yeah. Remember that time at the zoo?"

"That *was* a close one, but you made it." Marie was planting an important thought in Mitchell's head: *You handled it in the past; you can handle it now.*

Empathy and facts.

3. *Assure your child that you will be there for him.* He need not face his fears alone. Marie walked with Mitchell as best she could. "It's not my choice. Here's my number; call me if you need to. I am being careful to make certain we have time together about this." Marie also made the unspoken pledge "If it's important to you I will not treat it lightly."

These three steps—empathy, balancing fear with facts, and the pledge "I will be there for you"—work regardless of age, for children (and adults!) of all ages experience fears and terrors. Unfortunately, in children we tend to trivialize and discount fears which, in adults, we would call paranoia.

The preschooler often fears monsters or a bogeyman. The title of a "Calvin and Hobbes" cartoon book is *Something Under the Bed is Drooling*. It's a universal though transitory fear in kids. So . . . when the child wails in the night, are you going to stick your head in the door and yell, "That's stupid. There isn't any monster. Go to sleep!"?

How about coming in with a flashlight and going through all the closets: "See? Nothing here."

That doesn't work? Maybe you missed a spot, or maybe monsters are immune to flashlights. Perhaps you might say, "I used to be afraid like that. I decided as I got older that there aren't any monsters after all. The important thing is you're at home, you're safe, and we're here for you. We won't let you come to harm."

The antidote, again: empathy. Balancing fear with facts. The pledge either spoken or unspoken: "I am with you and will remain with you."

Children must learn to cope with the fears of everyday life if they are going to find their sense of identity on schedule. Unmet fears can hamper the exploration and independence which build identity. A few examples: By fearing to leave Momma's side or to go outdoors, Victor Kolbin is unable to explore his world and come to terms with it. Moreover, his excessive (for his age) dependence upon Momma weakens both his boundaries and hers; their ponies will wander into each other's corrals.

Joey Trask admitted a very common teen and preteen fear: ". . . my classes. If I mess up, man, that's it. I'm afraid I'll look like a stupid slug in front of the others. I'm scared to study, 'cause if they know I study and I still louse up, they'll *really* think I'm an oyster."

Fears such as this one are no less irrational than bogeymen, and they're common, paralyzing fears in kids. Again, empathy (Taking a test is really tough for some people, even people who know all the material. Educators have a term for it: *test anxiety*), facts (You're smart enough to pull it off well; I've seen you in action before), and that pledge (I am here for you) are the keys.

121

With this same approach you can teach your child to grieve. Grieving is the most important part of dealing with any of life's many losses, big or small.

Teaching Grief

As Dr. Hemfelt and Dr. Warren talked about the importance of grief recently, they agreed that the worst disservice modern Americans have done their kids is to fail to teach them, primarily by modeling, the ways of grief. As a result, Dr. Hemfelt finds that grieving is a key process in his work with adults, and Dr. Warren works on that aspect more than any other when helping children.

How can our innocent children grieve? The same way adults do. The steps in the grief process are:

- shock and denial
- anger about it all, with acting out
- bargaining and magical thinking ("If only this turns out well, I promise to do so-and-so")
- sadness and depression (depression in adults is usually the mopes, a draining of energy and enthusiasm. In children it may erupt as rage or a sullen attitude or belligerence)
- resolution and forgiveness; a coming to terms and acceptance

Grief is one of the few common threads children of all ages share. It's necessary, for life is a constant process of loving and losing; the child repeatedly leaves one comfortable niche to embark on a new level of living, as we have seen. The old familiarity must be grieved. While it is not impossible for children to learn to grieve on their own, hardly ever do they learn in a vacuum, unguided. This they must learn from you, perhaps by modeling, perhaps through play.

Children experience grief as three components: fear, anger, and sadness, usually in that order. In counsel we address those three components and in doing so lead the child through the grieving process. The goal is to teach the child to handle life's woes by grieving.

Although the grief process is similar in adults and children, because children think differently and usually have not built up such a heavy crust of denial as adults have, we work with them a little differently.

A good case in point is divorcée Lida Armstrong's family. Although her sullen Sarah was our identified patient, we asked to see Pete as well, for we always consider one child's problems to be a matter for the whole family.

Lida talked to Dr. Warren prior to setting up an appointment schedule for herself with Dr. Hemfelt. "Pete really took the divorce well. He sort of said, 'It happens,' and went on with his life. Hardly a ripple. No depression, no acting out to speak of, no anger or sadness. Pete just cruises through life," Lida said. "I don't know if it's good or bad, but it sure is peaceful around the house. Now Sarah, on the other hand—boom city."

"It's probable that Pete has taken the divorce altogether too well. If he's buried his anger, fear, and resentment—and nearly every child of divorce has those feelings—you can be assured they will surface one day, and almost surely not to his benefit."

"It's over with now. What can I do about it?"

"We can help him grieve his losses."

The Fear Component of Grief

Usually Dr. Warren's office, with its two walls of windows, is an ocean of sunshine. Today a heavy rain with dense clouds had muffled the brightness down to somber grey.

Jennifer Newport curled up in her favorite overstuffed chair, her chin on her knees, and stared out the dull windows, in an uncharacteristically pensive mood. "Yeah, I guess I feel afraid sometimes. But I don't like to think about it so I don't, except at night."

"What do you think about at night?" Dr. Warren broke into a package of cheese and crackers, spread one with that useless little plastic knife, and offered it to Jennifer.

She accepted it absently. "Thanks. Mostly about Mom. I'm afraid she won't come home. You know, some people stay in nut houses their whole life. Or maybe she won't be the same.

And I don't know what Dad'll be like. He's been yelling and snapping at everything that moves. Mostly Brian and me. Mostly me. What if he stays like this? Stays mad?"

Dr. Warren slowly wagged his head. "That's a big load of worry and fear to have to carry, a really big load. And none of it's silly. It's all serious stuff. I feel very sorry with you that this load's been dumped on you. Incidentally, it's not a nut house. I know people sometimes spend their whole lives in nut houses, but this is a hospital that specializes in treating drug dependency, and your mom will be home soon. I can ease that one little bit of fear, at least."

Jennifer was expressing one of the components of the grieving process in children—fear. We help first by giving the child permission to fear. A simple "It's OK to be afraid" gives that permission. So does allowing children to voice their fears without putting them down.

After giving permission to be afraid, either verbally or by simply listening, we let them know we'll be there for them. We resolve this component exactly as with any other fear— empathy, balancing the fear with facts, and communicating the promise, "I'll walk with you."

Specifically, we help the child deal with the fear part of grief by asking three questions: What has happened to me? What might happen next? If this will hurt me, can I prevent it or control it? Every child's fears differ; none are alike. But they all find their basis in these three questions. The child probably does not have enough self-awareness to articulate these questions. So we lead them on gently, as you want to do with your own children.

Dr. Warren asked Pete Armstrong about his parents' divorce. "What happened in that situation exactly? Can you tell me?"

Pete rambled on and on about the divorce. Some of his facts were accurate or close to it. Most were not. Some aspects were pure fantasy. Dr. Warren did not interrupt or interject until he had heard the whole picture. He was not at this time seeking truth. First and foremost he wanted to know how Pete viewed it—what Pete was thinking. Only after Pete had expressed his feelings could Dr. Warren trim off some of the misconceptions, add touches of reality (this will be much harder for you because you are so close to your children and their problems). Dr. Warren does *not* expect Pete to agree with his views and opinions. He voices them and moves on.

"What might happen next?"

As before, talking about it (or with small children, acting it out through play) provides resolution. As Pete explored aloud what might happen next in his life because of the divorce, his imagination waxed wilder and wilder. Dad might die (a distinct possibility, considering his line of "work"). Mom might go off and get married and abandon the kids, as the father had already done, in effect. Pete feared his friends would see the real Pete, the sad kid down inside, and not like him anymore—thus the happy-go-lucky exterior.

Again Dr. Warren carefully heard Pete out without making comment; the point of this was to get Pete to voice his inner terrors. Externalizing his fears—that is, bringing them to the surface and speaking them aloud—was what Pete needed, not another dose of adult-think. Frequently, when children hear what they're thinking in this way, they themselves come to realize that their fears are groundless or perhaps even foolish.

Kids don't want to hear the answer to question three. It is: they can neither prevent nor control what happens outside themselves. *"But,"* Dr. Warren always says, "nothing will be so bad that you can't find someone to share it, to walk through it with you."

Generally, Dr. Warren does not use this as an opportunity to explain how magical thinking doesn't work, that parents will do what they will do and the child cannot change anything. Rather, he introduces the need for and value of an adult journeymate.

It comes as a bitter blow when children realize they are virtually helpless to control what happens to them. Pets and people die. Parents separate. The family rips up roots and moves a thousand miles. Life goes horribly wrong. They need an anchor. Solid ground.

Pete talked a long time about the way his mom and dad

argued so violently and so often. To his mind, though, attachment through conflict was better than no attachment at all. His kid-think searched desperately for the magic formula of behavior or attitude that would bring the family back together. Talking, talking, talking with Dr. Warren, he came to realize nothing would do that. It wasn't going to happen. One of his worst fears was true; his terror was capped. But he had Dr. Warren to lean on.

He also had God to lean on. Jesus promised, "I will never leave you nor forsake you" (Heb. 13:5). Dr. Warren introduces the love and nurturing of God not because it's a pat answer to get parents off the hook, but because it's true. Human beings fail; God does not. We move away from Him but He does not move. Children frequently understand these aspects of God better than adults, for children see in black and white more than in shades of gray; an all-knowing and all-loving deity, a magnification of pseudoperfect parents, makes sense to them. Jesus told His followers, "Unless you . . . become as little children, you will by no means enter the kingdom of heaven" (Matt. 18:3).

"Pete," Dr. Warren asked, "you mentioned going to Sunday school. Have you talked much there about Jesus as a comforter?"

"I quit going. It got boring."

"Mmm. That's too bad . . . that you feel bored about Jesus, I mean. He's the most exciting person I've ever met, and I've met some amazing people."

"You talk about Him like He's real."

"You heard the story that He was dead and came back to life, that He was resurrected, right?"

"Yeah." Caution tightened Pete's face.

"So since He didn't stay dead, He's still alive. A normal human body gets old, so a normal human body won't last. He couldn't stay in a normal body. But that doesn't mean He's not available."

"What body does He stay in then?"

"We don't know. We do know that He promised never to forsake us, and if He promised that to everybody all at once,

He can't be confined to one body, or He could only be with a few people at a time. That's what preachers mean when they talk about the Spirit of Christ. Alive. With us. But not confined to one place."

"And He's gonna take away my fear?"

"He didn't promise that. He promised me He won't forsake me. And He doesn't."

Dr. Warren does not seek here to conquer fear the way you might attempt to allay a child's fear of monsters under the bed. Rather, he seeks to bring the fear to the surface so that it might be recognized. If children do not process their fear they often get stuck in it. They may become withdrawn, laden with phobias, trapped in a fantasy world.

A very sad case in point: A client, Jane, brought her eight-year-old son Stephen in when he refused to go to school or wear anything red. Jane reported he quit associating with friends and rarely left his room. She feared he was losing his mind.

For two sessions Stephen refused to speak or even to pick up a toy. Stephen watched as Dr. Warren played alone, making *brumming* noises as he drove trucks around in the rice box, telling stories to himself at the dollhouse, punching the punching bag. Not until the third session did Stephen begin responding at all.

The horrifying answer to question one—what happened—came out by bits and pieces. Stephen had witnessed a hideous accident; his mother, backing out of the driveway, ran over his two-year-old brother. It had happened more than two years before we began seeing Stephen. Jane had assumed, because he cried a long time, that Stephen had grieved it through. He had not; he was stuck in the fear component.

Dr. Warren helped him break through that by talking about the three questions and dramatizing them in play. Once the fears were resolved, Stephen moved rapidly to the next component of the grieving process. For Stephen, as with others, that component was anger.

The Anger Component of Grief

As Beth pointed out, Whalon Trask, though he did not realize it, had never given Joey permission to be angry. Yet children need that permission. Anger is the most misunderstood of the components of grief. As with fear, you can grant permission by allowing it.

Children eight and younger express anger in nonverbal ways. Talking about it won't help them a lot.

You remember that Regina Kolbin, seven, was referred for counseling when she set fire to the family's doghouse. Her mother, Melanie, asked over and over, "Why did you do it? You had to have a reason."

And little Regina quite honestly replied, "I don't know." Not only did Regina not know why, she could not have verbalized it adequately had she known.

Dr. Warren's task was to help Regina recognize her anger, even if she couldn't talk about it. During an early session he sat quietly beside her at the dollhouse as she put the daddy doll through its paces. She picked up the little plastic sofa and threw it. She then picked up the bed and threw it.

Dr. Warren entered the play scene with a boy doll, as a visitor. He asked, "Oh, wow! Is your daddy throwing them around?"

"Yes, he's really mad. He doesn't like them!"

"Why?"

"Because Grandpa does."

When James Kolbin came in to take Regina home, Dr. Warren talked to him privately for a few minutes. "Can you tell me something about your living room sofa?"

"It's one of those Victorian settee things in powder blue. Why?"

"What significance does it have to your father?"

"Dad gave it to us." James frowned, pausing, as some wild thought passed across his face. He shook his head. "No, it can't be. We never discussed it in front of Regina or anything. There's no way she could know."

"Know what?"

"Dad came by one day and said our furniture was junk.

Well, it wasn't. It was Scandinavian, really nice stuff. Melanie and I both like ultramodern. Lots of glass and chrome. A few days later this furniture arrives. Dad had bought us a whole new living room set in sort of phony country style. Even gave us kitchen stuff with those geese with bows around their necks. He said the place needed some charm. I can't tell you how much we hate that furniture. But we never mentioned it to the kids."

"You didn't feel you could refuse?"

"He's already changed his will three times. None of us kids dare cross him."

"I think we've uncovered a source of your daughter's anger. She's carrying yours."

When we talked earlier about playing with your child, we mentioned that your child may shock you with some of his or her imaginative play. Victor, the Kolbin's four year old, buried all the family dolls deep in the ricebox. Jennifer Newport loved car crashes and on one occasion tossed all the family members except the girl off the dollhouse roof. All were intuitive expressions of anger.

We help children come to grips with their anger by again asking three questions. This time the questions are: (1) Why does this have to happen to me? It's not fair! (2) Why can't life be easy like it used to be? Why must I face all this? and (3) What am I supposed to do with my anger?

Children are almost never savvy enough to realize these are the questions they are asking deep inside. Dr. Warren usually prompts them with something like, "If that [whatever the situation is] happened to me, I'd think it wasn't fair. I'd be wondering why I got picked, why it happened to me." Putting the words in their mouths sometimes helps them hear what they're thinking.

To Pete Armstrong: "If this all happened when I was five, I'd feel like punching something or somebody. I'd be really angry at the whole world." Dr. Warren plants the seed that anger is not wrong. He doesn't usually wait for a response, but in a sense talks for his young client, giving voice to the unspoken feelings.

The answer to that first question usually does not

satisfy—"You're right; it isn't fair. You have a right to be angry. Now you have to find some way to move on. It happened. It's a mess. We must make the best of it." And always, always: "I won't abandon you. We'll see this through together."

In responding to the second question, which asks, in effect, "Why do I have to grow up?" we again can offer no comforting thought.

To Pete, Dr. Warren also offered this: "A part of growing up is feeling frustrated. Let's work on it together." Again, there's the concept of journeymates.

Older children, once they've come to recognize their own anger, may themselves ask the third question, "How can I express it?" The channels children would intuitively pick have been closed to them in this civilized world of ours. They can't go around hitting people to vent their ire or destroy property or throw sharp sticks at small animals. Yet, as long as anger is expressed inappropriately, such as Joey's acting out, or not at all, like Pete, it cannot help the grieving process along.

Dr. Warren, on a case-by-case basis, helps children redirect their anger into wholesome and helpful channels. The channels are age-dependent. Small children such as Victor and Regina might sublimate anger with energetic, perhaps even violent, outdoor play. Grade-schoolers Jennifer's and Pete's ages can work off anger in team sports and some extracurricular activities. As children get older, verbalizing their anger is the goal.

Finding the Words

We help older children, especially, put their anger into spoken form. Simply talk it out. What are you angry about? With whom are you angry?

Joey Trask showed up at his session one day wearing a T-shirt with a skull on the front. Blood oozed from the grinning mouth and eye sockets and puddled near his biker belt buckle.

"Where on earth do you find those shirts?" Dr. Warren asked.

"There's a head shop downtown with them."

"You're not allowed to go down there."

"Yeah, but my friend Chuck is. I give Chuck some money and tell him to find me something really gross. He's good at it."

"He's a genius at it. Tell me some of the things you got angry about yesterday."

"Nothing."

"Nothing at all?"

"Went pretty smooth."

Dr. Warren nodded. "Get your test back?"

"Yeah." Pause.

"Well?"

Joey shrugged. "She didn't think much of my answer on the essay question, but I did OK on the rest of it. Only one wrong out of fifty."

"Mmm." Dr. Warren pursed his lips for a moment. "You know, I talked to a writer once, at a meeting. She said that when you write something it's very personal because it comes from inside you. And when an editor rejects it, your head knows that the rejection is strictly for business reasons, but in your heart you feel rejected personally. Now I remember writing essay tests. When a teacher corrected or rejected my answers, it really hurt. It shouldn't have, but it did."

"Yeah, I guess that's so."

"If I got a good test back with a rejected essay part, I'd be angry, I think."

"Yeah." Joey's face darkened as the anger started to surface. "I bet she didn't even read it. She says when I get my hair cut and quit being a punk I'll do better."

"That sounds familiar."

"Whaddaya mean?"

"Who else says that?"

"Oh . . . yeah. Dad. I never thought about it. She sounds a lot like Dad does."

"And you're angry with your father," Dr. Warren pointed out.

"You saying it rubs off? The anger, I mean?"

131

"Sometimes. In fact, many times. Other people treat you the way your parents do, and you get mad at them, not because of what they're doing, but because you're mad at your folks."

"It's sin to get mad at your parents," Joey protested.

"It's human to get mad at your parents. It's sin to stay mad at your parents. When the apostle Paul said, 'Do not let the sun go down on your wrath' [Eph. 4:26], he meant to work through it and put it behind you. Don't hang onto it."

The more we talked along that vein, the more comfortable Joey felt in discussing what he had been convinced was sin.

Children who can't speak the words sometimes find they can write them. Frequently Dr. Warren will ask an older child to write a letter to his or her parents. The letter is certainly never to be mailed, and Dr. Warren need not see it unless the child wants him to. Usually, though, the child asks the doctor to read it.

Sarah Armstrong wrote two letters, one to her mother and one to her father. Within a sentence or two of the "Dear Mom," she began to condemn her mother for the divorce. She went on for four pages, listing her reasons for being angry. Many had nothing to do with her mother; she was angry and fearful about the new and heavier responsibilities of growing up. She fumed at the imperfections of her parents. She vented her rage at many injustices she saw around her, none of them concerning her mom.

The letter to her father started out with praise and admiration—how handsome he was, and how victimized he had been in this family. By page two, she was talking about how his drug problem worried her. She feared he'd cook his meth wrong and blow himself up. She knew that sooner or later the police would take him. She knew, too, that if he was high when they closed in, there would be a shoot-out. By the end of the letter she was expressing violent rage toward her father's neglect and toward the mess he had made of his life and hers.

Dr. Warren sealed the letters in an envelope, put her name on them, and asked her to sign the envelopes across the seals. He put it away in his desk for the next week.

Finding Other Ways

Small children just aren't able to verbalize feelings. We've learned that, for the very young, finger painting is an excellent anger expresser. Usually the children lean toward red and black, the anger and fear colors. They can get into the process of expression up to their elbows, literally, for finger painting is a marvelously physical medium. And, of course, we draw pictures.

Some small children express their anger with the punching bag in the corner of the playroom. They stand on the platform beneath it, don the big gloves, and flail away. Children, especially small ones, are very physical people anyway.

Unhooking Hang-ups

These are not the hang-ups the sixties jargon talked about. We mean here the way children (and often adults too) get all hung up on anger and fail to procede further with the grief process.

Dr. Warren watched Joey jump three of his men in a game of checkers. "So when your dog got hit and killed, you got angry?"

"Yeah. I mean, the jerk must have been going fifty down the side street. He only missed me by a couple feet."

"And when your soccer coach—what's his name again?" Dr. Warren took off one of Joey's third-row pieces.

"Hank Sprague."

"That's right. And when Mr. Sprague blamed you for the loss, you got mad."

"Yeah."

"No sadness? No blues?"

"He was a jerk."

"It seems to me that everything comes out the anger door for you." It's an observation Dr. Warren often makes of children. "When you feel sad, you get angry. When you feel scared, you act angry."

Joey absently fingered the chains around his neck. "Yeah. I'd rather be mad than sad. It doesn't hurt as much."

It doesn't hurt as much. Adults avoid sadness for exactly

the same reason. In fact, adults—parents, teachers, and others—unknowingly block the grief process in children by cutting off or redirecting fear and anger. Many parents feel somehow threatened by an enraged child—loss of love, loss of respect, all sorts of nasty ramifications come to their mind. Besides, it's easier to be angry. But when a child gets stuck on the anger stage, as Joey had done, the blockage inhibits any further progress in the grief process.

We try to shake kids out of this hang-up by the same means we used for both anger and fear: permission to go on to the next stage.

The Sadness Component of Grief

"It's just not fair!" Sarah Armstrong yelled. "Pete gets to go outside and shoot baskets and I have to do the dishes. Maybe I'd like to shoot a few baskets, too, you know."

"I understand how angry you feel," Dr. Warren agreed. "There's a lot of sadness too. You're saddled with more responsibilities simply because you're older. More is expected of you."

"That's not fair either."

"And it's sad. Also, it's sad when a kid can't have the kind of happy relationship with her parents that she sees other kids have. Your mom's busy and depressed; your dad's absent, and he uses drugs. And there you sit in the middle. I feel very sad with you."

"I don't have time to be sad. Angry feels better."

"For a while, yes. But eventually it eats you up. Sadness pulls anger's teeth. I'm not sad for you. I'm sad with you."

Sarah looked at him a few moments. Her eyes darted away. They glistened. The tears came—half a box of tissues' worth.

We introduce the sadness component by asking four questions: (1) Does anyone know how sad I am? (2) Does anyone else feel really sad also? (3) Does anyone else care about how I feel? and (4) Will it ever feel better? Does it ever go away? We usually give voice to these feelings because the children cannot articulate them. And usually, we frame the questions in an empathetic way—a way of feeling along with the kids, rather than preaching.

For example: "If I felt this sad, I'd think no one else could possibly know how bad I feel. Does anyone else appreciate how you feel, do you think?"

The answer almost always comes back, "No. No one knows."

This opens the opportunity for us to assure children, "I know. I understand. You're not alone."

When posing the question "Do others ever feel this sad?" we start with something specific. "Do Mom and Dad ever feel sad about things?"

"Yeah, I guess so."

"What things, do you think?" And we launch into a discussion of things that make any person feel sad, Mom, Dad, or child. The object is to ease the child's feeling of isolation.

If children were to understand themselves well enough to ask their parents, "Do you care how I feel?" the parents would certainly say, "Of course!" Parents convey the feeling, though, that they don't care much because they rarely take time to listen and commiserate. Listening takes a great deal of time. Sometimes it doesn't seem important. It is. It is.

Until you can answer the child's fourth question, "Will it ever go away?" and expect the child to believe you, you must have the child's trust. That comes from being a faithful journeymate in the painful pilgrimage of sadness.

Once the child is introduced to the previously hidden sadness within, we encourage its expression in several ways.

We Give Permission

As with fear and anger, the way you allow your child to be sad is to give permission. "It's OK to be sad" is necessary. We almost always overemphasize this permission aspect. You may well have to also, particularly if in your family, sadness was previously cut short, buried, or denied. In several ways during the session mentioned above, Dr. Warren was opening the door to Sarah's sadness, giving her permission to be sad, by empathizing, by encouraging her to talk about it, by not objecting to the thoughts she expressed.

There Is No One Way to Express It

Talking about the sadness in her heart was one way Sarah expressed it. The tears were also an honest expression. Frequently among our child patients, tears are the only expression they can make.

Sadness Needs a Journeymate

Lida Armstrong, at first, was not a good journeymate for Sarah because Lida was not adequately dealing with her own anger and sadness. She had not processed the loss of her marriage and happiness. Until she dealt with her own feelings and could then reach out to Sarah, Dr. Warren became Sarah's journeymate.

This did not mean that Dr. Warren always wept when Sarah wept, always moaned when she moaned, and always agreed when she complained. Dr. Warren did, however, repeatedly remind her, "I am not sad for you. I am sad with you."

Sadness takes time. A true journeymate is willing to stop at all the stops along the way for as long as it takes. Picture your child's progress through this part of the grieving process as a walk along a nature trail. There are numbered markers here and there along the way, things to think about and be reminded of. The journeymate will not hurry the child along. A white cross beside the trail may mark a loss. We can stop there, perhaps talk about it, perhaps shed tears, perhaps offer nothing but silence. Silence in its way is an expression of sadness also.

This means that as a journeymate you must be willing to talk about some things over and over as the child works them out. And that means patience.

The Parents' Healing

As children are being led to ask themselves, "Who am I inside me?" the parents' healing begins with essentially that same question. They, too, must learn effective grieving.

Rob Newport moved into his period of sadness, by chance, about the same time Jennifer did. One evening, Brian and Jennifer shared clearing-the-table duties after a particularly glum and quiet dinner. Rob went into the living room and sat down. Jennifer could not say why she did it, for she had never done it before, but tonight she silently crossed to her daddy and climbed into his lap. His arms closed around her; they had never done that before. She sobbed. He sobbed. They wept together.

"That moment," Rob said days later, "was the first moment of my life that I truly became a daddy. And the pain of so many lost years made me all the sadder."

CHAPTER 8

The Parents: Who Am I Inside Me?

Rob Newport started the engine, but he didn't drive away just yet. He looked one more time at the big hospital doors that had closed between him and Alice. She was in there now. Six weeks, her doctor suggested. It would probably take that long to dry her out. He let the air conditioner do its thing a few minutes and sat in the parking lot, thinking.

Drug addict. Alice. No. Drug addicts are those shabby jerks on the streets downtown. Drug addicts are people in opium dens, people who hold up convenience stores, hippie types with scroungy hair who wear spike-studded collars like cartoon bulldogs.

Not clean, well-groomed, educated homemakers who have everything they could want or need. Not suburban mothers of cute kids. Not his Alice. Yet, he had seen her lab workup, all the junk in her veins.

Why? Anything she wanted he gave her. Nice home, pretty clothes, a free hand with the checkbook. He worked hard and provided well. He was the kind of husband and father any woman would yearn for, solid and responsible. How could she?

Disbelief set fire to rage. How could she! Rob Newport folded his burly arms across the steering wheel, buried his head in them, and wept.

Kids can't really heal until their parents do.

Almost invariably when parents bring their family in to either Dr. Warren or Dr. Hemfelt, their order of priorities is:

1. Fix the kid who is messing up.

2. Well, OK, if you want to tinker around with the marriage a little, we suppose it won't hurt. Might do some good.

3. Fix me personally? I don't need fixing. It's the kid.

And absolutely without exception, the reverse is the correct order of priorities:

1. Heal thyself.
2. Work on the marriage.
3. Now help your children resolve their own problems without pressure from above.

All the generational levels, as represented by that three-dimensional chessboard in Chapter 1, must be taken into consideration if you would ease your child's hurt. Concentrating all your efforts on that bottom surface won't gain much as long as zingers from the other two levels can intrude at will, unexpectedly, and mess up your game strategy. Again, a child's behavioral problem did not begin with him.

Throughout this section we are looking at ways you can lead a child to understand and deal with the person and hurts inside, deal with family relationships, and finally tackle the outside world. Whether or not the family works as a group, either by using this book or seeking counsel, the child can profit from the help you offer.

But the best interests of the child are served better by far when the whole family makes constructive adjustments.

"I don't need help," you insist. "I bought this book in order to help my child get through life happier."

Possibly. But if your child is carrying someone else's pain, that someone else is probably you. By examining yourself you can indeed lift weight from your child's shoulders, without placing it on your own. Also, you may discover hidden pain you have carried for the previous generation.

If you have been dealing with your own codependency through counseling or by reading books, such as *Love Is a Choice,* you may already be familiar with some of the concepts discussed in this section. One warning: Any counseling or reading you might have done on your own probably did not involve your child directly. By working through this section after reading about the child's discovery of "who am I inside me?" you will clearly see the relationship between your codependency and the problems of the child who carries your pain.

For your child's sake and yours, let's begin.

First Things First

There's soapstone, and there's granite. Soapstone carves quite easily as stone goes, and polishes to a soft, marbled glow. Granite also yields itself to the carver's tools, but it sure hates to. Cutting, shaping, and polishing take immense effort and go slowly. Rob Newport was soapstone. Whalon Trask was granite.

Dr. Hemfelt sat pondering the differences in stones as he watched Beth and Whalon Trask seat themselves in his office. When Paul Warren referred the Trasks, he explained a bit about what he thought was going on. After the initial appointment with them, Dr. Hemfelt agreed with Paul's assessment.

Dr. Warren felt the parents, extremely reluctant to say goodbye to their little boy, were unconsciously trying to hold back his emergence into adolescence, a thing that cannot be done. This generated a lot of anger on both sides. Anger must have a way out, and it was being vented through Whalon's intransigence, Beth's unpredictable mood swings, and Joey's defiant behavior. Dr. Warren felt that Beth had a lot of her own anger to add to the ugly pot. If you add enough new heat to a situation already seething, something will erupt. The pot was boiling over.

The session began routinely as Dr. Hemfelt asked the questions he always asks about family relationships.

He frowned. "Beth, do I understand you correctly that you are the go-between, so to speak, between your husband and son?"

"Well, uh, I suppose you could call it that. I see Whalon's point. I agree with him for the most part. So it's not that exactly."

"And Whalon, you don't talk to your son at all to speak of; except, I suppose, 'pass the salt.' Things like that."

"Joey knows what I think of rock music. It's filthy. I won't have a relationship with anyone who listens to that music. If he wants to talk, he can turn off his boom box."

Dr. Hemfelt could see that Whalon had left Beth the job of straightening Joey out, giving her the battle plan and telling her to do it. It goes without saying that each day was blistered by arguments and friction.

He asked Beth, "You say you agree with your husband for the most part. Where do you disagree?"

"Joey is so lonely, moping around all the time. Whalon says he doesn't believe me, but I'm sure what Joey needs most is Whalon's love and attention."

"Well," grumbled Whalon, "he can have it when he stops playing that music and gets back into sports and cuts his hair."

Impasse.

Impasses such as that must be dissolved first. One way is to identify them for what they are: nonsense cycles.

Breaking the Nonsense Loop

In counsel Dr. Hemfelt sometimes uses a silly little exercise with profound implications. With the focus outside himself, the codependent seeks change in others, always in others. "If only *you* would change, we'd get along." To help parents realize what they're actually saying, Dr. Hemfelt asks them to engage in an exchange something like this:

He: "I'll change if you'll change."

She: "I'll change if you'll change."

He: "No, I'll change if you'll change."

She: "Oh no. I'll change if you change."

He: "No, but I'll change after you change.

She: "I'll change if you change."

This endless, nonsensical circle, a vicious circle in the truest sense, graphically illustrates for the parents why change will probably never come. Someone must take the first step. No one can expect a child, a natural follower, to take a first step that the parent, the leader, is unwilling to make. The exercise shows the parents that change must begin "with me."

Variations include: "I'll stop hurting you when you stop hurting me"; "I'll give in if you give in."

You can see the cycle at work between Whalon and Joey. Now ask yourself, "What cycles function in my most important relationships, particularly those between me and my child?"

Why do such cycles develop and flourish? "Stubbornness," you might say—or fear of losing something valuable. True. But there are deeper causes, to be exposed and destroyed as healing proceeds. That healing process involves five steps: (1) breaking out of denial, (2) examining your own childhood, (3) saying goodbye to things that provide no true security, (4) washing out the pain through grief, and (5) building a better you by reparenting the little child deep inside yourself.

Step One: Breaking Out of Denial

Examine the things that have happened, and are happening now, in your life. Pick one situation and we'll label it X. X may be constant frustration with something, frequent arguments, disappointment, or loss. X may well be an addiction or compulsion—rage, alcohol and tobacco, drugs, absolute control over everything, work, shopping, extremely

---

Five Steps to Healing the Pain a Parent Carries

1. Break out of denial.

2. Look back at your childhood.

3. Say goodbye to false security symbols.

4. Grieve out the pain.

5. Become a nurturing parent to yourself.

---

rigid religious views, cleanliness, constant thoughts about food or weight loss/gain, intense involvement in another person—any of these, and others as well, may have slipped silently over the line from "healthy and desirable" into "addictive."

Your addictions and obsessions may until now have been neatly hidden by layers of denial. Given voice, denial says:

- "Yes, but my intense need to clean is not important. In fact, it's very good."
- "My spending habits aren't as bad as a lot of other people's are."
- "It's so-and-so's fault that I get so mad I go into a rage. The ball's not in my court. Until so-and-so changes . . ."
- "His alcoholism will get better with time. He's a sensitive man. He'll realize."
- "This Valium thing isn't much. It could be licked in a day, were I to try just a little harder."
- "My sexual compulsion ended a long time ago. It's over with now. Forget it. I did."

These are all statements of denial. If X ever caused you pain or loss, or is doing so now, or if X is absorbing much of your life, X must be dealt with. None of the above arguments is valid.

Rob Newport claimed, "I can't believe it! Alice addicted to drugs?" Rob finally let the truth sink in as he left that hospital parking lot. He had taken the first step in the process.

Beth Trask realized. "We considered ourselves a picture-perfect family. Everyone else did too. It took Joey's rebellion to show us our misery. I buried so much so long and never knew it. I can't believe I did that."

The roots of denial, and the dysfunctions that denial hides, all go back, way back. The dysfunctions fill unmet needs from long ago, but obviously they're a poor way to fill anything. Next, let's dig out the roots and examine them.

Step Two: Look back at Your Childhood

Bad sector. Bad sector. The computer user hates those two words. It means a sector on a disk in use is damaged. The whole sector is out of commission and sometimes the whole disk. All the data on the sector and usually all on the disk is lost, beyond retrieving. Lost childhood is a bad sector in the disk of your life experiences.

The abuses and dysfunctions discussed in part 1 do far more than hurt some tender feelings. You'll recall that as a child grows, he or she must complete certain developmental tasks. If these tasks fail to find completion, the rest of development suffers. Another way to describe this missing growth phase is "lost childhood." Quite literally, a part of childhood, almost always a necessary part, has been damaged or destroyed. If you the parent suffer any codependency problems, you have some bad sectors to root out and restore.

Review in your mind the abuses we talked about in part 1. Did you suffer physical or sexual abuses? How about the passive forms of such abuse? Were your parents rigidly authoritarian? Hard, tight boundaries permit no growth. Were they extremely lenient? The absence of boundaries damages just as much. Verbal abuse? Or its opposite—the distant, withdrawn parent? Did your folks confide in you adult-to-adult, treat you as a pal or even as a parent? Were your parents divorced? Did you lose one to death? Did one parent or both succumb to addictions?

At the clinic we have adopted this premise:

Nothing happens by accident or in isolation.

An acting-out child is almost invariably mirroring the broader pain in the family. When Junior kicks the school principal in the shin while Mom, chronically depressed, lies asleep on the sofa at home, the two events are connected.

As you look back on your childhood, how do you know what constitutes "excessive fighting and arguing" as opposed to "normal fighting and argument?" Where is the line between eccentricity and either passive or active abuse? Your child doesn't know, because to your child, whatever your family is, is normal. "That's the way families are because that's the way my family is."

You, though, know better by now. You've seen enough families other than your own. You know to an extent what they do and how they function. You have at least a partial handle on what is normal and ordinary and what is not.

Dr. Hemfelt tackled this lost childhood business with Beth and Whalon Trask, Joey's parents, during their third counseling session. Beth settled into her cushioned chair; Whalon perched on his, bolt upright, looking irritated.

Dr. Hemfelt began, "Beth, tell me about your childhood."

She spread her hands. "What can I say? Totally normal. Good, God-fearing parents who loved me; my brothers were no brattier or nicer than any of my friends' brothers; we grew up fine . . . nothing out of the ordinary."

"Good. Whalon?"

"My father was an alcoholic. He walked out when I was eight. Mom did a lot of crying and we got on with our lives. Thanks to God, not one of us three kids ever touches alcohol. So your statistics about alcoholics begetting alcoholics are not always accurate."

Dr. Hemfelt nodded. "We were talking about active and passive abuse last time, remember? Let's look at pressure points in your childhood lives. Active abuses. Whalon, you suffered the abuses of your father's erratic behavior both before he left and after he abandoned you."

"Yes, but—"

"We're not examining the quality of them yet, deciding how bad they were, or recalling how we dealt with them. This is strictly an assessment at this point. Were the abuses present?"

"Yes, but—"

"Beth, any active abuses such as we talked about?"

"None."

"How about those subtle passive abuses?"

"None. Low-stress childhood."

Dr. Hemfelt put aside consideration of active or passive abuses for the moment and went on to explore the possibilities of emotional incest, of unfinished business, of negative messages.

"What do you mean, overt or covert negative messages?" Beth asked.

Dr. Hemfelt described how parents' messages such as,

"You're no good," "You'll never amount to much," might be spoken aloud, usually in anger, or implied but never verbalized. As he talked, Whalon became more and more agitated.

Finally Whalon exploded. "I can't see how this is getting us anywhere. Where are we going, anyway?"

"My eighteen-month-old son dropped a bucket of blocks on his foot Saturday," Dr. Hemfelt began. "He wailed, of course; it hurt. But even before the wailing started he kicked the bucket in anger. He's too young to build defense mechanisms against expressing pain or grieving it. He did what comes naturally to the grieving process, including getting angry.

"We wise adults use our logic and other powers of inhibition to bury unpleasantness. We squelch the God-given grief response. However, if we don't cleanse away the bad things, the abuses, the day-to-day problems and disappointments, they build up and split off, and the children pick up the pain. In other words, either you take care of it or your child will have to."

"That's nonsense."

"I watch it happening over and over in this office. It's difficult to accept, I agree, but that's the way it works. There are two reasons adults must learn to grieve. One is to purge the traumas and stressors of life. The other is to model good grieving for your child, because that's how he learns to purge his own pain. Children learn more from what they see than what they hear."

Beth shook her head. "If negative messages are what I think they are, Whalon is still getting them from his mother. I guess he reminds her too much of his father. She's always complaining that he's not raising Joey right and that he doesn't pay enough attention to her. And you get the feeling when she talks that whatever he does is never quite right."

"Those are powerful negative messages! What about you, Beth? You say your childhood was tranquil and I don't doubt it. What messages did you get?"

"Nothing like Whalon. Dad's a neatnik. Everything has to be just so. Mom keeps the house spotless, and he keeps the garage and yard in perfect order. Always has. So I suppose a message would be, 'Be neat.' That's not negative."

"Would you consider your parents' devotion to cleanliness a compulsion?"

"I guess, in a way."

"What effect did their compulsive cleanliness have on you kids?"

Beth studied her knees a few moments, frowning. "We kids washed things a lot. The car, the garden tools every time they were used. Every time my brother mowed the lawn—and that was twice a week in spring—he had to hose down the lawn mower afterward. We weren't allowed in the house if we had any dirt or grass clippings or anything on us. It was like we weren't welcome in our own home unless we were spotless. Dr. Hemfelt, kids aren't spotless."

"What else?"

She raised her eyes. "Neglect. I can't remember Mom and Dad doing something with us except a trip we took to the zoo once a year. That was our outing. The only one."

"Now, look!" Whalon fumed. "She said there were no problems in her childhood, but you're bound and determined to find one, so you keep prying until you find it, whether it's there or not."

"I mentioned that we adults are good at rationalizing and covering up pain in our past—neglect, as Beth so accurately put it. It takes some prying. Pain doesn't surface automatically when you call it. Beth did not have the nurturing she needed. Addictions and compulsions absorb tremendous amounts of energy. When her parents invested energy in one area they had none for others, in this case, satisfying the children's attention hunger."

Whalon still looked skeptical.

"If we don't face up to this pain from our childhood, we may be blind to the pain we carry as adults. And worse, blind to the pain we are passing on to our children."

Step Three: Say Goodbye to False Security Symbols

Goodbye? That's what little kids have to say to things as they're growing up. Aren't parents beyond all that? If only that were true! Parents, like every other human being, also face a lifetime of constant goodbyes, but the codependent parent even more. The codependent person tends to take everything to extremes. Love? Never was a relationship so intense. Work? Sixty hours a week, minimum, if you want to get ahead in this world. Recreation? Party hearty! Going overboard is the essence of addiction.

The first goodbye a parent must say is goodbye to any and all addictions, compulsions, or obsessions. Addictions possess an iron grip of their own, a siren call. They slip in and take over the moment, the day, the life. So long as you the

---

Goodbyes Parents Must Say

For strong, healthy improvement, you must be certain that you have made the appropriate goodbyes.

Say goodbye to:

- the illusion that every thing is OK.
- whatever pain and dysfunctions occurred in your family of origin.
- the false shame and guilt you have carried.
- any matters of unfinished business or split-off feelings lingering from your family of origin.
- the illusion that you can fix, change, redeem, or rewrite the history of your family of origin.
- your family of origin itself. These include the actual physical, emotional, financial, and spiritual goodbyes to each family member, living or dead.
- the notion that *anyone* (spouse, boss, church leader) can function as an omnipotent parent in your life.

---

parent are under the spell of your addictions, you cannot move on to healthy improvement.

Goodbye to Addictions and Compulsions

Alice Newport had to shake her drug dependency first for this reason: Addictions literally have a life of their own. So long as her prescription drugs held her, no argument, treatment, or persuasion—no matter how compelling—would get through to her. Her situation required professional help in a hospital setting.

Whalon Trask was addicted to control. The addiction arose from his chaotic and uncertain youth in a household headed by an irresponsible alcoholic. In his conscious mind he sincerely believed that when spiritual principles give headship to the man of the house, the man made every decision, tightly ran every detail of the show the way he wanted it, and shaped his home exactly as he felt comfortable. He was sincerely mistaken. His was the home of three divergent persons, not one, and he was not addressing the needs of the other two. Yet he would not, could not, loosen control.

Whalon's addiction held him in sway and he simply could not hear what we were trying to tell him, not even when Beth and Joey eventually realized what the issues were. There were several ways he might see his problem for what it was and amend it. Because he so highly valued the Word of God as a guide to living, Bible study about balanced authority and control and about sacrificial love could show him the light. There is an important plus here: the Holy Spirit leads sincere, searching study. The Holy Spirit is the best teacher for showing the way to more effective Christian love and nurturing. Also, observation might lead him to change; seeing positive changes in Beth and Joey could lead to change in Whalon.

Goodbye to Parental Protection

The second goodbye will be to your own parents, the child's grandparents. You may well consider dismissing this idea for any number of reasons:

- "Sorry. They died seven years ago."

- "Dream on. They disapprove of everything I like, including my spouse. We haven't spoken since I married."
- "Whaddaya mean, goodbye? We drive over to their place every weekend and holiday. Every single one."
- "Not until I can pay them back the twenty thousand dollars we borrowed."

You need to understand that saying goodbye to parents involves several dimensions. There's the residential goodbye when you move out. There's the financial goodbye when you cut the umbilical cord of the checkbook. If you've said these goodbyes, have you left home spiritually? That is, are your religious views genuinely your own, or are they simply an extension of your parents'? How about emotionally? You may be two thousand miles away, but are you emotionally on your own? There is a special irony you may face: While saying goodbye is always difficult, it is especially difficult to disengage from the painful memories of an abusive family.

To determine if you have a problem in this area, reflect for a moment. Do you continually call home to ask advice, touch base, feel out the parents on decisions you must make? A recent example in our counsel was Jane Blacklock.

Jane's husband, an air force captain, was stationed at Edwards Air Force Base in California. Her parents lived in Rochester, New York. Twice weekly, sometimes three times, Jane called them because she hated to write letters. They called her every Saturday morning when the rates were good. She ran all her decisions by them and made sure they were up to date on the cute things their grandkids did. They heard about the California sun, and she kept current on Rochester temperatures. Jane's head might have been in China Lake but her heart was in Rochester. She had never emotionally left home.

The next goodbye must be said to any false security symbols. What are they? Non-permanent things that define your life and supposedly ensure your future. Prestige, money, sexual prowess, even food, may rank as a god of your life.

Goodbye to False Security Symbols

Rob Newport boasted, "I have close to six figures salted

away in accounts and CDs. Nice cushion if home construction goes bust."

"What if the bank goes bust?"

Rob sobered. "I don't know . . ."

We asked Lida Armstrong what sort of security symbols she kept tucked away.

"None," she answered. But then she thought a minute. "You know, though, I have work clothes in my closet. These are suits, jackets, and dresses you'd use to dress for success in an office environment, especially mid-level management. I could work every day for a month without duplicating an outfit. I guess that's a security blanket, isn't it?"

It is.

A codependent person might make the spouse a sort of god of his or her life. We certainly don't recommend saying goodbye to that spouse and walking out. We do say that the spouse ought to be lifted gently from the pedestal and enjoyed for what he or she truly is: a sterling person. We're asking you to emotionally give up the unhealthy aspects of the adorer-idol relationship.

Goodbye to the Illusion That I Can Rewrite Family History

Was General George Custer a hero or a fool, a splendid officer of the United States Army or a martinet who deserved what he got? His widow worked tirelessly for many years to suppress any hint that Custer acted recklessly with his final command. Most historians today believe he was unfit for the rank he held and blundered fatally; Little Bighorn should never have happened. All Mrs. Custer's efforts came to naught. So will yours.

There are several ways clients in our counsel try to change their family history. Rarely do the clients recognize that this is what they are attempting.

The magical thinking goes like this, and hardly ever is it recognized, let alone verbalized: "If I can achieve such-and-such today, I will be fixing the problem that happened many yesterdays ago." This illusion, that the painful or unpleasant course of past childhood can be altered, forms the basis of many compulsions we find in parents.

Henry Gross is a good example. Henry came to us utterly burnt out after ten years as a pastor. The pastorate had once been his shining dream. Now he hated every minute of it. In counsel we learned that neither of his parents was a Christian. Henry's magical thinking: "If I can redeem my congregation, perhaps if I can save a thousand people, the spiritual emptiness of my youth will be filled. I will be saving my parents." He was trying to rewrite the spiritual story of his family life.

Goodbye to My Illusion That I Can Have an Omnipotent Parent

Wouldn't it be wonderful if you could always turn to someone who has all the right answers? Don't you need someone right up there with the flag and apple pie who can lead you down the right path when the way becomes confusing? And isn't it a rotten shame there is no such single human being!

There are people in our counsel who don't let the fact that human beings are fallible keep them from elevating a friend or relative to the status of demigod.

- "I'll ask Frank; he'll know. He knows everything."
- "My boss can get me out of this. He's a master at pulling the right strings."

You see, the danger in this thinking is that the adorer's boundaries fade and meld into the adoree's. Eventually, the adorer enmeshes into a person he or she perceives as godlike, but that person is fraught with human error. Carried to its logical extreme, that's what happened at Jonestown, Guiana.

Jesus Christ alone made no human error. He alone is perfect. Upon Him alone can you depend. All others will fall short, and unless your boundaries are very, very firm, you will fall with them.

How Do You Say Goodbye?

Knowing what to say goodbye to is half the battle; the other half is knowing how to do it. Here are some specifics.

1. Make an inventory. Be exact. Know precisely who or what you need to say goodbye to. For example, James Kolbin

153

inventoried his rageaholism. He knew from experience that simply telling himself, "I must quell my rages," wouldn't do a thing. Taken as a lump, an addiction or compulsion is virtually impossible to master. Broken into precise components, it's more manageable. James, therefore, made two lists:

His first list named things he would do to prevent a rage: consult this list before speaking; ask himself, "Am I really angry? Or is my anger masking some other important feeling?"; never speak without counting to twenty first; put his hands in his pockets when angry (so he would not fling them around); forbid verbal expressions like sarcasm, yelling, name-calling, and profanity.

The second list started with a reminder that it's OK to be angry and gave him alternatives to raging: tell someone why you're angry; leave the room and take deep breaths; sit down and write a letter to the offender; use the punching bag in the basement. Immediately after making his list, James went out and bought a punching bag to install in the basement.

2. Make yourself responsible to someone. This person can be a trusted friend, a pastor, a support group, or, for some, the confessional. Let that someone, whoever it is, know your problem and how you're trying to master it. Then report in periodically. Give that person blanket permission to get nosy and ask, "How's your such-and-so coming lately?" We find it best if the person trying to say goodbye to some problem or mindset calls his or her support person on a regular basis. A few moments' conversation suffices—just enough for both of you to know "all is well."

Support groups, such as Alcoholics Anonymous, Emotions Anonymous, and Adult Children of Alcoholics, are excellent aids for those with deep-seated, persistent problems. Keep this in mind, however: "No one can do it for me. But I don't have to do it alone." A prominent basketball player with the Dallas Mavericks was identified as having a drug problem. He sought treatment, returned to play, relapsed, went into treatment again, relapsed again . . . This man had the finest doctors, the best treatment centers, and a lucrative contract. His teammates, a good coach, and thousands of fans all rooted for him. He wasn't alone, but none of his friends and cohorts could do it for him. A support group won't solve your problems. It can only help *you* solve them.

3. Invoke God's help. Like support groups, God won't do it for you either, but He'll certainly enable you. Over and over, our patients express relief when we assure them that human will power is insufficient. "How many years have people told me, 'Just try harder.' I do! And it doesn't work." Don't get caught up in theological debates about whether this was what Jesus meant when He talked about His burden and His yoke. Don't worry about whether God already knows or should you ask. Put theology aside and talk to God as a little child would. In simple childlike prayer, tell Him what you need.

4. Find alternative coping mechanisms. Tailor them to your needs. A smoker switches to lollipops. A violent rage-aholic takes up stress relievers such as jogging or rowing. The recluse deliberately joins common-interest groups, such as bird-watching clubs or service clubs, in order to make acquaintances. Acquaintances? Yes. You need not gulp down the whole answer to a weighty problem at once, just as we wouldn't expect a recluse to leap right into a close friendship. An acquaintanceship is a good first step, a preparation for deeper commitment.

What hobbies and activities might help you? What relationships might you develop to complement or balance unhealthy relationships to which you're saying goodbye? Don't leave a void for mischief to jump into.

The next step toward improved health, then, is to flush away the residual pain. This step helps not only you but your children as well, for they are carrying it.

Step Four: Grieve Out the Pain

We shake our heads at the Near Eastern custom of hiring mourners to weep and wail. How phony! We sneer at the last century's Victorian preoccupation with death and all the overly sentimental schmaltz they associated with it.

Now, infinitely wise, we routinely prescribe mind-altering

drugs for the freshly widowed to ease the pain and lessen the shock. A few words at a memorial, and we quickly turn our backs on death and loss, lest it hurt too much. We do this to our detriment.

What is the alternative to grief? That bugbear "splitting it off"—ignoring, disavowing, minimizing losses that aren't minimal at all. Dr. Hemfelt likens it to the infamous Love Canal in New York, or any other toxic waste area. It doesn't go away just because it's buried. Sooner or later it will seep to the surface, or percolate down into the water supply and poison the whole place. Only grief, properly applied, can purge the toxin.

Your next step toward health, so that you can better help your children, is to grieve through all the losses of your life. Dredge them up, all of them. Catalogue them. Let them shock and anger you. That's part of it.

Keep in mind as you go, however, an insidious impediment to grieving—fear. Fears will try to undermine the process all along the way. Whalon feared expressing the emotions of grief. A person who sees himself or herself as a hero or a stoic suffers tremendous fear of being laughed at, misinterpreted, or even ignored.

A fear of retaliation might whisper, "If you let down your mask, what will others do in return?" What others do might be terribly unpleasant.

Many patients in our counsel fear getting in touch with their deepest pain. "If I start crying, I won't be able to stop." We have not yet had a patient so totally overwhelmed by nonstop grief as this fear threatens.

Most of all, people fear becoming vulnerable. "I was scared to death to take that first step," we hear. Think of a three year old on a slide. She wants the thrill of sliding down, but she's terrified of the slope. Either she climbs back down or she braces her feet against the sidewalls, slowing her descent to a gentle, jerking slip. Adults are like that. When a parent sits at the top of the slide, seeking courage to begin or continue the grief process, the unseen end yawns frighteningly far below.

Here is where a therapist, support group, or special friend

can offer invaluable aid, helping the parent down the slide while identifying and allaying fears. If you recognize these fears for what they are—artificial impediments—you can either deal with them or ignore them, at least in part. Here we go down the slide!

The well-known steps in the grief process are:

1. Shock and denial
2. Anger
3. Temporary depression
4. Bargaining and magic to get rid of it all
5. Profound sadness
6. Acceptance, resolution, forgiveness

It must all come. It may not necessarily come in that order, and parts of the process might repeat themselves. All, though, are needed.

Each major loss you must grieve and resolve. The book *Love Is a Choice*, by Dr. Robert Hemfelt, Dr. Frank Minirth, and Dr. Paul Meier can help you here. What losses are we talking about? Deaths. Divorces, both your own and your parents'. Debilitating diseases. Not only any and all addictions but also the misery and peripheral loss the addictions caused—lost love, lost happiness, lost work time, lost money, lost social standing, lost affections, to name a few.

Shock and Denial

Dr. Hemfelt worked a long time with Lida Armstrong, chipping through her denial. She refused at first to believe she still had not resolved the loss of her marriage. Hadn't she been in court often enough? Hadn't she shed enough tears? Hadn't she turned her life around sufficiently?

During her third session she repeated a protest she had made more than once before. "Dr. Hemfelt, it's not me who's the druggie. I didn't come home drunk half the time. Sure, I filed for the divorce, but it's not me who wrecked the marriage."

"I understand that," Dr. Hemfelt assured her. "When a person lives for any length of time in an unsatisfactory relationship such as your marriage was, that person is damaged also. We call it codependency."

"I know the word. But I'm not depressed."

"Are you happy?"

"Of course not! Randy's not doing his part to support the kids. I have to work and do everything else."

"Are you at peace with your divorce?"

"Randy won't let me. He keeps filing legal actions just to annoy me. I'd love to make peace."

"I'm not talking about legal action. I'm talking about yourself inside. Is your hardship, your divorce—and your ex-husband—still consuming your time and thoughts?"

"I suppose, in a way, but—"

"You're exhausted when you get home from work. Is the work itself that taxing?"

"No. It's all the other stuff I have to do."

"You're saying that all that other stuff is wearing you out even before you do it. You get home, pop a can of cola, and just sit staring at the wall a while, right? Worn out before you lift a finger at home."

"Yes, but . . ." She smiled. "That's exactly what I do. And I yell at the kids when they come around, until it's absolutely time I have to make supper."

"That's depression, too, Lida, deny it as you will. Depression is anger turned inward. You haven't properly grieved your losses, which is the only way to deal with anger. Now the anger is poisoning your whole system."

"That's crazy!" Lida fumed. "Of course I grieved. I cried rivers while we were married and oceans when we separated."

"Weeping is only one aspect of grieving. *But,*" Dr. Hemfelt said gently, "when you examine your own life and cry out, 'That can't be! No! It isn't so!' one of two conditions pertains: either you're right, and it really wasn't so, or you're in the first stage of grief—shock and denial—a necessary starting place."

The second stage of grief is anger.

Anger

Asked what anger looks like, you might reply: "Sure, I know what anger looks like. Anger looks like a big black Doberman pinscher snarling." Or, "My old man when he was boozed up. Major-league yelling and hitting." Or, "I see anger every time I get home five minutes late. It's silent and dark and brooding, a huge, heavy cloud. Sometimes she doesn't speak to me for hours."

The many faces of anger. Actually, those are only surface manifestations. Anger takes many subtle forms, some unrecognizable. Dr. Hemfelt frequently draws something like Figure 4 to show his clients where anger can go. Basically, anger can go in any of four directions. Turned inward it becomes depression, which, as you probably know, is epidemic in modern American society. Anger may explode outward, manifesting itself as that "acting out" we mentioned in Chapter 1. Jennifer Newport's hyperactive troublemaking is such behavior, as is Joey Trask's defiance. Acting out is the symptom that most frequently sends parents to counselors in frustration.

Anger also emerges outward in a subtle way not even the sufferer may recognize, as passive-aggressive behavior. An illustration of this is the case of Herb and Mabel. Mabel is, well, she's a rather demanding woman; in fact, quite a demanding woman. And Herb? He's easygoing, happy to a fault. Their daughter wasn't doing too well in junior high, and they, together with the girl, entered our counsel.

Herb's chronic tardiness became a standing joke with his support group. Herb always missed the first ten minutes. A couple of times, he never made it at all. At home he was late for dinner. He failed one month to make a house payment. Another month their electricity was cut off because he had simply neglected to take care of the bills in a timely way. His lackadaisical ways infuriated Mabel.

And that, you see, was the whole thing of it. Herb kept that smile, but his intense anger surfaced not as violent rage but as happy forgetfulness, unconsciously calculated to slap Mabel where it hurt most: right between her drill-team orderliness and her punctuality.

The only acceptable way to defuse anger is by grieving it and its root causes. Grief—a need and skill America has sadly lost—cleanses anger, eliminates it, prevents it from

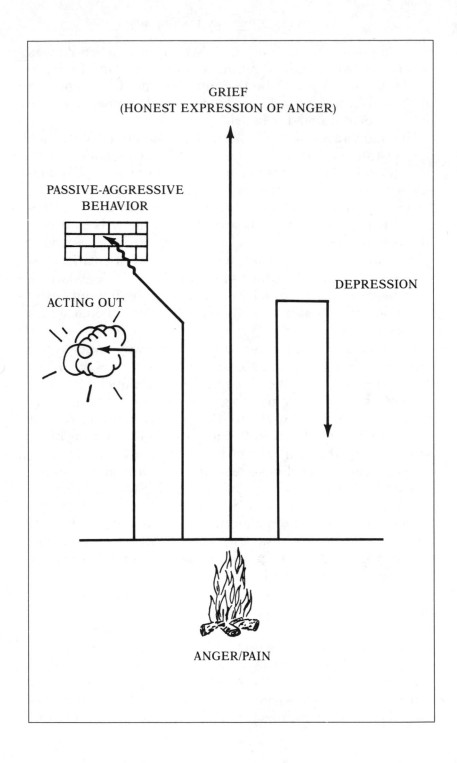

erupting somewhere else to cause trouble. Open, visible anger is a part of the grieving process.

Once past that shock, Rob Newport suffered through a terrible period of intense anger over what Alice had let herself slip into. He raged over the general unfairness of life. Just ask the kids.

"I sort of stay in my room when Dad's home," said Jennifer. "Is he always gonna be this way?"

"No," Dr. Warren assured her. "I know it's tough on you right now. It's hard on him, too, believe me. I'm sure it won't last. Hang in there. It'll get much, much better."

Beth Trask also found herself seething with anger. The more she thought about those years of denial, the way she had stuffed her feelings away and turned herself into a mindless robot, the angrier she got. Whalon in turn became angry about her anger.

He turned on her one morning at breakfast. "That's enough of this! You snap and snarl like a dog guarding a bone. I'm sick of it. From now on you're going to sweeten up."

A month earlier, Beth would have apologized profusely for her imperfection and seeming thoughtlessness, again cramming her feelings away unfelt. That was a month ago.

She sat down face-to-face with him and kept her voice as even as possible. "Have you ever noticed? Joey is not allowed to get angry. You don't like tantrums. It's not right, you say. Whenever Joey tries to express his anger you put the lid on him, always by getting angry at him for being angry. As if he weren't human like grown-ups."

"That has nothing to do with—"

"Please. I'm still speaking. You've done the same with me ever since our wedding. You are free to express anger, to rage. But I'm not supposed to have any anger. I'm certainly not supposed to rock your comfortable boat by letting it show. Those days are over, Whalon. From now on, Joey and I are going to be real people, with the same full range of emotions you so prominently display."

"You know I don't like—"

"Please don't interrupt. Anger doesn't mean we love you

any less. It doesn't mean we're not a happy family. It means we're human. I've been—"

"Of course you are. But I'd—"

"I'm not quite finished. I've been assured this won't last. And I believe it. It's not so intense now as it was a few days ago. But anger will continue to happen now and then. When it does I'm not going to bury it. We've put up with your ranting and snapping and snarling, as you call it, for years. I'm sure you're man enough to do as well." And she returned to the stove to turn his bacon.

Temporary Depression

In counsel with patients we always call this *temporary depression*. Many of the patients are already bogged in depression. "That I don't need any more of," they say. The beauty of this is that it's a healthy and natural part of grief, and it absolutely will not last.

If you are the adult child of a dysfunctional parent, you will almost certainly find blame surfacing in your thoughts. You tell yourself that whatever happened in the past must have been your fault. It's not a rational blame, but that doesn't make it any less painful. And it will intensify your depression. Be aware of it.

Bargaining and Magic

"I'm too old for magic."

No, you're not. Lida Armstrong isn't. She left the laundry for another day and played a game of Monopoly with the kids after school. She won by two thousand dollars while eating Girl Scout cookies (the shortbread ones). When they played Monopoly again on Sunday, she found herself getting out the Girl Scout shortbread cookies. Hey, it worked once! (If you *really* want to see serious magic in action among persons over age twenty-one, visit a bingo parlor sometime.) When she examined her motivations closely, Lida found herself battling other more serious problems through using magic.

- "If I only nag harder, Randy might go into treatment."
- "Maybe if I just nag less, Randy will quit causing so many problems."

- "I know. I'll make a pledge with God."
- "I now know why Sarah is so sullen, but if I change my ways, she'll be better and we won't have to go through this."
- "If I take a more forgiving attitude, I can sidestep some of this pain and travail. I just know it. It's all in the head."

In the head. Many of the patients we counsel try to intellectualize their way out of the grief process at this point. Sadness is a no-no in our society. Sadness makes those around us uncomfortable. And it certainly doesn't feel good to us. Lida, like others, wanted a quicker, less painful way out. There isn't any. There is no magic step you can take to change the people around you. They don't change until they find motivation for change within themselves.

Profound Sadness

Darla, in her twenties, came to us to master her food addictions, which had put nearly a hundred pounds on her. For years she had maintained a solid stoicism about the sexual abuse in her late childhood. She was tough. She was smart. She could handle it. We worked with her for weeks, chipping away at the denial. Her losses—of virginity, of innocence, of self-esteem—and the betrayal she endured finally broke through. Oh, did the sadness pour out! Her rhythm and tone of weeping sounded exactly like that of a six year old. When she attempted to speak between sobs, her voice was the high pitched wail of a small child.

When a person regresses like that in grieving, they are usually going back to the latest safe age they can recall. Some of our patients go into a catatonic depression, signaling that the latest time they actually felt safe was in the womb. Darla's abusive uncle joined the family when she was seven, began to talk to her about "secret things" soon thereafter, and commenced overt physical sexual abuse when she was ten.

Rob Newport had maintained a rough, terse demeanor throughout the first of our meetings. Something happened in one of the sessions and, neither of us can say what it was, broke through the tough shell. A word, a thought often does that, even though you can't even remember what it was an hour later. His anger, his secret bargaining had done its work. As the dam of his sadness broke, he whispered, "I did this, I helped do all this. And my kids . . . And Alice . . . And I . . ." He had wept privately before. Now he went public, this time with Dr. Hemfelt as his journeymate.

Acceptance, Resolution, Forgiveness

Until the buried toxins of hatred, anger, and unfelt feelings are washed out by sadness, true forgiveness cannot occur. There is no shortcut here.

In the hospital prior to her release, Alice Newport sat with Rob and Dr. Hemfelt in a joint session.

"Rob," Dr. Hemfelt asked, "can you forgive Alice?"

"Yes." He hesitated. "But I'm not sure I'll be able to make it stick the next time we get angry."

"A good answer. Let me explain this about forgiveness: to forgive does *not* mean you endorse the other person's actions. It doesn't mean you agree with what they did. Also, you don't have to forget. Of course you may if you wish, after it's been dealt with, but it's not a necessity for forgiveness. One more thing: healthy forgiveness is for your benefit even more than for the recipient. You must do this for yourself even more than for Alice."

Lida Armstrong faced a far more difficult task of forgiveness. Randy was not even beginning to deal with his drug problem or illicit lifestyle. He promised no hope for the future. Randy promised only more pain. Lida could not have forgotten if she wanted to, because Randy was continually reopening the wounds.

And it would not be in Lida's interests to forget. Herman Wouk, in his epic *War and Remembrance*, wrote, "The beginning of the end of war lies in remembrance." His premise: Should the nations forget the abuses of war, they are bound to repeat them.

Lida can spend a lifetime in anger and resentment, or she can, each day, reflect on the injustices, the anger they generate, the sadness, and then accept that it happened and forgive the transgression. Only if she resolves her problems in this way will she find peace within herself.

The fifth and final step of healing, becoming a nurturing parent to yourself, is such an important one that we will devote the next chapter to it. To see the need and wisdom of it, consider: How can you be an excellent parent for your child if you haven't learned to nurture your own needs, to be a good parent to yourself?

You as parents cannot give away to the next generation that which you do not possess. Only by grieving out the pain of your own difficult childhood and by discovering how to become a nurturing parent to yourself can you impart the gift of nurturance to the next generation.

CHAPTER 9

Reparenting the Parent

An apocryphal story begins with a young mother preparing a ham, scoring it and studding it with cloves, cutting the ends off it, and skewering pineapple rings to the top.

Her small daughter asked, "Mom? What are the cloves and pineapple for?"

"For appearance and flavor. Also, fresh pineapple juice is a natural meat tenderizer."

"Why cut the ends off?"

"Because my mother did." And she put it in the oven. Later, out of curiosity, she called her mother. "Mom? Why do you cut the ends off your ham when you bake it?"

"Because mother did. I suppose they dry out or something."

A few days later this young mother went to visit Grandma in the nursing home. She told her about the chain of questions. "Grandma, why do we cut the ends off a ham?"

The old lady laughed. "I don't know why you people do. I did because the ham was always too big for my roaster."

Cooking tips (and ham tips) aren't the only things passed from generation to generation. Parenting techniques, both the nifty tricks and the errors, do too. Hardly ever does anyone question whether some particular method works, let alone how well.

Many good books offer suggestions for dealing with parenting situations and crises. But when we talk here about nurturing yourself, we are discussing the step preceding the point where the parenting books begin. Once you learn to be a good parent to yourself (in a way, you're using yourself to practice on), you are better equipped to be a good spouse. That further solidifies the marriage bond and equips you to be an effective member of a good parenting team.

We will examine first the nuts and bolts techniques of re-parenting, as it's called, and then how to reinforce these techniques so that they become a part of your everyday life.

The Repetition Ghost

Think of this whole grieving process as a reverse trampoline. You plummet downward in the grief process and hit an emotional bottom. *Bowaaang!* Now you're rebounding, headed up. You've purged the negative, and now we'll replace it with positive. We could call this stage "establishing a new identity."

This step is essential, because you either purge and replace the negative aspects of your own childhood, or you condemn your children to repeat them.

Beth Trask shook her head. "Dr. Hemfelt, you can't believe how I hated the way my mother was so clinging. It was as if she burrowed right into me. She shared all her secrets and expected me to share all mine. She gave herself permission to come into my room any time she wanted. I even remember once saying something like, 'Mom, shouldn't you knock first?' And she said something like 'Oh, nonsense. It's only me.' And as much as I hated it, I thought that's the way things were with parents and kids. I didn't see it as something unusual or damaging."

"Today we'd call that violating your boundaries," said Dr. Hemfelt.

"What shocks me most of all is that, now that I look at my past for what it really is, I see that I've been doing that with Joey. He must hate it as much as I did. Probably more; he's a boy."

A major part of your own recovery will include new parenting techniques. Like Beth, weed out the things you remember disliking in your own childhood, knowing that you're almost certainly repeating them. And they aren't any better for your kids than they were for you.

The first phase of this step is to engage in positive self-talk.

Positive Self-Talk

Positive self-talk is simply the opposite of the negative messages you've rooted out of your past, messages unique to your situation. You alone can say what they are. People who know they've been parenting poorly have a particularly difficult time here. Alice Newport, whose prescription drug abuse galloped out of control for so long, needed a lot of positive change, a lot of positive reinforcement. People like Alice need the new message, "I can do a better job parenting," reinforced many times in many ways.

These are some of the positive self-messages adults in our counsel have had to devise for themselves. Perhaps they'll help you get started with yours.

• "I deserve to live."

Every human being can make that claim, but many codependents don't believe it down deep inside. Believe it.

• "I deserve a measure of happiness."

Persons with codependency problems feel responsible for all the ills and dysfunctions in their families (both their present families and their families of origin). Denying themselves happiness is one way in which they punish themselves for the false guilt, the imagined blame.

Lida Armstrong thought about the way her life had gone so far. "I think I'm guilty of that, Dr. Hemfelt—sabotaging my own happiness. I knew Randy had a drinking problem when I started going with him. I told myself he'd shape right up as soon as he became a family man."

"In our counsel we find that kind of situation is very common. You'd be surprised how many people constantly sabotage themselves because they agree with their lips that they deserve happiness, but they don't believe it in their hearts."

"How can I convince my heart?"

"Tell it that happiness is a part of the complete experience of living, and it's wrong to cut out part of that experience. Tell it that our own government is founded specifically for the pursuit of happiness, among other things."

"I never thought of that!"

"Bring your self-blame up to the surface, as we have been

Five Steps to
Help Yourself Grow

To nurture yourself as a parent—that is, to reparent yourself—you want to hold on to what was good and positive in your past and replace that which was negative. To do this:

- Give yourself new messages of worth. Lay it on thick. You deserve it.

- Give yourself new emotional permissions. You've been clamping lids on things that need to be released.

- Open yourself to new experiences (take healthy risks). Expanding horizons and learning to make decisions is as important to you as to your kids.

- Accept nurturance from support groups and individuals.

- Maintain your improvement through a lifelong commitment to healthy reparenting.

doing, and examine it for what it is—false guilt. That is perhaps most important. And, you've been taking another very important step already; you are thinking about where your life has gone so far. You're considering how you might have sabotaged it along the way. That insight will show you if this particular problem exists for you, and therefore if you have to strengthen the new messages you give yourself."

• "There's nothing wrong with (fill in the blank: sexuality, success, anger, me)."

Much of the early history of psychiatry focused on the issue of suppressed sexuality. Persons may similarly suppress success, sabotaging themselves as they climb their chosen ladder to achievement. A lot of people suppress anger, to their great detriment. It's not civilized or it's not appropriate or it's threatening to others or it's not Christian—so many reasons to hide anger.

All these problems have a common source: the person believes, in either head or heart, that he or she is wrong. Be very careful to draw the proper line between the thing itself—sexuality, success, anger, or other things—and the fault of wrongly using it. Sexuality is right when expressed with tenderness and respect within the context of marriage; success is right when its power is used beneficently; anger serves us well when it fuels change for the better.

• "I deserve close communion with God, not because of my worth, but because He loves me and wants that. His love, even if nothing else did, gives me value."

Christians with codependency problems sometimes get hung up on a performance-only relationship with God. We try to lead our patients to a more open father-child relationship with the heavenly Father, in which human beings are received with love simply because He loves them. Never do we condone sin, but we do distinguish between the act and the actor.

• "God wants me to accept His forgiveness."

"I should also forgive myself. I can do that. I can!" But it's very hard until guilt has been dealt with through grieving.

• "It's all right for me to take a position of authority, particularly with my minor children. In fact, I'm supposed to."

The Kolbins needed this message. James flew into wild rages, true; but in between times he was wishy-washy and nonauthoritative. Until the kids pushed him into a rage, he let them get away with anything. Melanie was very nearly as bad.

"How can I change?" Melanie wailed. "I've always been like this, even when I was a baby-sitter in high school."

Dr. Hemfelt replied, "You're not alone. We constantly counsel parents who have never made that positive self-statement. First you must know you're ready to accept loving authority over your children."

"For their sake, yes. I'm ready."

"Take the day a minute at a time. I know you've heard that advice before. It works here too."

"You mean, when I tell Gerald no, then I back it up."

"That's right. Case-by-case basis, from incident to incident throughout the day. It's going to be hard at first. The children have to get used to a whole new philosophy of being parented. To keep your strength up, you must constantly give yourself the positive message, 'I am the person who must help them learn good discipline by modeling. I can do it! I am supposed to assume the authority in this home during the day.'"

"It's going to be hard. You don't know Regina."

"I understand. Not just Regina. All three. Kids never give their parents any slack; kids push parents to the limit. Be glad they're testing their boundaries, because testing boundaries identifies and strengthens them."

And Finally: Maintenance

This final stage in the building of a new you also varies from person to person. Most people with serious parenting problems will find it very helpful to join and use a support group. An appropriate support group for this healing need is *not* the PTA or other service organization. Codependents by nature want to save the world and help everybody. You need an organization that succors you, not the other way around.

You are seeking nurturance, not another opportunity to serve. Join PTA as you wish, but look also for a parenting group that can reinforce your new decisions, attitudes, and behaviors. Examples are AlAnon, Parents Anonymous, Families Anonymous, Codependents Anonymous, and others. Find them in your phone book, or consult *Love Is a Choice*.

What you need is a family outside your family. Just as the nuclear family is the source of nurturing for its children, so your surrogate support-group family will nurture the fledgling new you.

This is the heart of reparenting. In a very real sense you need your own parent, a healthy noncodependent friend and confidant, who can nurture you so that you have the resources to nurture your children. This is a person you can go to for advice, for a few reassuringly honest words: "You're doing well with this aspect, but you still need to work on that aspect."

We normally recommend that you do not turn to immediate family members for this aspect of reparenting. The immediate family is, literally, too close to you in several ways. They know you too well to accept change quickly ("Oh, that's just Louie; Louie's always gonna be that way."). If you have codependency problems, it is almost certain other family members do too. Immediate family members may well have their own personal reasons to keep you the way you always have been. So it is generally best to look outside the immediate circle of family.

Lida Armstrong did not go to her mother, even though Mom lived right beside them in their duplex. Mom was developing too dependent a relationship on them; she'd make a poor journeymate.

Beth Trask didn't use her parents or in-laws either. Again, those people were too close to understand well what she needed. She went to a friend in the church who had a daughter Joey's age.

Alice Newport developed several close friendships in her support group, but those people were all at the same stage of growth as she. She chose as a recovery sponsor an older member of her support group whom she regarded highly, a woman who had gone through prescription drug abuse herself five years before.

Finally, keep in mind that grieving is a natural part of living and a necessary part of healing. Recycle through the grieving process as needed to deal with losses past and present.

Remember at the very end that you are doing this not just for your biological children but for the emotional child inside you, the forgotten sector, the lost child.

Now that you've explored your own childhood, let's look at what Dr. Warren does as he helps children answer the next question in their recovery process: "Who am I in my family?"

In this recovery journey, we must move back and forth across the three-generational chessboard: my childhood, my adulthood, my child's needs.

CHAPTER 10

The Child: Who Am I in My Family?

Melanie Kolbin was refilling her neighbor Jeanne's coffee cup as seven-year-old Regina came slamming in the front door. Jeanne jumped so suddenly she almost spilled coffee all over the kitchen table.

"I see school is out." Jeanne smiled self-consciously. "I guess I'm not real used to little kids."

"Mommy!" came Regina's high-pitched, whiny voice from the living room. "Vic is scribbling in my coloring book!"

Victor's thin little four-year-old voice howled. He began to scream angrily.

Two-year-old Gerald scrambled up into Melanie's lap.

Regina came running into the kitchen. She slapped her open coloring book onto Melanie's knees. "Look what he did to it!"

Behind her, Victor came barreling in, still screaming. He made a wild lunge for the coloring book. As Regina yanked it away, she accidentally hit Gerald in the mouth. Gerald started screaming.

Jeanne rose hastily. "I really must get going, Melanie. It was so nice chatting with you."

"Wait, Jeanne, please!" Melanie clapped a hand on Jeanne's arm. "Stop it!" she shrieked. "Just stop it! All three of you!" She dropped her voice. "Please don't go yet, Jeanne. Get out of here, Regina! Out! Go change into your play clothes. No, Victor! Cut that out. Nobody gets the coloring book. It stays on the table."

Regina didn't leave, but at least she quit arguing. She whined, "I want some cookies."

"Then go get some. Get a couple for Victor too. Just shut up! All of you!" She sat back, her nerves dancing on a razor's edge.

Victor climbed on a chair and up on the table, straining far enough to grasp the coloring book and pull it to himself. He snatched it up and scooted out to the living room.

Gerald's roar abated to a whimper. He squirmed in her lap.

"Jeanne . . ." Melanie took a deep breath and looked her neighbor in the eye. "Jeanne, you can't stand my kids, can you?"

Jeanne opened her mouth and closed it again. "I'm sorry, Melanie. It's true. They're totally out of control. It's a madhouse here."

Melanie took refuge in a lie. "But they're not all that worse than anyone else's."

Jeanne grimaced. "Melanie, I don't know how to answer gently. I—well, look at Regina. You asked her to change her clothes. She didn't. You asked her to give her brother a cookie. She didn't do that either. You haven't bothered to make her obey. Apparently the book is Regina's, but you don't seem upset that Victor took it."

"It's only a coloring book."

"But it's not *his* coloring book. A moment ago you told Victor no one would have it. He took it just now and you didn't reprimand him. All kids fight sometimes, but yours fight constantly. Except Gerald. He clings. There are no boundaries here, Melanie."

"Boundaries?"

"Limits. Lines. The line between obeying and disobeying doesn't exist here. Personal possessions represent another kind of boundary, between mine and yours. It doesn't seem to exist either. Gerald has no boundary at all. He just sort of meshes into yours, as if he were a part of you. I can't . . . I'm sorry, Melanie. I've said too much already. I really have to go now." And Jeanne, much flustered, made a hasty exit.

In the living room, Regina started shouting as Victor let out a keening wail. Gerald wriggled off Melanie's lap, heading for the cookies. And Melanie began to cry.

When Dr. Warren works with parents to help them in their role as journeymate, he talks to them about the developmental tasks children must make at each stage of growth. These tasks mold children's identities and serve as opportunities for them to discover who they are and how they fit into the world. The kids' boundaries protect their developing identities.

"The secret of growing up," says Dr. Warren, "is for a child to establish the proper boundaries and discover his or her own identity. If parents understand the necessary growth steps in each phase of their child's development, they can help the child mature successfully."

In this chapter we will look at the appropriate tasks a child must complete in each developmental stage to establish the proper boundaries between himself or herself and other members of the family. The question children unconsciously ask themselves is: "Who am I in my family?" or "What are my boundaries in relationship to my mom and dad, to my brothers and sisters?"

Picture a glass full of milk. The milk is the child's identity, the glass the boundaries protecting that identity. If the glass is cracked or broken, the milk inside is lost. In the same way, if a child's boundaries are broken or nonexistent, the precious identity inside is lost.

On the other hand, if the glass is closed tightly by a lid, the milk cannot be drunk and therefore has no purpose. It sours, unused. In the same way, if a child's boundaries are too thick, the gift of that identity can never be shared with others in the family. Neither can other family members penetrate those heavy boundaries to help the child.

Boundaries. Invisible lines that protect the special identity God has given every child. Dr. Warren's ultimate goal in counseling is to help children discover this unique identity and see themselves as God sees them, with both strengths and weaknesses.

After we've identified the growth steps, we will watch Dr. Warren counsel children who have not completed those steps properly. The journeymate-parent can use these same techniques to help any child complete the tasks within each phase.

Appropriate Boundaries

How do you build a skyscraper? Shave down to bedrock and lay your foundation. Put in the basement, which is probably the parking garage. Pause momentarily to wonder why they put the hollow, wide-open spaces—a parking garage—beneath the heavy superstructure. Build your first floor, with the workmen in bright yellow hard hats scurrying in and out.

You might put up a few more floors by working from the ground, but eventually you need a crane positioned on top of the work. The crane reaches down, lifting everything from ground level up to the floor in progress. When that story is completed, the crane literally jacks itself up a story and builds the next layer around its stilted feet.

Once the fourteenth story, for instance, is securely in place, the crane stands upon that floor to lift itself to the fifteenth-story level. Should the fourteenth floor be improperly built, or structurally unsound in some way, the fifteenth and all subsequent floors—and the crane itself—stand in peril of collapsing.

A psychologist watching a skyscraper's construction might say it is *epigenetic,* which means that the soundness and integrity of the upper layers depend upon the soundness and integrity of the layers beneath. In just the same way, the growth tasks of a developing child are epigenetic: each task is built upon a foundation of all the tasks previously completed.

The process of growing up requires the child to complete certain tasks, attach in certain kinds of bonds, and establish certain specific boundaries. In a healthy family these tasks, bonds, and boundaries fall naturally into line. In codependent and broken families, tasks, bonds, and boundaries are disrupted. When a growth step is damaged or wrenched askew, just like the skyscraper, everything that comes after will be damaged. If the damage of a missed step is great enough, the structure—the adult child—may well topple under its own weight.

In the end a well-made skyscraper assumes a strong identity. The Empire State Building. The Transamerica Building. The Sears Tower. The child's goal is also to achieve a strong personal identity. The child cannot establish identity without good boundaries. Conversely, the child needs identity in order to build sound boundaries. Left to his or her own devices, the child could never pull this off. But with healthy parents to provide appropriate boundaries and a healthy family to loan the child identity, as it were, the child possesses the tools to complete the tasks and bondings and emerge as a solid, happy adult.

As we explore these tasks and bonds, think about your children and your own childhood. How do your children reflect these tasks and bonds? What might they have missed? Picture the skyscraper rising floor by floor.

To make the following explorations more graphic, let's illustrate the child—yours or your own childhood—with an identity figure. The child starts in infancy with no identity to speak of, a hollow figure. Let us also use the figure's outline to show appropriate boundaries, broken for children with uncertain boundaries, perhaps double lines on a child who erects boundaries much too thick for the occasion.

Infants' Identity, Tasks, Boundaries

Identity: Fuzzy at Best

The thread that spins out the child's identity and relationships with the family begins in earliest infancy. Boundaries are fuzzy at this time; the baby's identity figure, empty. An infant's boundaries can be sketched as dotted lines, since the baby's identity comes from the family. Baby equals family, in fact.

Lida Armstrong realized this one day as she talked with Dr. Warren after her daughter's weekly counseling session.

"I remember when Sarah was just a tiny baby. She was serious then, it seemed. Didn't laugh a whole lot. Almost literally slept with her eyes open. She wasn't fussy, but she wasn't pleasant either." Lida handed Dr. Warren an old photo cube. "We were a family then." She sighed wistfully.

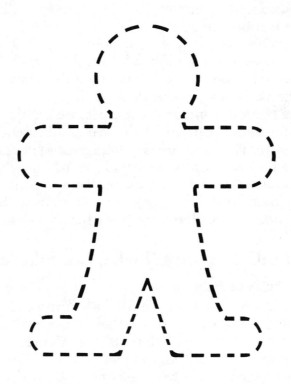

INFANT

Dr. Warren nodded. "Sarah as an infant was more deeply a member of the family than she would ever be again. We believe that infants can feel their membership in the family even before they feel any personal identity."

"Dr. Hemfelt was talking about identity. I hadn't thought about it that way; Sarah derived all her identity from Mommy and the family, right?"

"Exactly. I trust Dr. Hemfelt has shown you his gingerbread man identity figure. The baby's is empty. Any identity it enjoys is someone else's."

The Infant's Tasks and Boundaries

Why do babies cry immediately upon birth? You're squeezed like toothpaste out of a warm, comfortable home, somebody's about to do an Apgar test on you without your permission, you've just been swatted on the buttocks, and already you owe the government $6,493! Crying to fill his or her lungs is one of the few duties demanded of the youngest. The newborn's boundaries wrap in close around. The baby's horizons extend only as far as the milk supply.

The infant's duties are elemental: to express needs, to breathe, to grow. Yet even this tender child has a task. In a baby's first moments and first months the major task is to learn trust. Trust is the foundation of all future relationships, the solid base of all the rest of the skyscraper. As the baby's physical needs are met, the child gradually forges a powerful bond with mother.

Learning to Trust

Melanie Kolbin sat in Dr. Warren's office musing about Gerald's infancy. "He didn't just get this way lately; he's always been like this. He won't let me out of his sight. He screams if I leave the room and just keeps screaming. It's so exasperating. I don't use sitters anymore. They refuse to sit with him a second time; I even offer to pay double."

"You say from the very beginning. Describe what was going on in your life during his first two months."

"In my life? Well, uh, I came home from the hospital and, uh . . ." She frowned. "Not much. I was on medication a long time for a severe postnatal depression. James was having some problems at work. He's a neat person, James. I mean, he likes everything proper and neat and clean. Extremely orderly. And he had this supervisor who's a kind of casual slob. They didn't get along. But that wouldn't affect the baby."

Yes, it did, in several ways. The one that we're concerned with here is the way that, between James's preoccupation and Melanie's depression, infant Gerald's needs were met irregularly; sometimes quite well, sometimes not at all, sometimes tardily. Experience said, "I cannot depend upon others for the needs I can't meet myself." The baby never learned to trust.

Yet that task is the essential ground floor of the child's later identity (we'll show you how to build that floor in the next stage, if it was neglected in infancy). The thread of the baby's identity grows stronger as the child becomes a toddler.

The Toddler's Identity

When the child starts walking, an awakening concept of "Me!" expresses itself in a brand new word: "No!" The toddler's identity figure now possesses a very solid outline and is beginning to fill in with the discovery of his or her individualness. The parent of a two year old will be quick to tell you that the child is developing a little too much individualness.

Yet that's the toddler's most important task. The temper tantrum, as much as Mom and Dad bemoan it, is one way this youngster begins to establish some autonomy. The age pejoratively called the "terrible two's" is simply that time when a child first begins to test boundaries. Is Mommy or Daddy's "No" really no? How far can I go? Who's in charge here (I want to be!)? The tumultuous two's are a prelude to the heady exultation, "I am!"

Children bound out to explore their identity, yet they are intimately connected to Mommy. They begin to experiment while still safely attached. We call it tethering, for it's just

TODDLER

like a tetherball on a cord. At this stage the parent wants to avoid either cutting the tether or making it into a short chain. Preventing the child's exploration and discovery is the short chain error. To put down no boundaries, to let the child explore anything and everything without limits in a free-spirit attitude—the error Melanie Kolbin was making—is cutting the cord.

A child needs safe, definite limits in which to begin a life-time of discovery.

Then there is Gerald Kolbin, the two year old who panics if Mommy leaves him. Lack of identity for him has become a problem, for by his age, a toddler ought to have a definite sense of self. With this sense of self, of separateness, comes an acceptance of personal responsibility. The healthy toddler is not too young to learn, "I have some measure of responsibility over my own actions."

Gerald is learning, though. One moment he sat on Melanie's lap, and the next moment he squirmed to be let down.

Gerald's dad, James, watched impatiently. "Can't that kid decide what he wants?"

"Actually," Dr. Warren suggested, "he's doing exactly that."

"Deciding what he wants?"

"Making different decisions and testing the results, yes. To put it in technical terms, he's experimenting with extremes in an attempt to find the balance between autonomy and dependence. And he's beginning to develop his own identity. He's learning that he can control some things."

"How do we help him so we can get this phase over with?"

Dr. Warren chuckled. "Interesting way to look at it. The first and best thing you can do is try to look at life more from his perspective. Which is a good rule for dealing with all children, incidentally. Remember first that everything he encounters and feels is brand-new. He doesn't understand, for example, what winter and summer are because he's not yet experienced enough of them."

"Never thought of that. The kid's viewpoint."

"Small children aren't capable of moderation. Gerald especially will see only black and white, though it's true of Regina also. These wild extremes of clinging and breaking away are normal and necessary. Understand, too, that in the very young, such as Gerald here, 'individual' means nothing. If Mommy leaves, I'm annihilated. Short separations teach him that *Mom and Dad can leave me and come back. I'm not abandoned. I'm still me.* You can ease the trauma of separations with lots of reassurance beforehand and lots of hugs and happy talk upon reunion."

Melanie shook her head. "I just get so sick of the screaming, I haven't left him for months. Sometimes I think I hate him. Sometimes I think he hates me."

"You made an excellent observation. Another quirk in Gerald's thinking we call splitting."

"You don't mean splitting off, do you?"

"No. Splitting, as in dividing in two. This division is when the toddler sees Mommy as either all good or all bad. Good: Mommy gives me what I need, feeds me, holds me, plays with me; therefore she loves me and therefore I love her. But wait! Bad: Mommy just got mad at me, she failed to give me what I want, therefore she doesn't love me. Therefore I don't love her."

"I see!"

"So do I." James shifted in his chair. "If it's illogical and simplistic, Gerald will think it."

"Ah. Remember that we adults do exactly the same thing on a grander scale. Think of all the theologies that start out, 'If ours were truly a loving God He wouldn't let anyone perish.' Mommy is so much more complex than all-good/all-bad, and God infinitely more so."

"When does Gerald stop seeing me as two persons?" Melanie asked as she hauled Gerald back up on her lap.

"Still in toddlerhood. He eventually fuses the concept of a dichotomous, fickle caregiver into a single wise and loving Mommy. Gerald realizes, 'I don't have two mommies. Just as I have two ideas in me—yes and no—Mommy has two ideas in her.'

"And the same process occurs with Daddy. In fact, that fusion is a crucial milestone in Gerald's development. You see, boundaries become clear. I am me, Mom is Mom, Dad is Dad, and these siblings are occasionally a pain in the diaper. Gerald has found an identity of his own."

James nodded. "So why do we get so many boundary disputes?"

"Testing who's boss. The one thing you don't want to do is damage the boundary. It's pretty fragile."

"How would I damage it?" Melanie let Gerald down to the floor.

"For example, Gerald is throwing a tantrum. You say, 'Gerald, stop acting that way.' He says 'No!' and keeps on with it."

"Sounds familiar." Melanie grimaced.

"If you, Melanie, say 'Gerald, if you love me, you'll quit that!' you blow the boundary demarcation. Gerald was only testing his limits, a normal developmental task; love and lack of it is not at issue. So the issue of whether Gerald loves Mommy is something he shouldn't have to think about. All he needs to know is that Mommy loves Gerald. The adage 'It's not the child's place to be there for the parent' is as true at this age as any other. This gives Gerald freedom to be a child. You can't tolerate the tantrum—the line must be drawn—but the issue is boundaries of behavior, not boundaries of love."

"I see. I don't know how you guessed, but I do that sort of thing," Melanie admitted.

"You're the one who sets Gerald's boundaries—not so large that he feels abandoned or confused, or so tight and close he's strictly an extension of your will."

"I still don't know where the behavior line is, I don't think."

"I don't like to make specific comments because different families will want different parameters. Just know that Gerald's job is not to be good all the time and to avoid upsetting Mom and Dad."

"Well, he's certainly doing his job." James grabbed for Gerald as the toddler clambered from Mommy's lap to Daddy's.

"You see why, don't you? If he were good all the time, he couldn't test the boundaries and find his place. And that's his primary task."

Because of many problems in the Kolbin household,

and the high level of tension and irritability, Gerald didn't learn those important early lessons of trust, as we noted earlier. That only added to his tasks as a toddler. If his boundaries were not expanded appropriately now, his development would be all the harder as he grew. Therefore, we recommended to the Kolbins (now that they were aware of the problems in these lower levels of the skyscraper) to shore up the lower floors by doing the following to encourage trust:

- Meeting needs in a timely way.
- Talking and making your love and care obvious.
- Hugging when hugs are requested or indicated.
- Encouraging exploration: "Let's take a walk." "Let's see how many things we can find in the backyard. I'll go with you," or "Here's my favorite picture book. Want to read?"

At the same time the toddler begins to establish an identity, the child realizes he or she is dependent on both Mom and Dad. Now the toddler begins to seriously bond to the father as well as the mother. Daddy becomes more than a shadow in the background or a substitute when Mommy goes to the grocery store. The concept of family, grasped intuitively by the infant, becomes a practical reality to the toddler. Siblings have to pay attention to the toddler; now mobile, this tiny individual can run roughshod through their lives. He or she belongs.

In our imagined dollhouse, the toddler has earned a room of his or her own, with firm walls that both connect the toddler and separate the tiny person from the parents' rooms. The toddler still does not relate outside the family much; but inside, he or she is now quite at home. The toddler has begun the difficult task of learning to balance autonomy with dependency on other members of the family, a task that will occupy the child for the rest of the growing up process.

The Weighty Tasks of Preschoolers (3–5)

Parents usually claim that after two, three is a breeze, and it's not by chance. Boundaries are now comfortably in place.

Two year olds have learned the physical boundaries of their home—where they may play safely, where they must never wander. They know by now who's boss, and they're comfortable with that . . . most of the time. They have a name and a separate identity. With the first few floors of their high-rise securely framed, they may safely grow.

At one time we thought preschoolers vegetated, so to speak, growing physically, but not much more. Not so. We've discovered that the tasks they must master and the bonds they must forge shape the rest of their lives. The three to five year olds must discover the details of their bodies, figure themselves out cognitively, and work out their sexual role in life. Quite a tall order for a preschooler!

Preschoolers discover these details of their bodies—how strong they are, what they can do, what the various parts are like, almost exclusively by play and exploration. Manipulating blocks and other similar toys gives them insight into the physical universe and into their own capabilities. Children from outside enter their world and they, with Mom, venture out beyond the relationships within the dollhouse. There's a big world full of people out there. Preschoolers are soon up to their eyeballs in scary discovery and in the world of fantasy.

Fantasy

Beth Trask sat in session, shaking her head as she talked about Joey during his preschool years. "Spiderman. Joey got so into Spiderman. He spent hours trying to walk on the walls. I didn't mind Spiderman too much, but Blitz . . . Blitz had to go. That just wasn't normal. That was too much."

"Who was Blitz?"

"His imaginary friend. You know the Calvin and Hobbes cartoon with the stuffed tiger? That was Blitz only it was supposedly a person. I did everything but pull out a gun and shoot Blitz to get Joey to give up that nonsense. I was afraid of schizophrenia or something; you know, where the personality splits. It was that bad with him."

"How old was he?"

"Around four."

PRESCHOOL

Joey at four, replete with Spiderman and Blitz, was demonstrating how preschoolers figure themselves out cognitively. What seems like fantasy and nonsense to adults is simply the child balancing fantasy against reality, a natural and necessary process. The reality sifts out as the fantasy tells children something nonverbal about themselves. Spiderman can walk up walls; gravity prevents Joey from doing that. But it's fun to imagine. Things in imagination may or may not happen in real life. The thought processes ramble on, weaving in and out, defining the world and the child.

In the process, Joey was discovering not only himself but others. He was working out great mysteries of life—how other people are and how things happen. We adults are so accustomed to understanding the hard realities of the world around us that we cannot recall that tender age when it was all brand-new.

From this age and well into grade school, youngsters like Joey use fantasy extensively in the task of sorting out themselves and their world. Parents tend to disregard little-child fantasy. Some may condemn it as being untruth.

"Now you know that's not true! You do want to always tell the truth, don't you?"

Well, no, not especially. Reality to a child this age is highly subjective and truth is what you make it. Fantasy and imagination weigh quite as heavily as fact. With time and maturity, they will draw a stable line between fact and fiction. At this age the line, while clear, shifts easily. Parents can subtly control where the shifting line rests through interacting with the child and through play.

Fantasy. It's the path to reality, since children do not figure out the world by direct observation or by parents' lectures. The part of the child's brain that processes these functions is not well enough developed yet. But the creative part of the brain—that's a different story.

Consider the effect of a simple fairy tale such as "Little Red Riding Hood." Even when punished for lying, the child fails to understand that falsehood is wrong. But that child knows the wolf is very mean and very, very wrong to lie to Little Red Riding Hood. And that wolf is very, very, very wrong to try to eat the little girl and her dear old granny. Right is brilliantly right and wrong is clearly wrong—in story. This is why we use play so extensively for communicating abstracts.

Lecturing also does practically nothing to instill a sense of responsibility at this age. Chores, however (such as keeping his or her room in order), and personal skills (such as handling velcro shoe closures, if not laces) do. They serve another purpose also. They are accomplishments. And accomplishments help build identity.

Lecturing may not work but play does. Dr. Warren suggested that Melanie Kolbin try some play therapy of her own with Victor.

"Hi!" Melanie picked up one of those people made out of a round wooden bead and a wooden-block body. She put it in a wooden-block-with-a-hole-in-it car. "I'm driving up to your filling station to put gas in my car. May I?"

Victor set his little wooden person in his own wooden car. He drove toward the gas station they made from a few blocks. "Uh huh. Do you want the fancy gas or the cheap gas?"

"I don't know. What kind does Daddy buy?" Melanie asked.

"He buys the cheap gas. Here. Use this." Victor manipulated Melanie's car, putting it beside the upright block pump.

"Thank you. Glug glug glug glug. There. I put the gas in. I take care of my car myself because I'm big. Big people take care of their own things."

"Uh huh. Now I'm gonna get gas. Here I come." Victor drove his own car to the pump. "Hummmmm. Mommy? How come when Daddy takes care of the car he gets oil all over the driveway?"

Identity: "I Will Grow Up!"

The preschooler's identity is now rich enough that he or she can make an amazing discovery: "I won't be little forever. I can see myself growing. I'll grow up." With that revelation comes a most curious and necessary twist of

191

childhood thinking. That twist showed up bright and clear in the Kolbin family.

Melanie Kolbin described the situation to Dr. Warren. "Victor, our four year old, has become very attached to me. Not just attached. Possessive. He physically pushes his daddy away from me. We're watching TV on the sofa and Victor squeezes between James and me. He wants to sit beside me in the car. Last week he said he was going to marry me and James just blew up. I don't know how to handle it."

"Would you say Victor was acting like James's rival?"

"That's it exactly!"

"Yes, that is it exactly."

Curious and most necessary is this brief, intense rivalry that happens to the preschooler. First comes the revelation that he will not remain a preschooler forever; he will be an adult someday. Next comes the decision that when he grows up he will marry Mommy. (Girls decide to marry Daddy.) He may well become intensely jealous of his rival. But then he intuitively observes that Mommy is firmly married to Daddy. That marital unit is not only strong, it is very safe for the child for this reason: with Mommy being Mommy and Daddy being Daddy, and with the marriage solidly in place, the child is free to be a child. The outer dollhouse wall can stand up to any gale. Subtly, unconsciously, the child's determination shifts. He cannot marry Mommy; she's unavailable; so he will marry someone like Mommy.

The process seems so simplistic, yet it is critically important, as we shall see. The preschooler has begun the important task of answering not only the question "Who am I?" but also "Who am I going to be?" Without some answer to these questions, the rest of the preschooler's growth will wobble dangerously.

The Tasks and Identity of Grade-Schoolers (6–12)

On the African veldt, beneath a burning sun, lion cubs scrimmage and fight, then fall asleep draped all over each other. Under the back porch, the latest litter of puppies scrimmage and fight, then curl up together. Parents see their children squabble viciously with each other and cannot understand how the kids can be best friends with their enemies five minutes later.

The grade-schooler—we'll call this age group "she" for convenience, but boys are quite the same—is a competitive, sometimes belligerent, explorer. Probably no one noticed that her boundaries have enlarged immensely. She dresses herself, may even get her own breakfast. She sallies forth alone into the world. She spends time in school and more time with non-family members after school. She develops powerful bonds with like-sex friends outside the family. The grade-schooler needs to succeed in three areas now, two of them brand-new to her: to look successful to her parents, to be successful in the eyes of her peers, and to be accepted by an adult or adults other than the parents—a teacher, for instance. Her boundaries are being established and tested in other arenas now. All the squabbling and sparring serves this child the same purpose that it serves lion cubs and puppies. It answers the important question: How do I compare with others? What are my strengths? My weaknesses? The answers to these questions help her to further define who she is. Again the child is facing the all-important task of learning more about herself, which she began way back when she was a toddler. If she did not complete the beginning of that task then, she will not be able to reach greater understanding now.

Nine-year-old Jennifer Newport had problems in this developmental level which we learned as we counseled her family. Her older brother Brian made all A's; her mediocre report card did not impress her parents. In some ways she reflected her father, who tended toward bombast and, at times, boastfulness. She bragged outrageously—"My dad owns the Dallas Cowboys"—so much so that her classmates laughed at her. She made no firm friends her own age, and her bragging and hyperkinetic activity turned off the adults as well. Because her foundation of trust was shaky from the very beginning, she clung to Mommy in strange situations, at times reacting to so simple a new situation as a different

GRADE SCHOOL

Sunday school class with wailing and panic. Jennifer was getting none of the nurturing she needed from parents, peers, and other adults.

There is a dark side to answering the question "Who am I?" By comparing oneself to others, the grade-schooler may find that she does not like the answer. One day in a class of twenty third-graders, the captains choose sides for kick ball. They pick the best and strongest first. Then they pick others, first this team, then that team, one at a time . . . . Two children are left. The next to the last is chosen. And our third-grader is the last. Nobody wants to be last.

For every winner there is a loser. Much as adults detest seeing children sorted and categorized through competition, it is a necessary growth step. The grade-schooler cannot answer the question "Who am I?" until she knows her own strengths and weaknesses, for that particular combination makes her unique. "I may not be able to kick a ball well, but I'm a good speller, and the kids cheer me for that," perceives the grade-schooler.

Competitions can be controlled. When there is genuine peril, such as when a child is hopelessly outgunned by the class bully, she must be protected. But in the tussling inherent in this age group lies the key to healthy self-realization, even for the losers. Natural competition cannot be sidestepped, or an important step in the growth process will be stunted. The next stages of development will have been built on shaky ground.

One other thing about the grade-schooler: It is now that she must realize that life is inherently unfair. Consider these complaints Jennifer made:

"Aw, Mom, Brian [age sixteen] gets to stay up. Why can't I?"

"My teacher always picks Jeff to erase the board because he can reach higher. I could stand on something."

"How come Marjie's mom lets her, and I can't?"

"You spent all that time with Brian and none with me!"

In counsel we suggest that parents offer justice instead of fairness. In the example above, Brian happened to need the extra time spent on him. Jennifer should be assured that when she needs it, extra time will be given her also. Fairness cheats as often as it benefits. If Jennifer and Brian go to bed at the same time, Jennifer isn't getting enough rest and Brian is unfairly sent to bed before he needs to. Much as children continue to complain about unfairness, they can grasp the actuality that what may seem on the surface to be "fair" is not the best for them.

As a bottom line, we advise parents to assure each child that they are doing what is best for that little person now and in the future. Each child is an individual with unique needs that will be met, and "fairness" is not always the best way to meet them.

Identity and the Early Adolescent

The boys-are-scum girl takes up boy watching. Your twelve-year-old son comes home with one ear pierced. Telephone receivers become surgically implanted to sides of heads. Study sessions mix algebra and necking in unequal proportions. Malls become the native habitat of a kid who five years ago whined continuously when Mom dragged him from store to store.

"Ah, to be young again!" Don't you believe it!

The early adolescent takes a giant step when he begins to depend less upon his parents for his primary support and more upon his peer group.

Some parents, like Beth Trask, live in terror of that peer group. "What are those kids teaching my Joey?" she moaned.

"Every child must make this change," Dr. Warren replied, "regardless of its dangerous possibilities. I can give you this assurance, however: It's not so much what Joey is learning, which may be minimal, but how well Joey is growing. We call it individuating. Becoming your own person. Moreover, his allegiance goes to the group as a whole, not to individuals. That's why he says, 'I want to think for myself,' and then thinks and dresses exactly like his friends. Emotionally he's not quite capable yet of one-on-one supportive peer relationships."

EARLY TEEN

"Oh yes, he is." Beth grimaced knowingly. "Barry Gardner. He's the Young Life leader; Joey went to Young Life Friday nights. Joey idolized Barry. Whatever Barry said or did, that was gospel, literally."

"For example?"

"When Joey began losing interest in church, Whalon explained the importance of worship, over and over. Fell on deaf ears. Then Barry mentioned it once and all Joey could talk about was how important worship is. That kind of thing."

"Could we call Joey's fixation on Barry an infatuation?"

"Frankly, doctor, I'm afraid so. A boy with a crush on a man. That just terrified me. Naturally Whalon wouldn't permit that kind of thing to continue. I mean, Barry is too immature himself to be a youth leader, and Whalon told Joey so. But Joey didn't listen, as usual, so Whalon made him quit going to Young Life."

Beth and Whalon Trask did not understand an essential growth step in early adolescents. With the parents taking a secondary role and the peer group assuming ascendancy, there is a void; the child still instinctively needs interaction with a person, not a bunch. That interaction takes form in a massive, nonsexual attachment. The object of this temporary infatuation may be an entertainment figure or athlete, but most usually it is a person the child knows: a teacher, the older sibling of a friend, whatever—of either gender. The feelings last only a short time in all their glorious, painful intensity. Then this first taste of attachment outside the family fades, leaving the early adolescent confused, perhaps, but a bit wiser.

Because Beth and Whalon were overly enmeshed in Joey, wanting to keep him as he was, they, and Whalon in particular, felt threatened by Joey's relationship with a young man. We find this frequently in counsel. When Whalon broke off the relationship he so feared, he inadvertently cut off an important growth step in Joey's life.

Dr. Warren told Beth Trask, "You must remember that relationships outside the family are very new to Joey. He's experimenting, groping, finding his way. It's all a part of building a healthy identity and good boundaries."

"I don't think I understand this identity and boundaries business. Or maybe, what I think they are isn't the same as what you think they are."

Dr. Warren smiled. "Well put. My identity is all the little packets of information I've learned about myself over time. What I can do, what I cannot, what I like, my physical strengths and limitations and on and on. Call those packets of information ponies. My personal boundary is the corral in which those ponies are kept. The corral and the ponies grow as I grow. If outside circumstances keep my corral from growing, the ponies cannot grow. If—"

"What would keep a corral—a boundary—from growing?"

"Oh, for example, I very commonly see cases where the parents are too protective; they don't let the child step out and explore. If my boundary is too weak, fallen down in places, the ponies will wander off; then I'll experience doubt about my identity. Or my ponies will get mixed up with those of someone else who also has weak, fallen-down boundaries. We call that enmeshment; the identities become confused."

"Strong fences make good neighbors. So the stronger the boundaries . . ."

"Not necessarily. A child may erect boundaries so thick that new ponies cannot be brought in. If any ponies die, and we do lose information about ourselves when circumstances change, the herd grows weaker. No new blood coming in. Joey has adopted ponies you don't like. My job is to learn why he chose those ponies and whether he really wants them."

Those Imperfect Parents

Around late grade school age, Joey Trask saw evidence that his mom and dad made a few mistakes now and then. He ignored it. He was out to please them, not evaluate them. As a teenager, he can't ignore it any longer.

For example, Whalon yelled and hollered about the lousy way the lawn got cut. "Look at the little tufts of grass here and there. It's a mess. Go do it over again."

"I didn't do it. Mom did. She says it's that way because the blade needs sharpening."

At that point, had Whalon admitted error and apologized to Joey, a lot of fence would have been mended. But it never occurred to Whalon that he himself was less than ideal as a parent. No recognition of error, no apology. Instead, he berated Joey, a strong young man, for letting his mother mow the lawn. That was Joey's job. The fact that Joey was in school when Mom mowed the lawn was not, in Whalon's eyes, of any note.

Joey knew injustice when he saw it. And as he told Dr. Warren about the incident, tears appeared briefly in his eyes. He did not, at this point, admit sadness or sensitivity. That would come later.

Lida Armstrong told Dr. Warren about her own frustrating problem. "The divorce has been final now for six years. Six years that Randy never once paid for any of the kids' needs. When I tried to garnish his wages in the beginning, he got himself laid off. Do you know what hurts me so much?"

"The reason you are here, right? Your fifteen year old, Sarah."

"Right! Sarah puts that jerk right up there beside apple pie and the flag. I raised her. I broke my back and arranged the sitting and held her head while she threw up and did all the parenting things. Randy did nothing. Still does nothing. And to hear Sarah talk, he's perfect."

Divorced parents, particularly the custodial parents, find this phenomenon almost universally. During early adolescence the child of divorce slowly grasps that the custodial parent is not the paragon the child had always assumed. That parent is harried and insensitive at times. That parent makes mistakes. But the intense desire for perfect parents will not die. If this parent is flawed, the other parent must be the perfect one.

Lida fell short, so to Sarah Randy is obviously the perfect one.

"Sarah says she wants to go live in his home and go to school near his apartment. When he says he doesn't want her, she thinks he's just trying to be nice. She thinks he doesn't want her sleeping on the floor and stuff. She's deliberately blinding herself to reality.

"He doesn't want her. When the kids are there he practically ignores them. The only reason he wants visitation rights is because he knows I don't want him anywhere near the kids. It's a spite thing and Sarah twists it around to make it look like love. It's just not fair!"

Life is inherently unfair.

Teenagers tend to polarize everything. Sarah, by making her father all good, made her mother all bad. She doesn't want her mother picking on her dad. She doesn't want Lida dragging him into court. Sarah is caught in a hideous unconscious dilemma. She's angry with both parents for being imperfect. She's angry because they separated. But she can't express any of that anger toward her dad for fear she'll lose him completely. The link is too tenuous already to risk damaging it further. So she vents it all on Mom. Lida Armstrong is catching all Sarah's pent-up anger because Lida is available and she's the only safe outlet.

Dealing with Disillusionment

Sarah, Brian, and Joey have three options for dealing with the conflict between the beautiful myth and the ugly reality. Only one option properly resolves it.

The first bogus option is to let it fester. Sarah was taking this way out. She became agitated, even explosive, about how bad her mom was, and how seriously she was being wronged. Year after year, into adulthood, this can go on unresolved. It will enter the intergenerational network as unfinished business to plague Sarah's children.

The second option can be called cheap forgiveness. Brian was using this one, Dr. Warren learned. No grieving, no working it through; just forgive Mom her drug use and forget about it. After all, they didn't mean to be imperfect, they didn't intend to make all those mistakes. Again, because the issue was put aside without true resolution, it will cause serious problems in the next generation as unfinished business.

The only option a child has that works well is also the most difficult: Work through the pain and grief of having suffered under imperfect parenting, then forgive the parents for wrongs both real and fancied, out of love. Only then is it comfortable for the child, and for the child's children, to move on. Many say that this is the final stage of leaving the dollhouse.

Major Errors Parents Make

What do parents do that's so terrible, besides being imperfect? Parents can err in their relations with their teenagers in two extremes: *overprotect and underprotect.*

Overprotect

A recent case in our counsel is a classic example of overprotection. Joyce and Riley Kimball read all the books on building self-esteem in youngsters. They knew how important a solid sense of self could be. But their son Lane was, frankly, quite lax about getting his homework done.

Before the end of Lane's freshman year in high school, Riley was helping him with assignments, regularly completing the homework Lane left unfinished, writing reports and papers Lane simply didn't have time to complete. Riley just knew that if Lane's grades were to drop significantly (let's not even breathe the word *failure*), his self-esteem would be destroyed.

By Lane's sophomore year, Joyce was working at it along with Riley, and Lane neglected to come to the table while homework was in progress. When the Kimballs came to Dr. Warren near the end of Lane's sophomore year, the parents were still doing their son's homework, but now Lane was refusing to take it to school. So either Riley or Joyce would drive over to the school each day and give the homework to the teachers. Sounds unbelievable, but it's true!

"If we don't do this, Lane'll fail, and his self-esteem will be crushed forever." Overprotection. The Kimballs were not allowing their son to fail at fifteen when it was still safe for him to do so. They had obliterated the boundaries between parents and child, between the parents' job and the child's responsibilities. Lane is now repeating his sophomore year. And he's surviving the shock of having to take some action on his own behalf.

Underprotect

The opposite extreme is to exercise no guiding hand. "It's part of the parents' job to watch us and make sure we don't make mistakes," opined Gregorio Munoz. "Why wouldn't mine do that?"

Gregorio was overstating it slightly, though not by far; no parents can guarantee their children make no mistakes. But his parents were so wrapped up in their own issues of unfinished business that they didn't want the hassle of confronting their son, of setting the boundaries. Now Gregorio, at fourteen, was sitting in the judge's chambers of juvenile hall, facing arraignment for attempted rape, while his mom sat weeping and wailing in the anteroom.

Gregorio didn't know what the word *rape* entailed exactly. He knew only that at first Arleta was willing to try something new, and then she changed her mind. He knew Mom didn't like him smoking, but she never mentioned the cigarettes she occasionally found in his pockets on laundry day. He knew Dad worked two jobs to make ends meet, so Gregorio didn't really expect his father to do things with him, or sit him down for a father-son talk.

That day Gregorio Munoz learned the specifics of the facts of life not from his parents but from the judge and the public defender, with occasional words of wisdom from an assistant D.A. He also learned firsthand the meaning of the words *probation, personal responsibility*, and *mercy*.

Later Adolescence—Angst to the Max

Maturity brings with it a natural yearning for a greater independence. The adolescent is taking, essentially, the first full steps to membership in the world at large. If all has gone well so far, he is nearly prepared to leave the dollhouse.

All the testing, the self-exploration of the previous tasks, simultaneously come together and blow apart here. The body continues its physical development. The need to expand boundaries continues apace, but in all this lurks a wild card—burgeoning sexual maturity.

For males, this same repetitive, yet still not fully answered question "Who am I?" becomes "Am I who I think I am?" Boys who grew up being boys suddenly doubt their untested masculinity. One reason boys so commonly drop away from church at this age is the demasculinizing nature of Sunday school. Just as the boy's juices get flowing, the Sunday school teacher (usually female) preaches that sex is wrong. Premarital sex may be wrong, but sexual feelings are natural, and he must learn how to handle them. More doubt and guilt intrude. Here is where parents should communicate that these new sexual feelings are not wrong in themselves. Sin and error come in expressing them wrongly.

Exploration takes a whole new direction—figuring out the opposite sex. To guys, girls are a different species, with unfathomable thought patterns, likes, and dislikes. And that is quite true. Girls hunger for idealized romance. Romance is the farthest thing from guys' minds. Girls' sexual drives are diffuse. They're not interested in sex itself but in the accoutrements of romance; the perfect atmosphere, the undivided attention showered by the admirer. The myth of the White Knight is alive and well.

Lida Armstrong giggled. "My Sarah is fifteen now. Recently she went out on her first real date, to a party. She primped like you wouldn't believe. I know how it goes. I remember. Boy, do I remember. I found out later that the boy's older brother coached him in advance, because I know this would never occur to a kid that age. Fifteen-year-old boys are absolutely anti-romantic, you know?"

Dr. Warren smiled. "I know."

"This boy brought a bouquet of flowers. OK. Most guys bring flowers for the girl. He pulled out one flower, an orchid corsage, and gave it to Sarah. Then he turned and handed the bouquet to me, her mom. Hey. I'm thirty-four, and I'm not immune to romance yet myself. I melted like margarine in the microwave."

204

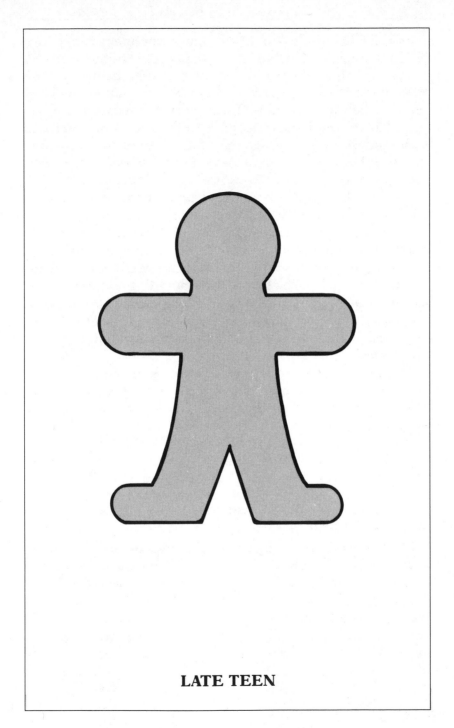

LATE TEEN

As their hormones direct the massive changes that turn boys into men, male teens' thoughts become highly focused. Sexual activity—kissing, touching, nuzzling, being with, ultimately to brave the act itself—literally consumes their interest. When by force of will they beat it down, it lingers on the edges of their mind, leaping to the forefront whenever sights and sounds suggest it. Even if no sights or sounds suggest it, it hops into mind anyway. Boys in monasteries have the same thoughts as boys in public schools.

The list of odd differences goes on and on. Both the girls and the boys must sort all this out. They do the sorting by interacting. They date, hang around together, talk, misunderstand one another, say one thing and mean something else, fail to communicate, declare the opposite sex hopeless and then hungrily seek further contact. All this is necessary and natural. We find that children who do not learn about the opposite sex by trial and error while it's still safe to do so have problems later on when trying to understand and communicate.

Mid-teens not only polarize, they oscillate. They cast everything in black and white and then keep jumping from black to white and back again. They're groping for the boundaries, in essence. One way to locate the dollhouse walls is to bounce off them.

Teens also, as parents quickly notice, become intensely self-absorbed. "You don't understand," wails Sarah. "You've never been in love!" These thoughts and feelings are so new, so intense, so compelling that surely no one else ever experienced them this strongly.

If, back there at the beginning, the preschooler completed his tasks, and the grade schooler completed hers, the adolescent's tasks, though onerous, will fall into line.

But what if they don't? What if, in this series of tasks, one was damaged or omitted? Guilt is a condition that can stifle your child's growth, although you may not even realize it exists. We will explore next the ways you can free your child of this destructive force.

CHAPTER 11

Helping Your Child Deal with Guilt

The thrill of victory—The agony of defeat. The intensity of brilliant minds locked in a cosmic power struggle on the gaming table of the universe. Sudden death in the play-offs of life! And here sat Dr. Warren on the floor of his office holding a lousy two-three domino, with no chance of playing it anywhere on the board.

Jennifer Newport sat cross-legged on the floor opposite him and carefully chose a domino from her hand. She laid her double four crosswise of Dr. Warren's two-four. "Why do I have to go to Sunday school?"

Dr. Warren ran a four-six out from the double. "I go to Sunday school and church because I want to, in order to worship God. Tell me some reasons you think you have to."

"Mom and Dad make me." Six-five on the four-six.

"Besides that."

Jennifer giggled as she saw that Dr. Warren was forced to go to the bone pile, that cluster of face-down dominoes off to the side from which you always randomly select the wrong one.

"Because good people do." The smile faded. "But Brian's not good; I mean, he's not good all the time; and he goes. And if Mommy was good she wouldn't have to be in the hospital for drug abuse."

"I've been told Jesus Christ came into the world to save sinners. If everyone were good to start with, He wouldn't have to. Everyone makes mistakes. Everyone does wrong now and then. That's what sin is. I go to church because God loves me and I want to show Him I love Him back." Dr. Warren's third draw was a five-one. He played it.

"I don't know if I love God or not. I don't understand about love. Sometimes when Daddy gets home and he's not

207

angry, I think I love him. Or when I snuggle up in Mom's lap, it's so neat. And then sometimes when Dad yells at me, I'm so mad and scared of him at the same time."

"That's love."

"All of it?" Jennifer played a one-three. She had one domino left.

"All of it."

"Daddy comes home earlier now so that Mrs. Bomberg can leave on time. He says they can get along without him after five. I'll be so glad when Mom gets home. When is she coming home, do you know?"

"I'll ask. I believe Dr. Hemfelt will be scheduling a joint family session for all of you shortly. It won't be long now." Dr. Warren played his three-five.

With unabashed glee Jenny-Jo plopped the five-one on the last remaining double opening. "I had it all along," she gloated. "You were doomed!"

No Wall Street broker plays the game more avidly than your average nine year old. In a sense, Jennifer's inborn desire for competition intensifies both her family role and family friction.

After their session (Jennifer won two games of three), Dr. Warren spent a few minutes talking to Rob Newport.

"Jennifer's doing better in school. Her teacher made a point of saying so." Rob was grinning. "Mealtime is the most peaceful it has ever been. Jenny-Jo," Rob crowed, "is shaping up."

Much of the behavior shift resulted simply from the change in her parents. The old tensions, the carefully hidden secrets in her house, had eased. Having grieved so deeply—a first in his life—Rob was better able to take a personal, emotionally involved role in the family.

Alice had not yet returned. When she would come home, the family would rock again as roles shifted and, perhaps, old patterns reemerged. Things were nowhere near perfect. They weren't even good yet. But they were already so much improved that Rob was bullish about their future.

Jennifer, to that point, had been Dennis the Menace to Brian's Clark Kent. Dr. Warren now had another consideration, which he kept to himself. Were tensions really easing, meaning that the roles had lost their intensity, or were the two children swapping roles? Either could happen, for Jennifer was at an age particularly vulnerable to unfinished business and split-off problems. Brian could become the scapegoat simply because Jennifer was shedding that role in favor of a role more nearly Hero. He must keep a close eye on the situation over the next few weeks.

In the first interview a few short months ago, all the family members had agreed that Jennifer was the problem. Drs. Warren and Hemfelt were discovering that at most she was a very small part of the problem. But the false guilt—"This whole mess is my fault! It's all my fault!"—had to be overcome. It wasn't going to be easy.

Assuaging Guilt

Guilt. Every child we've cited in this book had to deal with guilt in one form or another. Guilt can either shut down the grief process or trigger it. Wise parents must know that guilt is lurking in the shadows and be prepared to help the child resolve it if possible. For the very young, there is no way to resolve it. Your task as journeymate is simply to mark that the guilt is there, to understand.

Seven-year-old Regina Kolbin completed the barn she was building of blocks. "Mommy and Daddy were going to get a divorce once."

"Why?"

"Because I was a bad girl."

"But they didn't." Dr. Warren watched her sit back to admire her barn. A month ago she would have destroyed it.

"No, because I didn't want them to."

At any age, the child feels responsible for just about everything bad happening in the family. And she also feels confident she has the power to correct it. Be alert to that way of thinking in children.

Four-year-old Victor Kolbin could not articulate his feelings. If he could, we believe, he would have felt the reproach that he was the cause of everything that happens. That false guilt remains unless it is addressed at a later age. Treat it as you treated fear—empathy, followed by facts, and the assurance "I will be here for you."

Dr. Warren asked Pete Armstrong, eleven, if he felt any responsibility for his parents' divorce.

Pete shook his head. "Nah. When I was little I was sure I was the one who caused the divorce. Mom kept saying over and over that I wasn't, but I knew I was. Finally, I guess I figured it out on my own that it didn't happen because of me."

"Are you at peace with that now, that you didn't cause the divorce?

"Yeah." He paused a moment, thinking. "But I was always annoying Dad somehow. He'd tell me I was making too much noise, or I had to go blow my nose 'cause my sniffing was driving him nuts, or I was underfoot, or something. I was never what he wanted. If I could have shaped up better when I was little, maybe they'd still be married."

Older children, Pete's age and up, mature away from the conviction that they are the cause of everything. Yet the fiction persists: They could have altered the course of history had they only done something differently back then. Logically, therefore, there must be something they can do right now to force a happy ending. Along with the guilt, they end up with an overburdening feeling of helplessness, for they can *not* change their parents.

Global Guilt, False Guilt, and True Guilt

Global guilt is that feeling in the very young, children the ages of all three Kolbin kids, that the child is the cause and the answer to everything under the sun. There's not much you as a parent can do to reduce this feeling, but fortunately, the kids usually outgrow it.

False guilt and true guilt, though, relate to boundaries in relationships. Consider the contrast between poor and good boundaries:

Poor boundaries: Sarah Armstrong was the heroine of the

family, making good grades, being deadly serious about life, giving the family a good image. It didn't work. The family broke up anyway. Obviously she hadn't done enough. Her identity figure, damaged by codependency, could not perceive that she had no responsibility for her parents' actions. "I am them and they are me. It's my fault."

The subject of boundaries came up naturally during Sarah's fourth session with Dr. Warren, allowing him to help her begin to understand them.

"Dr. Warren," Sarah protested, "I hear what you're saying, but you just don't understand. We were getting along all right until Mom filed for divorce. We were getting along."

"Do you know why your mom did that?"

"She said she didn't want us living with Dad when he got busted. She said it was making us sick to be around him. We did all right."

"And you're sure that there's something you can do to make it come out right."

"There has to be," she murmured. "There has to be an answer somewhere."

There is an answer.

Good boundaries: I am me and you are you. My identity figure has a solid line around it, and I am responsible for what goes on inside it. I cannot be made responsible for what happens outside that line—for what other people do.

Dr. Warren found an opportunity to bring that lesson home to Jennifer Newport one day as he engaged her in a hot game of Monopoly. She had two hotels and he had none yet when he bumped the board. Playing pieces tipped and rolled all over.

"Jennifer, now look what you've done!"

"Whaddaya mean?! I didn't touch it," she howled.

They repositioned the pieces as best they could remember and continued.

"I need a double." Dr. Warren rolled the dice. "Now look what you did! A three and a four. You messed up my double."

"Like heck I did! I can't control what your dice do!"

A few minutes later Dr. Warren came around the corner onto Jennifer's Illinois Avenue.

"Three houses," she chortled. "Seven hundred and fifty bucks!"

"I'm too far behind. I'm doing this." He picked up two of her houses and tossed them back in the box. He craned his neck to read her deed. "One hundred dollars. That's more like it."

"You can't do that!"

"Yes, I can because I'm an adult."

"Then I'm gonna."

"You can't. You're a kid. I'm bigger. I do what I want, and you can't make me be fair if I don't want to."

Jennifer stared at him, crushed, on the edge of tears.

Dr. Warren returned her two houses to the place they ought to be. "But I will be fair, because it's the right thing to do. I wanted to make a little point you may have missed. You don't have any control over me, or over your parents either. You can't make me be fair, and you can't make them be fair. Is that true, do you think?"

"Yeah. All I could do is quit. And even if I quit you'd make me play if you wanted to finish the game. And you'd cheat. Why did you say I bumped the board?"

"To show you I can put blame anywhere I want to, but that doesn't mean it's true. And I accused you of messing up my double. I can accuse you, but that doesn't mean you could do it, even if you wanted to."

"Yeah, I see. But . . ." She took a deep breath. "No, I guess there aren't any buts."

"You're absolutely right. In this game I have the power and you don't. It's the same at your home. You couldn't make your mom misuse drugs if she didn't want to, and there isn't a single thing you could do to make her stop while she was doing it. You couldn't make your father come home from work and play with you, any more than you could keep him out of the house. Do you see my point?"

"Yeah, but if I . . ."

"If you what?"

"I don't know."

"Nothing. You could do nothing. Grown-ups will go their

way and do what they want. Brian too. Now let's finish the game the right way, without cheating." And he sold four of his houses to raise the seven hundred and fifty dollars.

These concepts—that Jennifer's family are responsible for their own actions—were half the picture. Through the rest of the afternoon, Dr. Warren concentrated on the other half.

The rest of the lesson is best couched in positive terms. "Jennifer is not responsible for Brian's actions" is negative. "Brian is responsible for himself" is positive. It's a giant step (and yet such a small one) to the next level: "Jennifer is responsible for her own actions. Only Jennifer can change her inside and make the decisions inside herself."

And Jennifer had reached an age where she could begin to grasp abstracts such as these. Younger children cannot. Grade-schoolers are the first age group who can really reach our ultimate goal of attachment with autonomy. Jennifer knows she is still dependent, but she can take an active part now in her own future. That's new. It's exciting. And frightening. Jennifer's relationship to her family has taken on a whole new dimension: personal responsibility.

Personal Responsibility

Joey Trask showed up one day with those torn jeans that were so popular for a time. He shook his head. "These things are the pits. See how my knee pops out when I sit down? Really uncomfortable."

"I have no sympathy," Dr. Warren answered. "You're the guy who controls what you wear. If you want to wear them, you put up with a cold knee."

"Not just cold, man, it's . . . I see what you're saying."

"You control all of what Joey Trask thinks and a lot of what he does. You cannot control what your mom and dad think or what they do. See what I meant about boundaries?"

"Yeah. I can make them mad, though."

"Sure. They make you mad too. The next question you ask is, 'What good does it do to make them mad?' Does it make you feel better or happier? Does it get you ahead in life? Only you know the answer, because only you know what's going on inside Joey."

"So it's my fault if I make them mad."

"It's your fault if you *deliberately* make them mad. When you wear that shirt, for instance, just to make your Dad angry." Dr. Warren frowned. "What color is that, anyway?"

"Puce."

"I believe it. Just to make your Dad angry. You have the power to do it or not. If you do it only to make him mad, that's not very smart."

"What do you think I should do?"

"Think. Ask yourself, 'Is this what I want? Am I doing what I think is right for me?' "

"You think I oughta cut my hair?"

"I think you oughta realize you have the responsibility to choose your hairstyle, and it's a responsibility worth considering wisely. I won't tell you what to do because I'm not you. I don't know what's inside you."

"You got a better idea than most, Doc."

Age of Responsibility

Although the very young, such as the Kolbin children, make only the most elemental of choices—obey or disobey, for instance—grade-schoolers can be responsible for more complex decisions. By the time they reach their teens, children such as Joey Trask have enough control, enough personal responsibility, that they themselves stand a chance of breaking the chain of codepedency, whether their parents heal or not. Older children can make the choices that will influence their own destinies—and the generations beyond.

Understanding what they can and cannot control will not come easily for them. For example, many children of alcoholic parents pledge: "I'll never become like that!" Most, however, break that promise to themselves within a few years. Although they may understand in theory that they cannot control others, their lives are governed by the pressing need to fix Mom and Dad, to make the past better and the future comfortable. So intent are they on controlling others that they don't make the right decisions for themselves.

Those right decisions are: "I can talk about my feelings. I will assume responsibility for my own behavior. I won't blame others for what I do."

"Right here and now is the moment to break the cycle," says Dr. Warren. That's the challenge he offers children as the end of counseling nears.

Personal Responsibility Will Break the Chain

Joey Trask scuffed into Dr. Warren's office and flopped into his usual place, the side chair. "Hi."

"Hi. Here's your sketchbook back. Thanks for sharing it."

"Sure." Joey accepted his sketchbook.

"What's up?"

"Dad says he's quitting this stuff. You know?"

"He asked me for a meeting following your session. I assume that will be the topic of discussion."

"So I'm going to quit too." Joey licked his lips and shifted in the chair.

"Why?"

" 'Cause. I just want to."

"You know that's not a good enough reason in here. Why?"

Joey squirmed some more. "Hey, if Dad isn't going to change, there's no use, you know? Some of this stuff we talk about in here, it really hurts. Why should I go through the pain and stuff when Dad isn't gonna bother?"

"Good question." Dr. Warren nodded. "Do you really want to know why, or is that another of our rhetorical questions?"

"Yeah. I really wanna know why."

"When you first came, it was because your father and mother wanted to modify your behavior in certain ways. Right? But in the last few sessions, you've been gaining some insights into how your particular family operates. What have you found?"

"You want me to go through all that?"

"I know you've been thinking about it a lot, and you're a smart kid. Yes. Go through it."

Joey studied Dr. Warren a moment, probably framing his answer. The boy wouldn't have noticed that he was meeting Dr. Warren's eyes squarely now or that he sat straighter lately. He licked his lips again, one of his nervous habits. "That first day when Mom said, 'I want my boy back,' it seems to me she was really saying it. She wants me the way I used to be. So does Dad. The little kid who does everything perfect, whatever Dad wants, you know?"

"I agree with you completely."

"It seems to me they want me to go back to being cute little Joey. They don't want me to grow up. When we sat and you talked about it—when you explained it that way—it clicked. It made sense for me. That's really how it is, and it explains a lot how they act. I guess Dr. Hemfelt was saying the same thing to them."

"Can you make them change their minds and welcome your growth?" Dr. Warren asked.

"No."

"How do you know?"

"That story you told about King Canute making the tide stop. I liked that one. I got to thinking about it and decided yeah, that's right. I never could make them do what I want."

(In the story to which Joey referred here, Canute, an early king of Britain, so fell in love with his own political power that he was certain he could stand on the seashore, command the tide to stay out there, and it would. He almost drowned.)

"Do you see why they might feel that way—that they want to keep you from growing up?"

"I dunno. I suppose it looks good on the outside. I mean, when the rest of the world was looking at us, here was this perfect little family with everybody towing the line and looking neat and clean. I suppose they like that. I suppose it's comfortable for them, you know?"

"A few weeks ago your parents forced you to come here. Now stop and think what you were saying just now. You've developed some very deep and mature insights into what makes people tick. We're examining your parents primarily,

216

but this sort of insight works with all the people you'll meet as an adult."

"Yeah, but . . ."

"Also, now you can see life from your parents' perspective. Which is to say, you can see from someone else's point of view. That's something many adults never learn to do well. You've come a long, long way in a few weeks."

"I guess so. But . . ." Joey's voice trailed off.

"So who benefits from these sessions? You or your parents?"

Joey stared at infinity beyond Dr. Warren. "You're saying I should stick with it because it helps me and don't worry about Dad. Is that it?"

"Yes, but I'd phrase it a bit differently. It's impossible not to worry about your dad; I know I still worry about my dad now and then. You know your dad can benefit by sticking with it, just as you can, and it's sad when he fights it. But you have the idea."

"But I can't make him do it."

"Right. You're not responsible for him. And he could make you come but he can't make you derive any benefit from these sessions. That you have to do yourself, if at all, and you do it splendidly. You are responsible for Joey Trask. You can make a difference in Joey's life. That's the most important lesson you've learned."

"Dad's pretty disappointed in me, isn't he?"

"I'd say perplexed. He used excellent parenting methods to raise you. They worked very well on a growing little boy, but not so well on an adolescent approaching adulthood. He's confused and upset that they aren't working the way he wants them to."

"I wish he loved me."

"He does, Joey. In his own way, he does very much."

"Not like you. You don't expect me to get a haircut before you'll care about me, you know? And some weeks I wore some of the wickedest stuff I could find in my dresser, just to see if I could get your goat, you know?"

"Like that bleeding skull T-shirt."

"Yeah! And you cared about me anyway. Even that time you said my T-shirt really offended you. You turned off on the shirt but not on me."

"And you haven't worn it since. I appreciate that. Thank you for being sensitive to my feelings."

"I threw it away."

"Your father loves you more than I ever will, because you're his son. He has certain preset expectations for all boys, not just you. It's hard for him to change those expectations. They color the way he thinks, the same as your attitudes color the way you think. Everyone's like that."

Joey tossed Dr. Warren one of his rare grins. "I keep trying to get you to bad-mouth Dad and you never do." The grin fled. "When we first came here I was sure Dad was going to win you over to his side, you know? Make you think his way. Then you'd both start working on me to change back to what Dad wanted. He did that with Mom and my soccer coach and the school counselor. Took me a couple weeks to see you aren't on anybody's side. I guess I have learned some stuff, you know? So I guess I'll stay with this even though Dad dropped out."

"That pleases me, for your sake."

Although Joey Trask opted to continue counseling apart from his dad's decision, Joey's recovery was still linked closely to the health of his parents and his parents' marriage. In the next chapter we'll look at the marriage and how to strengthen it. The parents' marriage is the foundation for the emotional security of the children in the next generation. Are the parents a team in the family?

If, like Lida Armstrong, you are divorced, please follow through with this next chapter anyway. There are three important reasons why: First, we will cover questions divorced parents ask. Also, this healing is as much for you as for the marriage. Whether or not the spouse refuses to cooperate, or even knows about it, the principles will benefit *you*. Third, these insights will help you reach the goal of this book, to improve your children's chances for happiness. Ideally, the spouse is an immense help; the marriage is a solid anchor. In your case, however, you personally hold the key.

CHAPTER 12

The Parents: Are We a Team in Our Family?

Whalon Trask glowered from his throne, the easy chair across from Dr. Warren, following Joey's session. "It's been a month and the kid hasn't changed a single thing. This isn't working."

"During the initial evaluation," Dr. Warren said, "I strongly suggested you and Mrs. Trask seek independent counseling. I understand you've been seeing Dr. Hemfelt."

"I assume I can be frank here."

"Absolutely. Without prejudice."

"I think the man's all wet. He was suggesting—didn't come right out and say it, but he was suggesting—that Joey's behavior is caused by problems between Beth and me. That's insane. Worse than insane. We don't have any problems. But the ideas he's putting out will cause nothing but friction in our marriage. Beth is content with the role God ordained for her as a wife and helpmeet, and the ideas that man is spouting can upset our relationship."

"I understand what you're saying. I hear it so very frequently. You have permission for frankness, Mr. Trask. Have I?"

"Certainly."

"You work for a large company, but you enjoy a certain autonomy. You can make major decisions that benefit both yourself and the company. Am I correct?"

"Yes. That's right."

"Would you change jobs for a company more important than the firm you now work for if you could not make any decisions?"

Building the Marriage Team

Steps to Take to Restore Union
in Your Marriage

1. Suspend the Blame Cycle.
   Suspend the impulse to focus blame on your spouse. Break the mutual blame cycle.

2. Acknowledge Your Contribution to the Pain.
   Each spouse acknowledges areas of personal dysfunction. Each shares in-depth. Neither person comments on the faults of the other.

3. Commit to Recovery.
   Declare what each of you is willing to work on. Be specific.

4. Yours, Mine, and Ours.
   Assess the degree of sharing in your marriage. Are your needs being met? Are your spouse's needs being met?

5. Loving Confrontation.
   Make sure you've suspended blame. Now address the problem issues that have surfaced so far. What do you want that you're not getting? What's missing in the marriage union?

6. Grieve the Losses.

   Mutually grieve the pains and losses you've discovered.

7. Give and Receive.

   Don't just talk about giving and receiving. Be willing to make concessions and to ask that your needs be met. Again be specific. Explain in detail what you're willing to give, and what you need to receive.

8. Adjust Boundaries.

   Make sure the relationships within your immediate family, with the extended family, with friends, with work, church, recreational commitments and such are all appropriate. Boundaries too tight or too loose become damaging.

9. Search Out Stressors.

   You can't eliminate stressors, but you can minimize them. Work on it together.

10. Deal with Special Problems.

    Divorced? Mate won't cooperate? The kids aren't responding? Figure out if there is anything you can do (there may not be), then either do it or grieve the situation and move on.

Whalon scowled. "No, I wouldn't. I don't see where you're going."

"Let's say you're forced to transfer. Now you have a prestigious position but no decision-making capability. How do you feel?"

"I'd quit first. What are you getting at?"

"You are very fortunate, Whalon, that Beth didn't decide to quit. A lot of women do."

"Say what . . . ?"

"Beth is your equal in intelligence and accomplishment. When she married you, she became an officer and the chief asset of the most important organization you'll ever be a part of, your family. Yet she makes no decisions, carries no authority. Dr. Hemfelt believes, as do I, that she has . . ."

"The husband is the head of the household. I make the decisions. She's happy with that; she knows what the Bible says."

"Do you believe in a literal Scripture, Whalon?"

"You know I do."

"Then read Proverbs 31. Don't insert your own thoughts and interpretations. Read exactly what it says and avoid reading into it what it does not say. Dr. Hemfelt believes Beth has split off her anger and frustration and Joey is picking them up. I think so too. Yours is a picture-perfect family, Whalon, and you try very hard to keep it running perfectly. Too hard. The control issue has become a problem."

"So now Joey's my fault."

"Not at all. I said at the very beginning we will not find fault or place blame. We're not placing blame. We are asking that everyone accept responsibility for contributions to the family pain. Are you?"

Whalon Trask sat silently a few moments, perplexed. Suddenly he shook his head. "No. The kid's hair is still a mess, he's still arguing with his mother, he still refuses to get back into soccer. You're not doing a thing for him. It's over. No more."

"That is your decision, as it always has been. I trust you're referring to your personal involvement and that Beth and Joey will make their own decisions about continuing."

"If it's not working, it's not working. I'm not going to keep paying for something that's not working."

"You realize you've just made Beth's decision for her—a personal decision, not a family decision—although she's a highly intelligent woman capable of knowing what she wants and making the choice herself. Do you see my point, Whalon, about the business of control?"

"I think you're both all wet."

First: Suspend the Blame Cycle

"Of course I'm a responsible person," claims the office wag. "Every time something goes wrong at work, they say I'm responsible."

Blame versus responsibility. A well-known John Bradshawism says, "No one is to blame. Everyone is responsible." Suspending blame is not the same as letting your spouse off the hook, letting the spouse deny responsibility for problems. Obviously, responsibility continues to lie somewhere. But the blame has to stop.

The codependent way is to ignore individual responsibility for one's own health and actions. The codependent leaps gleefully over responsibility and plunges straight into blame-slinging. It is so much easier to see how the faults of others are messing up an otherwise perfect relationship.

When the Trasks entered into Dr. Hemfelt's counsel, he asked them to explain the details of their family problems—what they saw as the causes of their woes. Were you to enter our counsel, we would probably ask you the same thing. To frame a theoretical response, picture in your mind exactly what the other family member or members are doing to upset the peaceful scene. You should write these problems down. Make certain these are all things that if eliminated would ease general tensions and not just someone's casual complaint (such as, "He doesn't put the cap back on the toothpaste").

When Rob Newport did this, he first listed Jennifer's whining and disruptive behavior. Then he detailed Alice's just-uncovered drug abuse. No wonder she never got anything done. No wonder it took her all day to do two loads of laundry and cook dinner. Next to Jenny-Jo and Alice, Brian looked absolutely saintly. Rob wished Brian were a little more eager to be a teenager, to go out with girls and get his driver's license, but what the hey; some kids are slow maturing. It certainly wasn't a fault. Dr. Warren called it a red flag. Hardly. Brian and Rob were the only solid members of the family.

After you've written out your blame list, set it aside. We hope you will be able to look at it later and see how it differs from the reality of your situation. For now, keep in mind that everything on that list is suspended; none of it will be assumed true, and temporarily no one will be held accountable according to this list.

Second: Acknowledge Your Contribution to the Pain

By examining yourself throughout these last chapters, you've gained some insight into your past, into the things that make you tick. We hope you've also seen how to give yourself positive messages and then put those messages into practical action.

In session with Dr. Hemfelt, you might be asked at this point to sit down facing your spouse. Then you'd be given the instructions: "Take the next fifteen or twenty minutes and tell your spouse about yourself. Not what you are so certain is wrong with that other person, but what the problems are with you."

The Newports did this when Rob joined Alice for a session in the hospital. Alice said, "You're aware that I grew up under a rageaholic, controlling father. You know how Dad can be. Remember how he absolutely exploded the time he thought you were neglecting Brian? What I've discovered is that sometimes when I think you're overcontrolling me, I feel confused. You explode like Dad does. I don't know if you really explode as my dad did and we have to set a boundary there, or if you're simply asking me to be responsible to you and I'm hearing Dad in my imagination. That's a problem for me, one of my personal dysfunctions. Am I hearing you or am I hearing my father?"

Rob Newport responded, as much for himself as for Alice, "At least there was a hand on the rudder in your home. I grew up in chaos. I mean, no control at all. You know how Grandma Newport can't decide whether to have corn flakes or oatmeal. She can't make heavier decisions any easier. Grandpa doesn't even try. We never had a decent vacation because they couldn't make plans or decisions. Dinner was a zoo with kids coming and going. Sometimes we didn't eat until nine at night because Mom was still thinking of something to fix until seven. I'm terrified of things not being in control. I don't know. Maybe sometimes I do overcontrol. I'm just so scared our family will become like mine was. Chaotic."

We find that just this step here can forge a dramatic reversal. Instead of attacking each other as antagonists, man and wife become allies; the villain is not each other but dysfunction itself. For once, husband and wife are pulling together for a common goal: healing the marriage. Even if that new bond doesn't magically appear, enormous relief pours out. Frequently Dr. Hemfelt hears a patient say, "If my spouse can change, that will be wonderful. But just to hear him acknowledge the role his past played takes a ton of bricks off my back."

Quite possibly, you have no spouse to do this with. You are widowed or divorced. There's no way you can sit down in front of that absent mate. Now what? You knew that other person pretty well. Sit down facing an empty chair. In your mind's eye place the spouse there. What would he or she say?

You can cop out on this and make it easy—and useless— by simply citing what you think the spouse's faults are. Don't do it. What would your spouse be saying about himself or herself from his or her viewpoint about his or her past? Stepping into his or her shoes may be quite an eye-opener for you.

When Lida sat down late at night with an imaginary Randy across from her, in her imagination's eye he wiped his nose on the back of his hand, an infuriating gesture he made a thousand times a day. Only that moment did she realize why: Snorting coke does irritating things to your nose. The rest of the "interview" would have gone better had Lida been able to put aside her animosity a little more. Still, it was a start.

Third: Commit to Recovery

In this third step, essentially, each spouse declares to the other what he or she is willing to work on. Where shall change begin? With me. How shall it begin? Let me tell you.

Having recognized his overbearing need to control, Rob agreed to let Alice remind him, "I think you're doing it again." He was, in short, willing to open himself to accountability.

Alice in turn committed herself to changing those negative messages recorded deep inside her. She had to consciously stop saying, "There it is again; his anger is just like Dad's." In the past she used drugs to get away; she had to keep reminding herself that was no way out. Instead she had to tell herself over and over: "I'm not going to let my feelings about Dad shape my response to Rob's anger."

Sometimes a couple in our counsel will put their commitment on paper, making themselves more obviously accountable. Depending on the severity of problems facing the marriage, one or both partners may also need to commit to the use of self-help groups such as Codependents Anonymous or commit to professional counseling. The bottom line is a commitment to work on oneself, whatever that requires.

Fourth: Yours, Mine, and Ours

The fourth step we recommend—assessing the degree of sharing—must come after the couple has agreed to suspend all blame. The blame step is essential, for only when you put all blame behind you can you launch into this step with any degree of success.

Sharing. How much is enough? How much is too much?

So often we find that the spouses have widely divergent answers to those two questions.

There was precious little sharing in the Newport marriage. Every night Alice had watched Rob come slogging in, eat dinner, plop into his chair with a snack, and turn on the TV. For the rest of the evening Rob played selector roulette with his remote control, snapping from channel to channel until he dozed off.

But if you'd have asked Rob, he would've said, "Share? I share as much as any husband. I share my paycheck. I come home instead of going out with the boys; a lotta guys do that, you know. I have a few buddies who go out with the girls too. Alice is lucky. We made love regularly until she quit wanting to, but I'm not running around on her."

Alice's side didn't sound a bit like Rob's. "I feel absolutely shut out. He doesn't say six words all evening. Sure, he's not out with the boys. But he's not here, either. He's in La-La Land there in front of the TV set. Or sometimes he brings home a video. But he never asks me what I might like." As Alice became more aware of her own discontent, she added, "Feeling shut out is probably the reason I shut down sexually." The two sets of feelings have much to do with each other.

This is why we routinely ask parents about their sharing patterns. Problems in one area spill over into all areas of the marriage. Again, this point can be easily illustrated with the picture of circles within a circle. The mother and father circles are agitated, closed in or spiking outward. The children are going to get tugged by the pressures in the relationships between four highly different people: Parents and children.

Sharing must be amenable to both parties in the areas of sexuality, money, authority, time, and emotional intimacy. Of these five, Rob and Alice did fine with money and authority. Alice flunked sexuality. Rob blew it with time and, most of all, emotional intimacy. Moreover, he destroyed Alice's sense of emotional intimacy.

In Rob and Alice's case, Rob explored reasons why he couldn't or wouldn't share time and emotional intimacy with his wife. Sometimes the reasons are deep and dark—

"I'm no longer quite certain I love her"; sometimes quite trivial—"I don't like the smell of that shampoo she uses." Often the trivial reasons mask the darker ones. Explore thoroughly as you work through this step. You may not want to write down an inventory of attitudes and reasons, but at least work through it in your mind, in detail.

If you did your homework well on steps one and two, especially the suspension of blame, you should do pretty well working this out. On your side is a factor we see over and over: Couples like to explore this sort of thing with each other and really get into it. They usually want very much to make it work.

Also, sexuality is a nice magnet that, given half a chance, will pull two parents together. It usually provides a fair degree of motivation to get beyond blaming.

Fifth: Loving Confrontation

Is there such a thing as loving confrontation? There can be, and you can do it, but it's scary. The preceding step explored where sharing broke down. Here we explore where the other person's dysfunctions might be causing damage. You, the spouse, are the best and the worst to reveal problems in your mate. You know that person well, perhaps too well. And you, whom your spouse should trust most, may be least trusted to say the truth. Move very carefully, weighing your words well. We are confronting out of love, not blaming as a means of discharging old anger.

In the case of Alice and Rob, Alice thought of Rob with his snacks in front of the TV set and called upon him to examine the possibility that he was an obsessive-compulsive overeater. Alice would have to walk an exceedingly fine line between nagging and enabling him to continue to overeat and deny his food addiction. Should she fail to speak, for she alone knew by living with him how much he put away, she would be encouraging his possible addiction.

If communication has been opened and blame suspended, Rob might hear her without considering it a personal attack or recrimination. There's no way to negotiate around this one; Alice must hit it square on.

Lida Armstrong has far more serious difficulties; there is very little if any loving left, the confrontations have already gone on too long, and Randy isn't going to sit and listen anyway.

"What are my responsibilities?" she asked. "It's not just the drugs. Sometimes he takes the kids when he's supposed to, sometimes he doesn't. He might show up and he might not. What do I tell the kids? Do I deny visitation? I just don't know what to do."

Dr. Hemfelt, approaching her questions with her in mind, and Dr. Warren, looking at it from the kids' needs, agree completely: The children need stability now, and either one of the parents attacking the other will damage the children. Foremost, whatever that ex-spouse is or is not, he or she is still the child's parent. The other parent must not expect the child to quit loving a parent simply because Mom or Dad did. *Don't try to snuff out the child's love.*

Usually, neither side is satisfied with the details of a divorce decree. But it serves an excellent purpose: it provides a solid framework for your children's lives. In Lida's case, Randy was to have the children the first and third weekends of each month. Sometimes he refused to take them when it was his turn. Other times he might show up to get them on Lida's weekends. We encouraged Lida to stand firm in following the decree requirements. It need not be cast in cement; there might be special circumstances—a circus in town, an unavoidable job demand (but *not* the reason: "I'll be cooking meth this weekend, so I'm taking the kids next week instead"). But a stable environment requires that the children's visitations be orderly and predictable. Lida should confront Randy regarding irregular visitation and insist he honor the written agreement, for the sake of the children's stability.

"Understand, these are not legal parameters. You should talk to a lawyer about legal ramifications of any of this," Dr. Hemfelt cautioned.

229

To confront Randy regarding his illegal practices is a choice only Lida can make. We suggested she make the children's safety her primary consideration. If his illegalities endangered their physical safety, she should immediately take whatever legal steps were necessary to protect them.

"Should I tell the kids about Randy's drug problem? I mean, the whole thing, even though I can't prove it?"

"Don't deny it. That's enabling," Dr. Hemfelt advised. "You can avoid acknowledging it in a blaming way, though. For example, we told a woman with a similar question that 'Your dad's a drunk' is deprecating. 'You dad has a bad problem with alcohol and it concerns me' is non-blaming."

"Above all," Dr. Hemfelt added, "keep in mind that you are not responsible for solving his problem. You are not his keeper. You are no longer his spouse. Make him take full responsibility for his own actions."

"What do I tell the kids when I'm so adamantly against what Randy is doing?"

"You tell them, 'I don't agree with your dad's behavior, but he is still your father. I know you love him, and that's proper. Love has nothing to do with behavior.' "

Lida leaned forward in her chair. "But do I stress to the kids that he's outside the law? Pete was asking about it. What do I tell Pete without tearing Randy down?"

"Acknowledge Randy's behavior, yes, but in this manner: 'You and I can't control his behavior. Only he can make himself obey the law. We can tell him we don't approve, but we can't tell him to quit and expect him to.' "

"No," said Lida sadly. "No. I gave that up long ago."

Sixth: Grieve the Losses

The sixth step towards wholeness as a parenting couple is an area you already know well: grief. You went through the process individually as you worked through the vicissitudes of your family of origin. Now think about what you have lost as a pair, the months and the years that locusts have eaten.

Rob and Alice mutually grieved through the emptiness of

their emotional distance, the lost delight that sexual expression can be, the frustrations and anger. So much. So much.

Rob claimed he remained true to Alice despite her sexual distance, and technically it was true. Emotionally he had mistresses, though—his work, his food, his TV set.

Another client, named Karen, explained why she sought a divorce from her husband of four years. "I found myself staying long at work, rather than going home to him. The better work looked, the worse he looked. Finally, I told myself, 'This is ridiculous,' and bowed out." There was no other man in Karen's life; her job played the role of gigolo. Such affairs, and also any affair in the classic meaning of the word—a sexual dalliance—must be expunged, forgiven, and grieved. It ruptured the family circle. It damaged and destroyed. Deal with it.

Alice Newport spent a week of her hospital stay explaining how Rob had driven her to an overuse of drugs with his constantly demanding attitude, his weight gain, his lack of attention and appreciation. She got *so tired* of waiting for that man!

She spent another week and more trying to come to grips with her own portion of responsibility for the dysfunctions in her marriage. Then suddenly during a group session she grasped just how much her dependency had cost her. Rob's distance. The children's lost nurturing. All the times she was out to lunch and missing the nuances and joys of life. The onerous financial cost. And the shame; the raw, unmitigated shame; her own and Rob's and the children's. It all burst upon her. She wept for three days.

How important is this grief? If we do not grieve out this past pain in the marriage, we will carry that pain, probably as deep resentments, into the future of the marriage and eventually into the lives of our own children.

Seven: Give and Receive

Everyone agrees that marriage is a process of give and take. Very few actually do it. Here you reactivate that principle of reciprocity. Remember how eager you were to give when the courtship was new, when the bloom still graced the rose? It's still just as rewarding, if you let it be.

In counsel Dr. Hemfelt gives a big pile of facial tissues to each spouse. "Rob, give a tissue to Alice. Alice, give one to Rob. That's it. Keep giving; as soon as you receive one, give one. How fast can you go before you run out? That's right; you never do. Now let's say that Rob says, 'I'm afraid my needs aren't being met, so I'm not going to give. I'm going to hoard. I need them. What if I catch a cold or something?' Alice gives you a tissue; that's right; and you keep it. Now how long before one of you runs out? Do you see the damage to the give-and-take that lack of trust engenders?"

What exactly might a couple give and take besides nose tissues?

Alice: "I want half an hour of your time and attention each evening, with the TV off. Not in bed, not during dinner. When you get home or after supper, sometime like that, but attention paid to just me."

Rob: "I'll check the TV guide."

This couple just illustrated the ground rules:

1. Be specific, as was Alice. No generalizations. Whether or not your partner can provide doesn't matter yet. Ask. Just acknowledging your need is helpful in itself.

2. Each spouse states clearly what he or she is willing to give. It may be all of what was requested, it may be none. The answer in either case must be honest. Rob didn't say, "I will," or, "I won't," because he wasn't sure he could deliver. The ball is in his court and he knows what his wife wants. Perhaps he'll prize fifteen minutes out of his work schedule. Maybe he'll even turn TV off for an hour. The groundwork is in place for a solution.

Rob: "I want your love four times a week, minimum."

Alice: "Oh, come on! Zero to four's a big jump! How about twice for starters? I'm not sure I want to commit to more than two, but I will promise that much for you, because I know you want it."

Give and take. Give and take. Being honest. There's the key. Make no idle promises.

Go back now, especially to the thoughts you had regarding

sharing in your marriage, or lack of it, and pick out other points of contention, other areas that can profit from this reciprocity.

The first six steps, which is to say the process through and including grieving, was the down. Give and take is the first of the up steps. From here on, it gets better and better.

Once this process begins to flow, a heady sort of excitement takes over. *The more I give, the more I get back.* That is one of the best ways to rejuvenate a relationship gone stale.

"But wait! No!" you cry. "You're making a mechanical monster out of something that ought to be spontaneous! If I have to ask for it, it's not from my spouse's heart. It's not real, not authentic if it's not offered spontaneously."

To which Dr. Hemfelt replies, "Fallacy!"

One of the damaging family myths we encounter in our work is, "If I have to ask for it, it doesn't count." In healthy, noncodependent families, people indeed ask, because nobody in those families is a mindreader. Men and women so rarely think alike. Frequently they want and need different things. There is no way they can perceive their spouse's needs unless those needs are voiced. Don't force yourself or your mate into a vain attempt at mindreading.

Eighth: Adjust Boundaries

A perfectly serviceable Tahitian house consists of four stout poles supporting a thatched roof and a platform floor far enough above the ground that the pigs have space beneath. The adobe walls of a classic hacienda in New Mexico are eighteen inches to two feet thick, effectively insulating the home from torrid summer days and frigid winter nights. And then there's your modern mobile home, and your basic igloo . . .

Because the symbol of your family is an imagined dollhouse, you can make it anything you wish, prosaic or romantic. In our eighth and ninth steps to wholeness, we're going to adjust the walls, whatever they are.

Too thick? Even adobe walls can be built too thick. Your family's walls are too thick if your family is your whole life.

When Mom and Dad have no close friends outside the family circle, when the kids are permitted no outside interests, when family activity is the only activity for parents and children, the walls are far too protective. The children's rooms cannot expand. For that matter, neither can the parents'. Shave the walls thinner by cultivating outside interests, friendships outside the family.

Too thin? When Dad is a workaholic, he's dragging his workplace inside, making the wall bulge outward. Any affair damages the fragile wall. The boundary is being violated. Thicken the wall by placing the family first, by immediately ending the affair whether it is one in the classic sense or an addictive love of work or food—whatever.

How thick the walls should be is in part cultural. Certain cultures and ethnic groups place a stronger emphasis on family than do others. Let your cultural priorities shape your family but not lock it into a rigid mold.

Ninth: Search Out Stressors

Related to all this is a search for stressors. What is putting pressure on your family? Over-scheduling and not enough time? Frictions that can be eased by a give-and-take session? Is Mom or Dad spending an inordinate amount of time rescuing or visiting an elderly relative? Let's ease off. Intense or demanding commitments don't affect one member only. Remember, every family member suffers impact. Jettison whatever obligations you must in order to put your family on an even keel.

Incidentally, this may well include financial stressors. We have advised more than once that a family move to a less costly home, sell the power boat that's draining two hundred dollars a month in payments, do without that four-wheel drive recreational vehicle. Simplifying, particularly for single parents, is usually a good thing.

Walls within the dollhouse require attention also. Draw again a picture of your family expressed as circles within a circle. Be honest; are you drawing some circles too close together for their own good? Too distant? The walls within may need considerable adjustment, particularly those of growing children.

Most of all, take a close look at intergenerational boundaries. Reviewing the aspects of emotional incest, do you see any of that present in your family now? Are your children assuming any adult roles? End that!

Brian Newport wasn't free to be a kid. He was shielding Jenny-Jo from both herself and her parents' wrath. He was constantly calming troubled waters. He had picked up the slack in the kitchen and elsewhere when his mom didn't quite cut it. When Alice went into the hospital, Dr. Warren strongly cautioned Rob, "It's going to be very easy to simply make Brian the baby-sitter. He comes home when Jennifer does. He's there. He's old enough. He's mature. He's cheap. I'm sure you're thinking it's his family duty to help out in this crisis, unpaid or nearly so."

"So why not?"

"Do you remember your thoughts when Brian was born?"

"Not exactly. Happy. Incredibly happy. I never mentioned to Alice but I really wanted a son. Bingo. Brian."

"Happiness. Yes." Dr. Warren nodded in agreement. "And a feeling of responsibility. I recall when my Matthew was born I felt an overwhelming sense of responsibility. What in heaven's name am I getting into? Am I ready for fatherhood? It's a heavy burden."

"Yeah." Rob smiled. "Yeah. Panic is another way to phrase it."

"Is that a responsibility you want to dump on a sixteen-year-old boy?"

"Brian can handle it. You'd be amazed how mature he is. He's even a pretty good cook."

"I agree he probably can handle it and school too. But I said, 'Do you really want to do that to him?'"

"I see your point. There's far more to housewifing than just watching the kid."

"True. So true."

Another area of intergenerational boundaries you should consider is that of extended family. Are grandparents intruding too closely, always ready to fill in, perhaps even meddling? Are they so distant that the kids haven't seen them in years? Any maiden aunts or down-on-their-luck uncles putting pressures on the system? Assess the pressures other family members are putting on your dollhouse, and ease those situations.

Take another look now at the blame list with which you started out the chapter. Think not so much about the items in it, but rather about your attitudes toward those items. How have your attitudes changed, for that is the crux of a marriage—the attitudes toward one another.

There are, however, problems that even healthy attitudes cannot surmount. Let's look at a few of them.

Tenth: Dealing with Special Problems

Beth Trask looked comfortable and settled in her over-stuffed chair in Dr. Hemfelt's office. Whalon looked decidedly unsettled. He fumed, "We've been at this for weeks now, and it's stupid. Just plain stupid. Passing Kleenex back and forth. Joey's still wearing those shirts and that long hair and he's still arguing. Passing Kleenex around isn't going to make him shape up. I told Dr. Warren, and I'm telling you, Dr. Hemfelt. No more of this. We're quitting."

Dr. Hemfelt sat back. "Have you both agreed to this?"

"We've been talking about it," Beth replied. "I can see what we're doing. It's starting to come together for me. I can see what's going on in our family better."

"It's silly and it's over. We just wanted to let you know. Whalon hopped to his feet. "Come on. Nothing personal, you understand, Dr. Hemfelt." He paused at the door.

Beth sat still.

"Well?" he snapped.

She studied the bookshelf only because it blocked her view of infinity beyond. "I'm thinking."

"You're not supposed to think!" Whalon froze. He glanced about.

Her voice purred, remarkably steady, "That, Whalon, is one of the problems."

Still visibly embarrassed, he muttered, "I'm going over to Plano to get those junction boxes for the church. You coming?"

"Not yet. Pick me up, please, on your way back through."

"Beth . . ."

Beth's voice remained firm and gentle. "I understand now. I can't control whether you keep with this or not. Probably if you drop out Joey will too. I can't control that, either. I need this. I'm doing this for me."

Whalon glared at her. He glared at Dr. Hemfelt. He left.

Whalon's attitude was no surprise to either of the doctors. Their work is not overrun with happy endings. People do drop out short of the goal.

We want to emphasize what we've said before in several different ways. Recovery for you and for your children is, in every case, an individual thing. It begins with you as an individual. And whether your spouse takes part or not, you personally and individually will derive great value. Healing is healing. Your children need it, as do you. None of us is unblemished. So pursue as best you can a path of recovery tailored to your needs and your limitations.

Lida Armstrong sat in Dr. Warren's office mulling over her own special problems. "Randy—my ex-husband—has been using court appearances to harass me. Thirty-seven appearances in the last two years. Know what he said? 'You can make your life a lot simpler by remarrying me.' 'On your terms, right?' I said. 'Right, because my terms are right and yours are wrong.' Can you imagine? I wouldn't give him the time of day, let alone engage in a save-the-marriage session. No. He's done too much to me."

"You've assured me your first interest is the children."

"It is!" Lida sagged back in her chair. "I understand the kids need a marriage as part of their lives. But the way things are now, or in the foreseeable future . . . ," she sighed. "I guess I'd better deal with the way things are now."

"Always a good idea."

"Then I have questions."

Dr. Warren smiled. "We have plenty of time. Shoot."

"First one. Randy has a live-in relationship with some woman. The children and Randy all know I'm dead-set against that sort of immorality. Do I halt visitation until he ends the situation? How much does that damage the kids?"

"That's a toughy." Dr. Warren thought about it a few minutes. "The relationship is confusing and discouraging to the children. I definitely would not halt visitation; that puts the onus on you. But I would insist they not stay overnight there. Knowing in theory about their father's intimacies and actually seeing them are two very different things."

"Minimize impact, you mean."

"Exactly."

"All right," Lida continued, "how about the rules? I mean, for instance, he lets them watch R-rated stuff; maybe even X-rated, for all I know. He says they can eat anything they want there—they're always holding it up to me. 'Dad lets us do—whatever.' I know the only reason he lets them have the moon is to make me look like the villain. I'm pictured as the old witch with the suffocating rules. What do I do?"

Dr. Warren frowned. "Remember, we're looking for stability. The rules in your home are yours; the rules in his are his. If you confront him, you should not say, 'I know you're doing this because you don't like me.' Rather, approach it as, 'The difference between your rules and mine is too confusing for the kids. We have to make some compromise here; bring the two sets closer together.' Then be ready to compromise somewhat."

She grimaced. "Easy for you to say."

Our Goal

The end of all this marriage mending and enrichment is to build a strong parenting team. If your circumstances require it, you may have to work on a strong one-person parenting team. The positive changes you are making in your marriage in this present generation will pay enormous dividends for your children in the next generation.

In Part 3 we will consider your work as a team. If you are a single parent, or like Beth Trask—a parent whose spouse is not participating—you will not be able to complete the role of your spouse completely. But Part 3 will offer you insight into what must be done and some ways to accomplish the job effectively. For now, let's focus again on the next generation and see how we might help your child improve relationships outside the family.

CHAPTER 13

The Child: Who Am I in the Community?

One of the wealthiest and most socially elevated of England's untitled families, the Nightingales, consorted with royalty. As befits Victorian gentry, Father spent considerable time sequestered in his study. He went to the club. He stood for Parliament. Mother ruled the two daughters, Florence and Parthe, with so iron a hand and so strong a notion as to what was proper, that when she forbade her thirty-year-old Florence to leave home and take nursing training, Florence almost didn't go.

Almost. At age thirty-three she finally left her parents' direct supervision in order to run a women's hospital in London. There she endured her trial by fire as cholera swept the city. What she learned in that hospital served her well a year later in 1854 when the secretary of war, a close family friend, asked her to go to Turkey. Hospitals there were receiving casualties from the Crimean conflict. They needed a nursing supervisor, Sidney Herbert said, someone to organize nursing care. She went.

Two years later England welcomed home a genuine heroine, and Florence Nightingale had become the stuff of history and legend.

In Victorian England the only proper way a girl of breeding could leave the dollhouse was through marriage. Florence never married, so she broke cultural precedent simply by walking out the door. She broke another by taking up nursing, a then dishonorable profession. By the sheer strength of her own image and character, as brought back by the Crimean veterans, she transformed nursing in the public eye into a respectable pursuit for dedicated professionals.

Most of our children will not leave home quite so dramatically as did Florence Nightingale, and the culture has changed. Today if a girl hasn't left home by age twenty-five, married or not, she's considered a bit strange. Setting out beyond the dollhouse walls is for most children the ultimate rite of passage.

You can expect certain characteristics of emerging independence to pop up in your early teen. Some make the transition from childhood (primarily within the dollhouse) to adulthood (primarily outside the dollhouse) smoothly. Children who carry our pain almost always do not. They rip themselves away violently, even as they yearn for the security of home.

In this chapter we will look at how parents can help their children walk out of the dollhouse door confidently and successfully. Now kids have an opportunity to test the boundaries they have learned inside, and the identity they have developed there, in the outside world. In doing so they will answer the question, "Who am I in the community?"

Five Principles for a Child to Remember

Dr. Warren challenges kids to take five principles they learn in counsel (as can you with your own children) through life with them: (1) celebrate your gifts as you accept your weaknesses, (2) balance new privileges with responsibility, (3) always answer the question, "Why do I do what I do?" with honesty, (4) recognize the power of your peer relationships, and (5) remember that what happens to you is up to you.

1. Celebrate Your Gifts as You Accept Your Weaknesses

In Chapter 7 we talked about grieving the sadnesses, the losses, the shortcomings. Equally important is celebrating the fun and exciting things, the gifts and talents. Unfortunately, many children, such as Nancy, have never been taught to celebrate the gifts God has given them.

Nancy was a charming, quiet little girl, very poised for only age eleven. She sat serenely with her hands folded as

Five Principles
for Children to Remember
as They Walk out the Door
into the Community

1. Celebrate your gifts as you accept your weaknesses.

2. Balance new privileges with responsibility.

3. Always answer the question, "Why do I do what I do?" with honesty.

4. Recognize the power of your peer relationships.

5. Remember that what happens to you is up to you.

Dr. Warren listened to a tape of her recent piano recital piece. The *Warsaw Concerto* rolled to its exuberant conclusion.

"Wow, Nancy!" Dr. Warren popped the cassette out of his stereo. "You're really good!"

"Oh, no! I wouldn't say that."

"Why not?"

"That would be conceited."

"What would you say?"

"I don't know. But not something conceited."

"If someone else had played that, would it be good?"

"I guess so." Nancy frowned. "But our pastor says we mustn't be conceited."

"Let's say you give a friend a special present because you like her so much, a very beautiful gift. And she goes around telling everybody, 'Oh, that's not a very nice gift.' How would you feel?"

"If she was really my friend she wouldn't say that."

"That's right, Nancy! God has given you a beautiful gift; that is, your talent. You're making the most of it, but you didn't manufacture your talent. God did. If you came in crowing, 'Boy, I'm the greatest piano player in America!' or something, that's conceit. But being pleased with the talent God has given you is honoring God. Celebrating it is perfectly proper, so long as you give credit where credit is due. Do you see?"

Children in particular (and frequently adults as well) fear celebrating personal accomplishments. There's even a school of theology which says that finding anything good inside myself is self-worship. We suggest that an attitude of that sort is actually self-centered, because the focus is still firmly fixed on the self; the attitude is egocentric. I am this; I am not that.

Children who are afraid of appearing conceited will frequently wall off their talents and bury their gifts, thereby missing out on the joy God intended for them. Rephrased, we help children see the difference between honest rejoicing ("I have been blessed!") and false pride ("I make the sun come up!" crows the rooster).

We urge children and adults regardless of their religious persuasion to focus on God, seeing gifts and talents as true gifts. The theologian who celebrates worthlessness says nothing good about either himself—God's handiwork, or God—the giver of the gift.

2. Balance New Privileges with Responsibility

In counsel we work toward two ultimate ends, which at the very end become one: We help children develop personal accountability by understanding themselves inside and by learning to weigh and balance duties against privileges. We then help them take those skills outside the home. Personal accountability comes only with strong boundaries. Whether teens like those boundaries or not, Dr. Warren tries to help them see such limits and bounds realistically. Joey Trask saw the light during one of their regular sessions.

"They never let me do anything." Joey had been going on for five minutes about his strictured existence. "Mom and Dad treat me like a baby. They just don't like to let me have any fun."

"Give me a for-instance." Dr. Warren sat back.

"Like I want to go down to the West End. Hey, everybody that's anybody goes down there. It's where things are happening."

"You're really angry about this. I can see how strongly you feel. Can you think of a reason your parents wouldn't want you to go, other than your belief that they don't want you to have fun?"

"No, man!" Joey waved a hand. "Everybody goes there."

"Almost everybody. I don't. Think a moment. Why do some people stay away from there?"

"You mean the night stuff? The gangs and stuff?"

"You read the papers, Joey. How much gang activity in that area in the last month?"

"Yeah, but that won't happen to me."

"Oh." Dr. Warren cocked his head. "Are you experienced in dealing with dangerous situations? Knives, guns, gang members, drug dealers?"

"Well, uh . . ."

245

"I suggest your parents are sincerely trying to act in your best interests. They may be concerned that you'd be over-whelmed. In over your head and they can't protect you."

"Yeah, well, maybe . . ."

"Besides." Dr. Warren smiled. "It's a lot better to tell the other kids at school, 'I can't go because my folks won't let me' instead of 'I'm really kind of scared to go there.'"

Joey broke into a self-conscious grin. "Yeah!"

In the very beginning of counsel, Beth Trask commented that every time they gave Joey a little slack, a bit more re-sponsibility, he messed up. Young Tiffany, currently in Dr. Warren's counsel, had the same problem.

"My parents keep grounding me!" fifteen-year-old Tiffany wailed. "Twice this month and it's only the twenty-third!"

"Tell me about the latest one," Dr. Warren suggested.

"I wanted to go to the movies on Saturday, but Friday a couple of us were driving around and Billy got a ticket. And when Mom heard about it, she grounded me. I wasn't the one who got the ticket!"

"What'd he get the ticket for?"

"Well, it wasn't a ticket exactly. I mean, he got that too. But he got arrested for driving with an open container. The ticket was for speeding."

"Beer in the car." Dr. Warren didn't have to be a lawyer to picture the scene.

"I didn't drink any, honest!"

"It's illegal to have an open container in the car, not to mention speeding. You and Billy both knew that, right?"

"Yes, but I didn't do anything. It was Billy."

"I believe you, and I understand your frustration. Now stop. Take your feet out of Tiffany's shoes and put them in your parents'. Look at the picture the way they see it. When your parents let you out, you get into trouble. Not yourself, necessarily, but you end up in trouble situations. Ever hear about double messages?"

"No."

"Double messages are when your words say one thing but your actions say something else. Not just kids do it; adults do it all the time too. With your words, you say you want your parents to let you make grown-up choices. But then you mess up, almost as if it were deliberate. This last time, for instance, you allowed yourself to be put in an illegal situation; your actions are saying, 'I'm not ready to take on adult responsibilities.' "

When parents' motives are discussed outside the context of anger (both the child's anger and the parents'), older children usually develop solid insights about themselves. Tiffany at fifteen was able to understand in the abstract, to see principles behind decisions. Jennifer Newport at nine would not be.

Joey Trask is just beginning to. He, too, displayed double messages. Dr. Warren explained double messages to Joey just as he did with Tiffany. But it took several such explanations before Joey could really grasp what he was doing. If your early teen misses, don't despair. It will come.

If your child is eleven years old or younger, philosophical observations will zip right overhead, miss completely. Children simply don't think that way yet. But the underlying principle is the same for both the Tiffanys and the Jennifers: *Decision making is a balance between duty and privilege. Jiggles in that balance characterize the emerging teen.*

For the Jennifer-aged child, saying, "I want you to make your bed when you get up each morning in order to prepare you for the day when you're on your own. It's a good habit to develop early" doesn't mean a whole lot. "You can't leave the house until you make your bed" means much more. It's immediate. It's not abstract.

Edicts of this sort do not smack of punishment, though a child may claim so. Punishment is inflicted from the outside; in other words, the locus of control is outside the child. The either/or edict places the locus of control inside the child. Do this and that will happen. Fail to do this and that privilege is withheld. The child determines the outcome.

The child learns self-responsibility step-by-step, by learning to make the small decisions first.

3. Always Answer the Question, "Why Do I Do What I Do?" with Honesty

When Joey Trask and Tiffany sent out those double messages, they were being dishonest, though they didn't realize it. Their mouths said, "I want more freedom!" Their actions, driven by forces beyond the conscious level, said, "I'm afraid to be out there free and loose!"

In counsel over a period of time, Dr. Warren encouraged Joey Trask to examine the motivations for that haircut, those shirts, the punk manner. Was he doing it to please himself or to irritate his father? Would irritating his father serve Joey's purposes well?

As he talked to sixteen-year-old Brian Newport, Dr. Warren again urged examination of motives.

"Brian? Have you ever thought about why you don't want a driver's license yet?"

Brian shrugged. "Insurance costs too much."

"Your father doesn't seem to think the cost is worth worrying about. Insurance is your only consideration?"

"I guess so."

Dr. Warren changed his tack. "I understand you'd like to go to Nepal someday. Why?"

"It's such an amazing place. I've read about it a lot—in *National Geographic* and a couple of those big coffee-table books. You're talking about a whole country a couple of miles above sea level and the world's greatest mountains. I mean, the greatest."

"Sounds fascinating!" Dr. Warren agreed. "Let's say your dad developed an interest in it too. Or he just wanted to get away from all his troubles for a while. If he offered to go and take you along, would you go?"

"You bet!"

"That would cost thousands of dollars for, essentially, recreation. Yet you're reluctant to spend a few hundred to maintain insurance with a driver's license. Can you think of other reasons you might not want to learn to drive?"

Brian stared at him a minute. He chuckled. "I should've seen that one coming. OK." He thought a few minutes. "I don't know. It's just that, well, it's a big responsibility. Your life. The life of everyone around you. It's scary."

"Now we're getting down to honesty."

It's extremely difficult to bare one's deepest motivations. Younger children cannot. But if the teen is ready to leave the dollhouse, he's capable of examining his reasons for doing things.

4. Recognize the Power of Your Peer Relationships

In the Australian outback, one man and a good dog can comfortably handle a thousand sheep. No worries, mate. All thousand of them move essentially as one big, wooly lump; get the front end doing what you want, and the whole lump follows through. Sheep follow like—well, like sheep.

Sheep and young teenagers share some traits, unfortunately.

There goes your sixth-grader out the door. She whines, "I want to make my own decisions. I can think for myself!" And then she dresses like everyone else in her class. She follows their fads, drools over their music groups, does whatever they do. A bunch of clones. That's thinking for yourself? Bah!

A child's primary support group before adolescence is the parents, followed closely by siblings, then extended family members. Someone in that circle will know the answers, will know what to do in a tight situation. That all begins to fall apart somewhere around the fifth grade.

The child now takes an intermediate step between depending on the family for answers and depending on himself or herself; the child latches onto a decision-making peer group. This is not a one-on-one thing. It's one-on-group. There is power in numbers, and all these people think the same way. That way is not necessarily the parents' way. It's not necessarily the sensible way. Privately, children may in fact differ strongly with the peer attitude. If so, the peers never find out. Thus, "I want to make my own decision" means I want to dress like every other kid in school whether I like the style or not.

This fact of early teen life especially tortured Whalon

Trask. He had no way of knowing Joey mentally might not be going along with the crowd. Whalon did not understand that this phase is as important a growth task as any other. He only saw the T-shirts and hair. He only saw Joey suddenly marching to another drummer.

Boy-boy comradeships and girl-girl friendships exert some pressure. But the boy-girl relationship is a roller-coaster ride.

The Added Power of Love Relationships

Age three: "Mommy, I love you!"
Age nine: "Girls stink! Yucch!"
Age twelve: "Ah, who needs 'em?"
Age sixteen: "Darling, I love you!"

What goes around comes around. Adults love to make jokes about teen hormones. Grade-schoolers love to tease. The only ones who don't think it's all that funny are the teens.

Teens' sexual development doesn't shoot straight up, like an arrow, in one direction. It's a roller coaster, up one hour and down the next, grinding along under the tight control of the drive chain one moment and flying uncontrolled the next.

Children who carry our pain, already suffering codependency problems, have it even worse. The throes of first love are painful enough for the healthy teen. "Never did anyone feel as I feel; never has anyone gone through this so intensely." And as a footnote: "Certainly not Mom and Dad." But the codependents' place of happiness and control lies outside themselves, in the object of their affections. What little control they might have had isn't there. Because a hallmark of codependency is to go to extremes, the roller-coaster highs are higher, the lows lower. For a teen, that's excruciating.

What's a parent to do? The parent with codependency problems already feels a love-hate relationship with the child: "I can't live with him, and I can't live without him." Of course you want the child to achieve independence. *But . . .*

250

Guidelines that worked previously work well here also. *First, let the child know you understand and empathize.* Let them know you see their point before making yours.

"Joey," asked Dr. Warren, "what were your folks like at your age?"

"I, uh . . . you know."

"What were their interests? When did they meet? Any clues?"

"Uh, I think they met at some sort of community thing. A picnic or something." He shook his head. "You know? I don't have the slightest idea. I can't imagine Dad being thirteen. He just, he isn't; he can't . . . you know?"

What Joey voiced so eloquently is the common feeling of early teens. Parents have always been parents and they always will be. Teen urges and needs? They just don't understand. It's a barrier you will surmount, if at all, simply by pointing out the obvious: you, too, began life as an infant and worked your way up.

Next, set boundaries. The teen leaving the house for a date should always have a specific destination and a specific (approved!) activity in mind. When the teen leaves the house, the roller coaster is probably at the low end of the ride. By the end of the evening, they will likely be topping out, headed for the "Wheeeee!"

Finally, be there for them. Some years ago, teen sobriety advocates suggested contracts to be signed between parent and child. If the kid hits big trouble, gets drunk, or ends up in the company of a drinking companion and needs a hand, he or she calls the parents for a ride home or whatever else is needed. In return, the parents stay off the kid's case. No questions asked until a more appropriate time. For some parents it's a drastic and necessary step. A much better step, however, is for the child to absolutely know, from childhood on, that a phone call to the parents is the first and best thing to do. That's another benefit of the pledge, "I'll be there for you."

Someone has to ride herd on the roller coaster, not to stop it, but to keep the riders in the car.

251

5. Remember That What Happens to You Is Up to You

This resolution is a variation on the duty-with-privilege principle. If you do so-and-so, such and such results.

Only after the child takes that long journey of discovery, learning what lies inside and how it works—grieving and celebrating what is found—is he or she strong enough to accept personal responsibility. The act of exploring inside brings the center of interest and control inside. This is myself. I can do this and that.

Children, particularly younger children, may not be able to discuss all this, but that doesn't mean they can't internalize it all the same. Even children Joey Trask's age and older may find it hard to put intangibles into words.

Balance between privileges and responsibilities, like the seesaw of balance between the dependence and independence, is a skill to be honed throughout life.

With the balances in mind, if not in place, with insight sufficient to know why he or she ticks, the child can at last shed the pain of others and embark on rewarding relationships outside the home. However young the child may be now, he or she is on the road to building relationships that do not simply gratify one's own needs but serve a larger purpose.

The Beginning of the End

Joey was wearing a plain yellow T-shirt today. He sprawled in his chair with arms and legs flung out like a Tinkertoy gone berserk. "I don't understand exactly why we're here. I mean, it's been a couple months and what are we doing?"

"What do you think we should be doing?"

"Aw, come on, Dr. Warren. I ask a question and you bounce it right back to me. I'm asking you this time. What do you want to accomplish? You keep asking me that. I'm asking you."

"My goal is to help you achieve what every thirteen year old deserves simply because he is thirteen: whatever happiness that being thirteen offers."

"Big deal. In a couple months I'll be fourteen. Then we start over, huh?"

"Hardly. You should know what's happening inside yourself well enough by then that you can achieve your own happiness."

He mulled that a moment. "Maybe so. Mom and I aren't doing too bad any more. Dad quit, but she's still going to Dr. Hemfelt and I'm coming here and it's easier now."

"Splendid. How are you and your dad getting along?"

Joey shrugged with false casualness. "Mom says he should talk to me, and he says he won't talk to anybody with hair like this. So we don't talk."

"Why *do* you wear your hair long?"

"I don't know."

"Not good enough. Everything has a reason, remember? Let's explore that."

Joey shifted his legs to a different configuration, still sprawled. "I guess to . . . naw. I was going to say, 'to make Dad mad.' I can do that without the hair."

"How do the girls like it?"

"Some of them do, some don't, I guess."

"How do you like it?"

"It's a pain to wash when it's this long, so I don't wash it as much as I should. Especially when I oversleep."

"So you're not doing it to please yourself at all."

"Yeah, I guess that's true."

The First Resolution

Along the final mile of our journey in counsel, we lead children beyond self-realization (always helpful in itself even if we get no further than that) into practical ways to put their new knowledge to use. You as a journeymate can do the same.

The first major resolution is: *Mean what you say and say what you mean. Make certain your actions say the same thing your words do.*

Poor communication is a major cause of friction. Often children, and adults as well, say one thing with their actions as they say quite another with their words. Helping the child to see what's happening and to avoid the trap does much toward helping him succeed in life.

The second major resolution: *What happens to you is up to you.*

This is the exact opposite of the codependency tenet that sets the locus of control outside oneself. "Mom did it to me . . . Dad made me . . . My friends made me . . . My brother did it to me . . . It's my teacher's fault . . . I have a lousy school."

As You Tackle the Job

Whalon Trask faced a daunting dilemma. As your child shrugs free of parental control and steps out into the big, bad world, how do you balance your personal standards of conduct against your child's changing behavior? Where is the line between "wrong" and "different"? When, if at all, do you let the child cross it?

The child constantly changes and adjusts to life at home as he or she grows within the family, for the child's thought patterns, skills, and interests change radically. If the parent does not keep up with these changes, adjusting parenting skills to fit the situation, friction such as the Trasks' develops. You can avert much of that friction, nip problems in the bud, and give your child a much better start in life by adopting some attitudes that automatically change and flex as the child grows. They are:

1. "I'll do whatever I perceive is in your best interest, both now and in the future, to help you walk out the front door successfully."

This was no pretty platitude for Lida Armstrong. Her commitment to act in her children's best interest cost her her marriage. The bitterest pill to swallow: neither child appreciated her sacrifice. Your child may well fail to appreciate your commitment to act in his or her best interest also.

Theologians often claim that God gives us not what we want but what we need. So shall you. But what your child wants and what your child needs may be two very different things. You can see the corollary to this: What your child asks for is not the primary reason to give or do something.

Six Parental Attitudes
That Will Help Your Child
Grow Up Successfully

1. "I'll do whatever I perceive is in your best interest, both now and in the future, to help you walk out the front door successfully."

2. "I will commit to setting clear boundaries and expectations."

3. "I will make every effort to understand your situation and your feelings as you leave this house."

4. "I will allow you to fail while it is still safe (while you still have your home to come home to). I renew the unspoken pledge: 'I will walk through this with you.'"

5. "I'm going to encourage you to have relationships outside the family, both with other adults and with peers."

6. "I will be committed to helping you understand that the secret of life is coping, not mastering."

Be prepared for flak as well as reward.

2. *"I will commit to setting clear boundaries and expectations."*

A most difficult task is building a child's boundaries, and it is the absolute best way to help him or her make the giant step into the world. When counseling children with problems—usually caused by poor boundaries or boundaries too thick, we teach basic principles that the parents can reinforce. They include the following, with which you are now familiar.

Duties are balanced against privileges; actions invite consequences. By giving the child a choice of actions, each with its attendant consequences, the parents can reinforce the cardinal rule: What happens is up to you. Good boundaries allow personal accountability.

We encourage the parents to insist their child also be accountable regarding integrity; that is, meaning what you say and say what you mean. This doesn't eliminate double messages, many of which are generated outside the conscious level, but it cuts down their number. Most important, it opens up responsible communication between parent and child.

3. *"I will make every effort to understand your situation and your feelings as you leave this house."*

The kitchen-to-dining-room door frame in a little house in Gonzales, Texas, is nearly black with pencil marks and dates. Every year or two, Mom would back her four kids up to the door frame and mark where the tops of their heads came. Then she'd enter the children's initials and height right there on the white paint, beside their marks. When at age eighty-four Mom finally went into a nursing home, her youngest son ripped out the door frame and brought it along, that she might keep it with her.

Parents truly enjoy watching their children grow. But there is a still a greater joy. Trying to understand your child's situations and feelings is not a skill you can ignore until the hour when your child leaves. It is a skill best nurtured from the child's infancy up. From this skill you will reap unexpected blessings. For as you get to know and understand your child better, you can take deep and genuine delight in watching him or her grow emotionally and cognitively as well as physically. No matter how much benefit your children will derive by being understood, you will derive more.

4. *"I will allow you to fail while it is still safe (while you still have your home to come home to). I renew the unspoken pledge: 'I'll walk through this with you.'"*

Perhaps you remember the case of Lane, who refused to do his homework. His parents did it for him for fear he might fail. Most parents don't work that blatantly to avoid seeing their children stumble, but in counsel we find all manner of amazing cases of a more subtle nature. We also find two different forces at work here.

Of course the parent who loves the child wants to see the child succeed. That's one force at work. We might call it the pep squad aspect. The other, more invidious force might be voiced as: "If my child fails, I will lose face before my friends. I can't bear to think what my friends would be saying if my little Johnny or Janie failed."

Stumbling quickly teaches the blind man where the curbs are. Failure may be an important teaching tool in your child's life.

5. *"I'm going to encourage you to have relationships outside the family, both with other adults and with peers."*

It's not just some ego trip that makes you as a parent want to remain the brightest sun in your child's sky. It is you who hold the attitudes and moral standards you want your child to hold. It is you who know the child's needs best; therefore you can serve them best. So it is terribly hard to gracefully step back and let other suns shine in your child's heavens.

Whalon Trask could not bring himself to step back. He discouraged Joey's outside relationships such as with the youth pastor Whalon deemed too immature. In Whalon's case the problem boiled down to a matter of control; he could not bear to relinquish it. What is the control situation in your own family?

The changeover will be much easier on you, as well as on your child, if you can accept that a hero of the child's own choosing will become the brief and momentary guiding light. Even more difficult to understand and accept is that inevitably your child will follow like sheep with a group you may or may not want to invite to a garden party.

You do correctly to forbid your child's association with an extralegal or illegal counterculture. We don't suggest that gangs are an option. We know from our experience, however, that the majority of parents view with distaste most peer groups. And yet, most groups are harmless, however different they may look.

Should you criticize your child's choice of appearance and friends? A limited bit of mild teasing helps the child's cause; it further separates the peer group from the adults. It helps you, too, to express some of your annoyance. Bitter invective and unrelenting sarcasm, though, work against you and honest communication.

6. *"I will be committed to helping you understand that the secret of life is coping, not mastering."*

Over and over we find the phenomenon repeated: kids are not interested in mastering their environment. All they want or need are the tools to cope.

We do not in any way promote mediocrity over excellence. That's not what is meant here. No person alive, however, can excel in every single area of his or her life. "Everybody is ignorant, only on different subjects," said Will Rogers.

Perfectionism is as much a compulsion as is any other. The child driven to excel where coping is sufficient will spend a miserable lifetime burning out.

In the end, coping mechanisms, such as grieving, become a form of mastery. "Life knocked me down, but I made it back up before the count."

The Essence of Healing

At Minirth-Meier we see as the essence of healing the ability to see yourself not so much as others see you but as God sees you. Without that insight, healing is difficult. The things to grieve and the things to celebrate together make the whole child, the child God sees. We try to make the child see himself or herself as God sees. This is the foundation of helping children shed the ill effects of codependency and cast off others' pain.

We have reviewed the pain that you carry from your own childhood, the remnant of that pain which has injured your marriage, and the legacy of that pain borne by your children. Let us turn now from individuals and look at the family as a unit—not a houseful of individuals (albeit healthy ones, now), but as an organism in and of itself.

PART THREE

THE FAMILY'S
ROAD
TO RECOVERY

CHAPTER 14

The Shape of Your Family

Nervously, uncertainly, Brian Newport glanced at Dr. Warren, at his father, and at Dr. Warren again.

Dr. Warren smiled. "Take your time. Think about it."

Brian led his father out into the middle of the open floor and left him standing there. He walked off to the side where all the furniture had been shoved, picked up a chair, paused, and put it down again.

He led his mother to the middle of the room and, after another moment's hesitation, positioned her just so. She stood four feet away from his father, their backs to each other.

He wasn't glancing about nervously anymore; he seemed to have forgotten Dr. Warren. All his attention now centered on his family and on the living sculpture he was creating. He led Jennifer out into the open space and placed her first here and then there. She whined a couple of times, breaking the silence that had been asked of her. Eventually he placed her not between his parents but beside them.

"Jen, you grab Dad's arm with your right hand there. Now take Mom's arm in your left. That way. Mom, no. You don't turn toward her. You keep looking that direction. Like that. Yes. Jen, you shake them. Jerk on them. Shake them hard. Like that. Right."

Jennifer yanked and tugged on her parents' arms.

"Now, Brian," Dr. Warren asked, "where do you fit in?"

Brian squatted down in a corner on his father's side of the room and hunched over.

"Before any of you move—Jennifer, you can quit shaking them—I'd like you each to look around. This is Brian's concept of what his family is. I want to commend you, Brian. It's very scary, representing how you think your family is in this way. It's revealing. Exposing. You did an excellent job by taking such great care, trying to do it the best you could. Thank you."

Alice sniffled. Dr. Warren passed her a tissue and she blew her nose.

"Rob, how do you feel about this sculpture?"

"It's disturbing. I'd say it even makes me a little mad. But I don't know why."

"Alice?"

"I never knew Brian felt this way. I'm all alone."

"Jennifer?"

"I don't know."

"Brian?"

He shrugged. "This is just how it feels is all."

"Remember your places; we'll try a variation on this a little later. Brian and Jennifer, will you bring out chairs for us, please?"

In instant motion, Jennifer bounded over to the side and came dragging a chair to Dr. Warren.

He set it in the middle of the floor and sat down. "When I ask a family member to build a sculpture of the family like this, I usually choose an older child. They have remarkable insights, although rarely can they express them verbally."

"What are you looking for?" Rob asked. He sat down near Dr. Warren. "Just the obvious? Like who's close to whom?"

"Yes. Relative positions can say a great deal. Who is close? Who is distant? Who faces whom? Brian placed you and your wife facing away from each other. Close together, but a world apart, literally; the circumference of the earth separating you. He thought about putting Jennifer between you; in a sense she has driven herself as a wedge between you. Instead he chose to place her between and yet outside. Think of this sculpture as a nonverbal statement."

Rob shook his head. "I'm surprised how powerfully it struck me. I'm usually not a mushy person."

"This is a whole different dimension of expression. We call it a kinesthetic expression of how the family functions."

Alice blew her nose again. Her makeup was smeared.

"Let's try another sculpture. Brian, if you would again." Dr. Warren stood up and moved his chair to the side. "Take your positions as you were, please. Now, Brian, if you can, change this present sculpture to express how you wish the family were. Tell me when you're satisfied with your new arrangement."

"I don't know. The way I'd like it best?"

"Or maybe the way you'd feel most comfortable in it. It's your choice. Whatever you think best. Take your time."

Brian didn't need much time. He'd gotten the hang of this. Now he positioned his mom and dad right next to each other. He placed their hands on each others' shoulders. They almost but not quite faced each other. He stood Jennifer in front of them, facing them to form a triangle. He laid their free hands on Jennifer's head.

"Me too?" he asked.

"Please."

Brian stood close to his father, holding his free hand. He let go of his dad's hand. He stepped back. He tried a position between them and backed out. "Jen, stand still. You're not supposed to be moving around." He stood beside his father, not too close, facing his mother, his hands at his sides. "This way."

"Rob? How do you feel?"

"I, uh . . . do you think we could ever get this way?"

"I'm confident you can. Alice?"

She sobbed openly. "I can't believe for all those years that I—that I . . ." She blew her nose in tissue number six.

"Jennifer?"

"I don't know."

"Brian?"

"It's scary, but it feels good. Is that silly?"

"Not at all. Beautifully stated. That is exactly what growing up is: very frightening and yet exhilarating. Rob, you'll notice that he is a part of the family and yet separate. It's the way he'd like to be, not the way things are now. You'll notice, too, that Jennifer is much calmer. That's no accident."

"I wanna do it too," Jennifer whined.

"I think that would be very enlightening. Let's do that."

The Shape of Things

You may wish to try this sort of exercise in your family. You may well find it revealing. Keep in mind, however, that no such device reflects "absolute truth." When we at the clinic employ the device professionally, we never let it stand alone. It is only one element in a great mass of data. So don't place weight on it that ought not be there.

We generally recognize that the youngest sculptor should be at least nine years old to work confidently. For a youngster, you might try coins. We use coins frequently, both for young children and for older clients who are sometimes a bit too inhibited to express themselves with full-size sculpture. Coins also work well for single parents and for broken families when not all the biological members can be in one place at one time.

Use quarters or half-dollars to represent Mom and Dad. Choose an appropriately sized coin for each child. Ask each person to arrange the coins in a pattern he or she thinks represents the family now. Talk about it. Why? How long has it been like this? Will it change? If so, to what? Then ask each person to rearrange the coins into a more comfortable configuration. Again ask why. Might it change? What would be the worst possible arrangement you can think of?

A girl of eight, when asked to structure the worst possible configuration of coins, removed all but the dime which represented herself.

"How did this arrangement happen?"

Here's how the child explained it: Mommy and Daddy got divorced and took her older brother, the nickel, with them. Both parents decided they didn't want her. When quizzed, the parents admitted they were considering divorce but couldn't agree on custodial arrangements. They adamantly insisted they had never, ever mentioned anything about this to the children. They were shocked that the mere thought of it had impacted their daughter so severely.

The coins and the sculptures, and perhaps at times drawings, accomplish two important purposes. First, they give visible form to the family relationships; they show how the sculptors view the family. More importantly, they give the family tacit permission to make the same kinds of changes, from what is to what ought to be, by showing what the family relationships can become. The idea of change has been given a body. It is no longer merely a concept; it's a viable goal to seek.

Always in counsel we pay close attention to the way a family unconsciously arranges themselves in a room, from their first appointment on. For instance, when the Trasks first sat down in Dr. Warren's office during that first session, Joey sat opposite them. No accident. And it wasn't by chance that Brian Newport sat close between his mom and dad while Jennifer took the odd-man-out chair. Dr. Warren keeps his desk shoved back against the wall behind him and sits out among the people he is talking with, on purpose.

Understand, again, that this is nowhere near foolproof. We counseled a ten-year-old boy who was at disastrous odds with his mother. Nonetheless he sat quite close to her. We learned later that the child was hard of hearing. He had to stay close to make out Mom's soft, light voice.

In therapy we may rearrange spaces and distances between family members deliberately. For example, one of us might alter the way a family is sitting by saying, "I'd like you two to move. You sit here; you and you sit together. Thank you." It's all treated quite casually. The therapist is using "structural family therapy," physically intervening to show the family nonverbally what a more satisfying structure might be. Yes, most families do pick up on the visual representation.

Sometimes we even ask a member to leave temporarily. What is the family structure without the eighteen year old to whom the parents cling so tenaciously? We show nonverbally by sitting the teen out in the hallway momentarily. See? The family remains a close family even after a member has left.

The goal, for us and presumably for you, is to get the family united in a healthy, honest vision of what is and of what can be.

Think back to when you and your spouse (or ex-spouse)

first became a couple. What family structure then, perhaps envisioned in an imaginary sculpture, influenced the way you treat your kids now? Your past influences the family sculpture that is your own family today. Once you have that structure clearly in mind, you can rearrange it to better meet the needs of you and your children.

The Making of a Parent

John kissed his bride. "I only ask one thing, darling. We eat supper when we feel like it, all right? Mom made my family be at the table on the dot at five. Every blessed day. Five. Dishes at 5:30, cleaned up by 6:00. Drove me nuts. Let's eat at 7:00 once in a while, huh? Please?"

John, who now eats anywhere between 4:00 and 8:00 P.M. illustrates one of the three common ways that young parents develop their parenting strategies. *Rebellious* is one of those ways, and it is not nearly so violent as it sounds.

- "Mom and Dad were so lenient with us that we felt lost. I'm raising my kids a lot stricter, let me tell you."
- "Assigning all those chores was OK when we were growing up on a farm. But my kids are growing up in a condo. I'm not going to do it like my parents did."

Another way is *compensatory*, pretty much accepting the parents' way while filling in where the young parents perceive a lack.

- "I like the way Mom and Dad sent us kids to bed by eight, and I'll do the same. But we never had any time together with our folks; I'll read a lot more, bedtime stories and Mother Goose and things like that before they go to sleep."
- "My parents thought fifty cents a week was plenty for allowance. Took us a month of hoarding to afford a fast food burger. My kids are getting a hefty enough allowance that they can buy something without having to save up for half of forever."

Finally, there's the *mimetic* way that new families develop strategies. They simply copy their parents' methods or, on occasion, copy those of a favored friend or relative.

- "Mom and Dad did it right; we all turned out pretty good. Why fix it if it ain't broke?"
- "I like the way Mom took some shortcuts to give herself more time with us. Hey, vacuuming the carpet was not the be-all and end-all of her existence. It's not going to be mine, either."

If these three ways worked perfectly, in a couple of generations we'd have perfect parents; as poor methods were abandoned and good methods preserved and improved. But they don't. Things go wrong. Parents try to do better but still make mistakes, or simply give up, burdened too heavily by other woes.

Every family has its little quirks in parenting—both ways that ought to be improved and also neat little tricks that work. In counsel we see all sorts of innovative parenting ideas that restore our faith in the resiliency of the human parent. We also see the sorry fruit of errors—children who cannot function well in society, who hold scant hope of happiness as adults.

Before looking at some parenting strategies that may well be new for you, let's glance briefly at a few methods that don't achieve what they should. They pop up distressingly often in our work at the clinic.

Things That Go Bump

Simultaneously, Mom hears: "Mom? I can't find my shoes." "I want my breakfast. I don't wanna wait any longer!" "Oh, incidentally, hon, the insurance man's going to be here this evening. We'll need all our medical records for the past year. See if you can find them, OK? I looked and I don't know where a lot of them are." "Gimme twenty-five cents for the fine on my library book, will you, Mom? And my report on rabbits was due last Friday. She says I have to finish it tonight if I want any grade at all. Know anything about rabbits?"

The Underorganized Family

If the chaos and lack of control in the underorganized family were the worst of it, living in this situation would still be a pain. Financial records in disarray, things lost, things not done on time, opportunities missed, constant upheaval, impatience, despair, anger. . . .

But all that inconvenience and loss is not the worst of it. The worst is that boundaries of all sorts have broken down, as well as the physical organization. The greatest need for a healthy childhood is healthy boundaries, appropriate bonding with different persons at different times of life. The chaotic family cannot offer them.

The child in such a family hangs constantly on tenterhooks. Will the things I need for school be ready in time? Will Dad come through when I need him? Will so-and-so remember such and such? No one in this family intentionally neglects the child's wants and needs. No one actually lacks love. It just doesn't all happen when it ought to. The rest of the world marches to a beat the chaotic family simply does not hear.

In the underorganized family, children must pick up the slack when parents fail. That's right: emotional incest. Kids find themselves meeting their own needs because the adults aren't doing it. Kids cannot relax and be kids; they have to worry about things they should not, at a tender age, be concerned with. Too often, the children are incapable of meeting certain of their own needs adequately. Trust, the foundation of all relationships, breaks down, brick by brick. Eventually the children learn they can trust no one to come through for them.

The Kolbins, for example, were chaotic. Reacting to his father Joseph's overcontrol, James wielded little. Melanie fought recurring depressions, which seriously blunted her ability to care for the kids.

The Overorganized Family

- "I bet she waxes her mailbox and irons her lawn."
- "Mom? My music lesson is over at 4:20 and I don't have

to be home 'til five. That's forty whole minutes. Can I go over to Leslie's then?"

- "He doesn't just clear his driveway when it snows; he shovels the street too."
- "Marly's teacher thinks Marly does all her homework in triplicate; one for her teacher, one for her files, and one for the Library of Congress."
- "Dad? If I get the lawn mowed and the hedge trimmed before 11:00 A.M., can I go to the matinee with Ralph? You can make Ritchie edge the flower bed, OK?"

Wouldn't it be great if your family always arrived everywhere on time, always had the correct change for the bus turnstile, always got the Christmas decorations up—and down again—at the right time, always had clean underwear in the drawer, always . . . *ad nauseum.*

We encounter families who do, but there is almost always a terrible price to pay. With extreme orderliness comes the rigidity necessary to keep the orderliness in place. To hold a diverse family in lockstep, particularly a family with small children, you need a strong authority figure at the helm. There is nothing wrong in itself with strong authority figures. But in a family situation, they almost always become the huge, powerful, bulging circle in the family circles-in-a-circle illustration, pushing on the others, applying far more pressure than necessary.

The essence of childhood is spontaneity and flexibility. The overorganized household has lost that. Here boundaries and bonds are so tightly set that they cannot change easily as the child grows. The kid can be a kid but can't be himself or herself. He or she is what fits in the family, doing what fits in the schedule.

If the essence of childhood is spontaneity, the essence of growth is to question, to try one's wings, and sometimes to fall clumsily in an attempt to fly. Why can't I stay out that late? I don't see what dancing has to do with being religious, and all the other kids are going. Becky's family plays Yahtzee with five dice, and they go to church. What's so wrong with games with dice in them? I don't like piano. Why can't I take guitar lessons instead?

In the rigidly authoritarian home there is no room for question. This is right and that is wrong. This is the way we worship; that is not. This is neat and clean; that is beneath the family dignity. Do it this way; any other way, no matter whether the results satisfy, is the wrong way. Children chafe, friction grows, all suffer.

Moreover, children can be very messy little creatures. They throw up at inconvenient times. In fact, they almost never get sick at convenient times. Children grow fussy and tired. Children get bored. They speak up at the wrong time and say the wrong things. They resist when it's illogical to do so. They break things and dig holes in the wrong places. They forget. Sometimes they wander off. Children who can't go potty before getting in the car have to go desperately fifteen minutes short of the destination.

By their very nature, therefore, children do not fit comfortably in an overly controlled household. They find themselves constantly in trouble for being children, and the resulting negative messages stay with them for a lifetime.

Joey Trask, as you may guess, grew up in a tightly structured environment.

The Distant Family

For one reason or another, parents with whom we deal sometimes consciously or unconsciously avoid a close emotional relationship with their children. "I just don't relate well to kids" is the frequent excuse. Many grown-ups find most children more annoying than most adults, not a problem in itself. But codependents by definition take life to extremes, including their hesitation or downright fear regarding emotional intimacy with unpredictable little people.

Several dysfunctional parental types emerge from this desire to avoid emotional closeness.

King and Subject

Both Whalon Trask and Rob Newport fit this category. Strongly authoritarian, they cruised somewhere above the intimate circle of the family in their own stratosphere of activity. When they saw some glitch in family operations, they descended with sweeping pronouncements to correct deviations and quell squabbles. They issued the orders and left it to their lieutenant, Mom, to see that the orders were put into practice. Even in casual family situations such as outings or devotions, they remained king, a cut above the crowd.

Circus Ringmaster

It starts so innocently at first: a birthday party for a gaggle of three year olds on Saturday, a nursery-school recital here, a neighborhood field trip to the fire station there. Then there's the dance lessons at age five because you wonder if your child has talent and all great dancers start early. Sunday school. Church with kids' church. Pioneer Clubs, scouting, school activities, and bingo! You're hooked. It's all for the good of the children; that makes it all worthwhile.

It's awfully easy to turn the family into a three-ring circus, with Mom and Dad feverishly both orchestrating the action and taking part in it. Anyone can fall into the trap, and we've already mentioned the prevailing myth, the bait for that trap—"A busy family is a happy family." In counsel, however, we find a very clear category of parents who involve the family in this attempt at perpetual motion for all the wrong reasons.

If Mom and Dad are busy with worthwhile projects—charity, church, work, political, or social action—they are, in their own eyes, setting a good example for the children. In truth, they are setting themselves apart from the kids, far enough to avoid that dreaded emotional entanglement.

Similarly, if the kids are up to their sweet little bippies in worthwhile activities, they won't be pressing close emotionally. They'll be too busy.

Not All There

A third situation that we find occasionally might be subtitled "the porch light is on but nobody's home." The parent has simply checked out emotionally. Physically, Mom sits at the kitchen table; physically, Dad is plopped down on the sofa with a book or a television show, but they remain detached, disinterested. The parent has erected a solid boundary, a wall to exclude unwanted intrusion. Because children live not in a world of things but of relationships, the emotional distance impoverishes them far more than adults can understand. This is passive emotional abuse, as we discussed at the very beginning.

Explainer

Distance of another sort results when the parent takes a "come let us reason together" attitude to child-rearing.

To two-year-old Joshua: "Quit running around in your diaper, and come get your clothes on. If you don't, we'll be late to Uncle Ed's and you won't have time to take a ride on Maxie. You want to ride on Maxie, don't you?"

Riding on old plowhorse Maxie is the farthest thing from Joshua's mind as he tears through the house giggling and making noise. His toddler brain cannot equate getting dressed now with riding a horse in the unforeseeable future. Mom cheerfully believes she's relating to her child in a meaningful way. In truth there has been no communication between Joshua and his mom, no fostering of their relationship.

When a small child asks why, he or she is less interested in an answer than in where the boundary lies. "Because" is just as good an answer for a preschooler as an explanation of why. For example, you have spent an hour in a playground area at the park with a four year old.

"Time to go home now," you say.

"Not yet. Two more times on the slide, OK? Just two."

Boundary testing.

"Now. I have to start dinner."

"Why?"

At this point you might explain eating customs and time constraints. You could launch into an explanation about how pot roast requires a minimum of an hour and a half for the meat to cook thoroughly and the flavors to blend. You could mention the time it will take to get home from here. Or you could say, "Oh, because. Let's see how many things that are red we can spot on the way back. Taillights don't count; too many of them."

Then you start back hand in hand, the four year old and you, and you let him find the red coat on that lady, the red car, the red letters in that sign, and let the child shift the game rules to yellow so he can count the golden arches you just passed.

Changing the Shape

There is a watershed difference between codependent families, whose children carry the pain of others, and healthy families, whose children thrive emotionally. That difference is willingness to adjust.

Healthy families ease comfortably into change when change seems wise; they are willing to grow and change with time as circumstances require.

Codependent families find themselves locked into one stage of growth, as for example, the Trasks. They rigidly resisted growth, not even realizing that was happening. The unspoken rule became, *Shut up and do it like we've always done it.*

The world, however, is not divided into two camps, the healthy families and the codependent ones. Each and every family is a mix of the two in varying proportions. Frequently in counsel we find an otherwise healthy family that just happened to get stuck in some phase and things started going wrong. These families respond quickly and well to counsel, even casual counsel. They are, you see, willing to change.

We shall devote the remainder of the book to ways in which you can change the shape of your family for the better. What constitutes "better"? "Better" is the ultimate goal of lifting the weight of our pain from our children's backs, thus letting them be children. Then they can pursue those developmental tasks so important to building healthy identities.

The Core of a Team

You, the parents, have undergone healing, learning about yourselves individually, grasping contentment and confidence more firmly. You've examined and redirected your marriage; strengthened it rather than merely patched it up. You are now in a position to understand the psychological mechanics of your children, who have been carrying your pain. The children, too, understand themselves better. We can now combine all of these powerful forces into an unbeatable unit, a healthy family.

The suggestions that follow are not intended to be taken in sequence. Seeing to all of them at once is best, but perhaps not practical. Review each suggestion thoughtfully. How does it apply to your family? Some will be important to you, others hardly at all, but how? Most important, as you forge this new team, remember that the kids aren't employees or chattels; they're team members. Include their ideas in your considerations.

CHAPTER 15

Putting the Team Together

"Dad? Can I go down to the mall for a couple of hours with Mary?"

"I don't know. Go ask your mother."

Out to the kitchen she goes. "Mom? Dad says I can go to the mall if it's OK with you."

"I suppose, if he said so."

"Can I have some money?"

"Use your own. That's why you get an allowance."

She hastens back to the living room. "Dad? Mom says I can go, but I need some money."

"Oh, all right. When is she gonna learn to keep a few bucks on hand?"

That's mild, lightweight manipulation. When parents separate, particularly in joint-custody situations, the manipulation becomes absolutely Machiavellian.

Children are born connivers, some more than others, and not surprisingly. A child is powerless in an adult world. The ability to connive, indeed the very ability to look cute, is about all the influence a child can wield. Theorists believe that this is one of the tasks of babies: to charm, to be cute and appealing, to thus encourage the parent-child bond.

And yet, a family is not a matter of "them the kids against us the parents." A family is "we," and sometimes even "we against the world." Parents, then, to provide a comfortably functioning family, must build teams, a team within a team.

First comes the A team, Mom and Dad united, to work as one when dealing with the kids. With the management team well formed and in place, the children are free to play their appropriate family roles, free to be kids. The A team works within the larger team, the family as a whole.

Building the A Team

The Rosses discuss their college-aged daughter, Tina:

"Good dinner, hon."

"Thank you. Marj was razzing me about empty-nest syndrome now that Tina's away at school. Frankly, I enjoy being just the two of us again. Leisurely dinner, not so many frantic emergencies when one of the kids needs this or that instantly."

"Speaking of Tina: She called this afternoon." Dad wiped his mouth and folded his napkin. "She was phoning from school. Reversed the charges."

"Really! She called me this afternoon too. All excited about her courses for next semester. Bought her books. Since she switched majors she seems extremely enthusiastic about her college work."

"I agree. It was a good move." He sat back. "She, ah, mentioned she didn't go to the hockey game last night. 'It was either spend the money for the parking or buy a cup of coffee this morning,' she said. And she giggled."

"I got the same pitch exactly, complete with the giggle. You sending her some money to tide her over?"

"I dropped a check in the mail for her. Not much. Parking and coffee money."

"Good. I wanted to check with you, whether you did, before I did. You'd think that in nineteen years she'd figure out that she can't play us off against each other."

"College students are only smart in some ways."

College students also prove that kids never outgrow some skills. The Rosses worked together; we suggest parents be careful to coordinate the A team.

When the A Team Is Only One Member

For a number of reasons, the marriage bond is of necessity the most important bond in any family. If you are a single parent, you are coming from behind when you do not have that bond available as a tool in child-raising. Single parents feel much, much pressure to not let the kids be kids. Everyone must pull an extra load, and that load is not appro-

Building a Working
Family Team

1. Coordinate an A team—the parents—within the family by opening communication between them and setting common goals.

2. Make the remaining family members part of the team by involving them in decisions and opinions.

3. Things to handle as a family team:

   • Identify addictions, compulsions, or excessive habits that appear to be growing in individual members.

   • Identify stressors—job pressures, time management, relationships with extended family and friends.

   • Handle identified stressors as a team.

   • Examine boundaries within the family periodically. Look at boundaries outside the family as needed.

   • Assess members' strengths and weaknesses periodically.

priate for youngsters. There are adjustments you can make and support is available (do not despair!), but we do want you to know you're working at a serious disadvantage so that you can compensate as much as possible.

Recognizing the A team is half the battle; melding them into a true, coordinated, well-matched team is the other half.

Coordinating the A Team

Gayle wants their young children in bed by 7:30. George, who doesn't arrive home from work until 6:00, thinks 7:30 is too early. He only gets to spend an hour or so with them. What alternatives does this couple have? Gayle and George should:

1. Argue about it in front of the kids so that the children know disagreement is part of marriage and parenting.

2. Flip a coin. Best two out of three, winner gets his or her way.

3. Look it up in a parenting book and go with what the expert suggests.

4. None of the above.

If the first answer said "discuss" instead of "argue" and the children were older, we might allow it. The second answer leaves serious issues to chance—not good. We like number three, since we're writing just such a book, but it's not the correct response. Every family situation varies, every collective family identity is different, and no single cookbook-answer will serve. Books—including this one— should be used for developing overall strategies and concepts, not for blindly plugging in automatic answers to each random problem of life. That leaves the last answer, none of the above, which in itself does not offer a whole lot of help.

We do have some suggestions, however. In private conversation George and Gayle should discuss the issue and arrange a compromise. Then they should present the children with a united front. Of course, the children may know there was disagreement. In fact, they ought to. Life is compromise and marriage is never 100 percent agreement. But marriage is also unity. The parents are thereby presenting a healthy model, teaching by example how to overcome disagreement.

Sometimes an unresolved problem calls for a united front when unhurried discussion simply is not possible. George has discovered that a dandy children's movie is playing at the mall cinema. He thinks it's perfect for the kids. Gayle feels that the five year old is up to it, but it contains too much sadness and too many confusing points for the three year old. They learn the movie will be replaced tomorrow. No time to maneuver; it's now or never.

Gayle explains her position, George his. The compromise: George takes the five year old to the movie and Gayle takes the younger child to the yogurt parlor for a treat. Then the two of them will pick out a kiddie video for rent at the video store. The movie gets out at 3:10, so the family will meet at the video store at 3:15.

Why didn't Gayle simply say, "You're the boss, dear," and let the head of the household get up with the little one when the nightmares arrive at 3 A.M.? In fact, in many instances she does say that. In this particular case, however, she knew the children more intimately than George did. The children and the parents all stood to benefit from her input. George, Gayle, and the three year old all slept well that night.

If you are divorced but, unlike Lida, still involved in a solid parenting arrangement with your ex-spouse, your children will benefit if the parents can coordinate. In a divorce arrangement, particularly with shared custody, children become masters at playing one parent off the other. That's all the more reason for the parents to keep close contact, at least as it regards parenting.

Keep frequent telephone contact if possible. Children's needs change quickly as they grow.

Lay solid ground rules to prevent the push and pull in which children specialize. For example, "Dad lets me," or, "Mom said I could," should never be taken at face value. Whether together or apart, parents should agree in principle to basic rules such as: Who provides how much allowance and when; who provides children how much freedom to roam and where; who purchases clothing and other essentials.

Above all, make certain the children are always under one

roof or the other. Children whose parents live within bicycle range of each other have been known to create a comfortable limbo for themselves, with ample opportunity for mischief. "I'm going over to Dad's," unless Mom checks up, is an open door to nonsupervision. The kid may not go to Dad's at all.

Involving the Whole Team

Family Relationships

You've been working at healing yourself, your marriage (if applicable), and your kids. This is an on-going process. Keep it going as you pursue the remaining suggestions.

As a part of this healing, it pays to look for trouble spots. One of the ways is by involving the whole family in ferreting out hidden problems.

Addictions

In counsel we get the whole family together for a session to talk about addictions, compulsions, and near addictions. You might well do the same. Now and then when we get input from all the family members, a sleeper shows up, so to speak. We're searching out the little invidious ones hidden in the creases of your life. For example:

"Ralph, what do you do for recreation? Have you any hobbies that we've not talked about yet?"

"I dabble in stocks and bonds."

"Tell me about it."

Ralph lights up, distinctly more animated. "I'm a long way from retirement, so I'm not interested in the redwoods—you know, the stuff that grows slowly. I want fast money."

"Which means penny stocks and junk bonds."

"Well, yeah, they call it that. Actually it's more complex than just snatching stuff to make a killing. You have to keep abreast of the industry—who's out to take over what, what leveraged buyouts are in the offing.

"Then you put a big chunk into one place, watch it rise, and grab your money. It's more an art than a science."

Clint, the seventeen year old, shook his head. "If that's an art, Pop, so is bingo. You're gambling, man. That's all it is, and it's scary to me. The market goes up, you go up. The market goes down, you crash and burn. And we get the flak. You run around the house yelling at us and raving. You're hooked on the action, looking for the next big killing."

Clint could see it. Ralph could not. Hopefully, at this point in his own recovery, Ralph could be honest enough to recognize his incipient gambling addiction for what it was.

Stressors That Warp the Family Circle

Again, listen to the kids as you talk about stressors in the family relationship. What factors are pushing and pulling at the family circle? What wolves are huffing and puffing at the dollhouse walls? Your kids might identify something others never saw.

The Newports were startled when Jennifer complained, "All the kids in my class go on vacations and then they tell about it in class. Our family hasn't ever been on a vacation since I've been in school." Rob and Alice had never noticed the lack of a vacation. But they certainly noticed that they had never enjoyed the stress relief that a well-planned vacation provides. About the time you read this the Newports will be in Brownsville, sport fishing and taking bird-watching hikes through the many reserves along the lower Rio Grande.

Parents often feel the push from people stressors. Parents are on a demanding point, responsible for the care of their children and also approaching the time when they must consider the needs of their own parents. Think of the grandparents who send these messages: "You ought to do such and such better." "Why don't you bring the children to visit us oftener?" "I don't want to be a burden, *but* . . ." Then there are all the other friends and relatives with unmet needs, unfinished business, and misplaced boundaries who impinge on time and energy.

These stressors were particularly grievous in the Trask family. Extended family, we learned, were pushing their own unfinished business and needs onto the Trasks, for after all, Beth and Whalon were such a stalwart and picture-perfect couple. From the Grandparents Trask came a parade of guilt trips. "You don't love us anymore." "You don't come by often enough." "If you loved us you'd do such and such." "After all we've done for you . . ." From Beth's mother, "You're our only child who isn't working. You have a duty, you know. You certainly wouldn't want nursing home care for me if you're at home all day and can come here to help me."

Besides, the Trasks only had one child, so it wasn't as if they were overburdened or anything. And because Whalon was a pillar of the church, solid and dependable, the church called on him constantly to fill emergency church needs. You could always count on Whalon. Beth ended up in the nursery nearly every week simply because she would do it and everyone else had some reason why they couldn't that week. It was so easy for the Trasks to slip into a codependent relationship with the church family as well as with the demanding grandparents.

The Trasks had to identify the stressors, then either eliminate their influence or determine specific methods for handling them. You must do the same.

Handling the Stressors

In the comic stereotype, Og the caveman defies fight-or-flight perils during the day as he tries to beat saber-toothed tigers to the kill. At night, however, he unwinds by relaxing and inventing myths for the kids, myths that will long outlive him, as a fire crackles merrily at the mouth of his safe, cozy cave. Primal stress relieved by primal relaxation (and possibly a primal scream or two). These days it isn't so easy.

Kids have to be taught coping skills; the skills don't come automatically in today's complex society, with its overkill of exotic stressors. Children learn by absorption, by watching the parents. In other words, you learn the skills first and pass them on.*

---

*We refer you to Minirth-Meier's book *Worry-free Living* (Nashville: Thomas Nelson, 1989). It contains a plethora of practical suggestions for taking pressure off, such as stress-reduction exercises and other coping methods.

A theoretical example of parental role modeling: Dad is enraged because he just learned on the phone that a business associate has let him down. He can scream and rant and drive his fist through the dry wall. He can yell at any kid who happens at that moment to walk into the room. Or he can roar, "I'm angry, but it has nothing to do with you, kid. It's something else." Then he goes outside to work off his fury, jogging, splitting firewood, pounding on a punching bag, whatever.

Dealing with recurring people problems takes more tact, more energy, and, in the end, will probably generate some flak. Whalon may have abandoned treatment, but he listened to the suggestions Beth made about the demands of their parents, as they discussed it one night.

Beth observed, "Every time we go over to your folks' house, they sit around all night criticizing Joey and what you're letting him get away with."

"Yeah. I'm getting pretty sick of it, but what do you do?"

"I suggest we phone more often—several times a week—and go over once a month at most. That way we'll keep good contact and avoid the hassle."

"The doctors tell you to do that?"

"Not exactly. Dr. Hemfelt and I were identifying stressors, and the parents are a biggie. He suggested a guideline; balance duty against stress. Find middle ground."

"What about your mother?"

"I already put our name in at Oak Point Manor. It's not a nursing home. She can live there independently, yet receive the daily assistance she needs." Beth paused. "Whalon, I really would prefer to bring her into our home. It's what I would consider the best solution for her. But she's so hard to live with. Always cranky and irritating. Stress again. Daily stress. I know it's all you can do to smile sometimes when she visits. Plus, she'd quickly tie us down. I may not have a career but I do a lot of volunteer work. I don't want to give that up."

"I don't want you to. It's valuable."

"It's not set in cement. If it doesn't work out, we'll figure out something else. But I'm not going to jump into a stressful situation so long as we can find some satisfactory alternative."

"Oak Point Manor sounds like a good alternative. Yes."

Did Whalon notice that for the first time in their marriage Beth had stepped out in a decision of her own? We still don't know, but we like to think he did.

Beth gave the church some dates on which she would be available for nursery duty. All other Sundays she worshiped at her husband's side. Frankly, she got the guilt-trip treatment from the nursery supervisor for a while. She stuck it out, and Whalon, impressed with her resolve and pleased that she made it a priority to join him, defended her staunchly.

Beth had set her boundaries and was defending them.

Examine the Boundaries

Lida Armstrong's problem with her elderly mother became quite thorny, not to mention stressful.

Lida, Sarah, and Pete Armstrong live in a duplex next to the aging grandmother. Grandma suffered a mild stroke some months ago, which partially disabled her. Now she repeatedly insists that Lida quit her job and stay home during the day. Grandma also wants them to remodel the duplex to permit access between the two units; and Grandma owns the building.

What is Lida to do?

Examining the boundaries in your family includes looking at extended family relationships. In a way, this complements the work you're doing when you examine stressors, for stressors are usually nothing more than boundary attacks.

In counseling we ask our families these questions: Does each person in the family have permission and opportunity to be separate and autonomous? Is each person's individuality respected in the family? Stress results when the boundaries are out of kilter.

We suggest that, in a group council, your family go through the positions one by one. Assess boundaries. I am the father. You are the son. My duty is to be there for you.

You do not have to be there for me. If you are eight, you will not be expected to be twelve. Neither will you be allowed to be two. Do the boundaries feel comfortable? Do the boundaries appear appropriate according to what you now know? Does each child have room to grow according to the developmental tasks of which you are now aware?

Draw an identity figure for each child. Put it on paper so you can look at it. How do your children's figures compare with what a figure ought to look like for their age? Are they developing a firm, healthy outline? You know them better than anyone else does. What do you see?

Not infrequently, we find that the parents' boundaries are impinging on the children's. If that's happening in your case, you can't see clearly just what your children's identity figures truly look like.

Consider the Newports. Alice had become emotionally enmeshed—call that emotionally incestuous—with Brian. She depended on him. He was her helper, her kid to be proud of. In the darkest recesses of her heart, Brian had replaced Rob as her source of emotional support. Brian was warm, Rob distant.

Alice engaged Jennifer in what counselors call "attachment by conflict." Jennifer's irritating, disruptive behavior, in a sense, held the family together; they were united in their efforts to minimize her irritation. Brian on his own tried to hold the family together, by helping, by placating, by making them all look good to the world. In no way could Alice have drawn an accurate identity figure for either child. So beware of this possibility as you work through these suggestions.

When parents' boundaries impinge on their children's, we often recommend periodic short separations. Phrased in the vernacular, we urge the parent to get away from the kid for a while. This is important, especially when the child, like Jenny-Jo, is difficult to live with.

Eventually, the Newports scheduled at least one evening weekly when they went out to do something or go somewhere without the kids. Brian did not baby-sit on these occasions. Also, the children were both sent away for a week in the summer to camps. These breathers gave Alice and Rob the space they needed to get a little perspective on their family.

Doublecheck Family Members' Roles

Mom and Dad have made decisions about how to be more effective parents. The old roles, though, might still be blinding them and getting in the way. When we as counselors gather a family together in a conjoint therapy session, we look for these old ugly roles to crop up, for we know it's far easier to make new decisions about nurturing children than to live by them. The head makes choices but the heart controls action, and rarely do head and heart agree. Old ways die very, very hard.

For example, Webley Washington was the third of Paul and Myra's four children, the kid who couldn't do anything right.

"Man," he complained, "my folks don't do nothin' but cloud up and rain all over me."

"That's 'don't do *anything*,' dear," Myra corrected. "Don't use double negatives."

Dr. Warren cleared his throat. "I believe one of your goals was to cut Web a little slack; not lean on him so hard."

"Well, yes, but he sounds like an ignorant old Alabama cotton farmer with those speech inflections. He gets them from his uncle."

"Uncle Walter grows cotton near Selma." Webley grinned. "The rest of the family don't hold much truck with him."

Myra sighed. "Do you see what I mean?"

"Are you setting him a good example with your own speech?"

"Of course, but . . ."

"So he knows standard English. And has correcting him done any good?"

"Obviously not. But . . ."

"You made new decisions. Are you going to stick with them, or are you going to return to the old ways?"

"Yes, but . . ."

Yes but—the call notes of the frazzled parent honestly trying to adopt new strategies. Since you, the reader, probably have no counselor looking over your shoulder, you must keep close watch on yourself. You have a powerful ally for change—two, in fact. First, now you know better how your family is functioning and how the kids think. At last you can see what's happening. Second, because you are effecting changes in your own life, the pains and pressures are automatically easing on your child. It's easier for him or her to relax the extreme behavior.

In Webley's case, the parents still saw the kid who couldn't do anything right. Mom was still intruding on Webley's space more than a child his age should be monitored. *And Webley was fulfilling their expectations.* Despite all the good intentions, the old role was still draping itself across Webley's shoulders. And why not? It was familiar, it was comfortable, it was the way he used to cope and meet the family's collective needs. The old roles and boundaries will remain a menace to growth and happiness. Yet with time, the new attitudes will become quite as comfortable.

But won't a child's true nature eventually express itself? A number of sad cases illustrate the response, "Not necessarily." Some have become the subjects of films. In the scenario, a child is mistakenly sent to a home for the mentally retarded. The child grows assuming he is retarded. This essentially normal youngster looks and acts retarded. He or she takes on the cultural characteristics of the immediate environment. Only if an outside observer—usually a social worker or foster parent—chances to see the spark will the child be helped to rise to the level of excellence that God intended. So will children in codependent families.

It's not easy, seeing your children for what they are. Here are some ways to avoid some common blindnesses parents sometimes end up with.

Assess Strengths and Weaknesses Periodically

There are, of course, strengths and weaknesses in every child and adult, special long suits and other skills that keep ending up half a brick shy of a load. As you assess the strengths and weaknesses in your children and yourself, you'll be looking not at roles but God-given talents. It's not easy.

Consider Joey Trask. His father is a jock, his mother well-conditioned—she watches her weight and jogs. And Joey just turned his back on athletics. Joey isn't cutting it, as they say.

Similar but even worse was the case of Marcus Russo. For thirteen years Marcus's father played basketball in the NBA. There was no career for women in basketball, but his mom went as far as she could go in NCAA sports. Marcus's sister and three brothers were active in sports, winning in track and field and (his eldest brother) football. Not Marcus.

Marcus's brother's football team went to the state finals and the family went too, to cheer him on. When his middle brother and sister took medals in the West Coast relays, the family watched proudly from the bleachers of Bulldog Stadium. Little brother already shines as a Little League talent. When Marcus and two companions won a grueling regional computer tournament, nobody was there to see them accept the prize. Marcus placed third in the state in advanced math at the state scholarship test finals. His parents might have gone to the presentation ceremonies—the tests are held less than an hour's drive from their home—but there was a Little League game that day, and . . .

Who in your family might be overlooked because their talents are not yours, their interests not yours, their achievements not touted by your world? Newspaper sports sections devote whole issues to school sporting finals and tournaments. Academic achievements, when mentioned at all, appear in the D section as a small item in local news. Art achievements go universally unnoticed. Don't let mass media sway you as you assess your children's strong points. Celebrate the differences!

Strengths and weaknesses have another dark side to them, one you must keep in mind. Children are masters at both finding and exploiting weaknesses. Jennifer Newport at age nine could find the vulnerabilities in Fort Knox. Cracking her mom was a snap. She knew intuitively that she could make her mother feel guilty and worked it into a power ploy.

290

Jenny-Jo's anger, frustrations, and impatience translated to Alice as, "I'm not a good mom or Jenny-Jo wouldn't be that way." Alice was an easy mark because she had such strong self-doubts to start with; she was all vulnerability. Rob on the other hand was so confident in his strengths that he refused to acknowledge vulnerability. He split it off, in effect, and you know what happens to traits that are split off: floating free, they're going to land in someone else's circle.

It's the job of every team member in the family system to avoid exploiting the others' vulnerabilities. The team is called to love each other, by God and by man, and exploitation is not the way of love.

Again, this is a subject to be taught by the parents through modeling. And the model will be unique to each family. Yours is the only family on earth with your particular blend of strengths and weaknesses. You don't have to discuss them. You do have to deal with them, compensate where needed; in short, keep your strengths and weaknesses both under control. In dealing with them, you give your children permission to be both strong and weak, to be both vulnerable and invulnerable. To be fully and wonderfully human.

The bottom line of all this assessment and examination is simple. What does God have in mind for you and for each of your children, individually and as a family unit? Only when every person can reach the level of achievement God Himself has in mind can that person be happy and satisfied with life. This cannot be learned from a book, for every single person is unique in His sight. You are. Your children are.

How do you get all this act together? One of several ways is the regular family meeting. We've found that in many instances it provides the forum that recovering families need in order to keep their new decisions and attitudes on track. Let's explore family meetings next.

CHAPTER 16

The Team in Action

Lida Armstrong settled herself cross-legged on the floor. She looked solemnly at her eighth-grader, Pete, and her eleventh-grader, Sarah, who were hunkered down in a circle with her. "I declare this war council in session."

Pete studied the carpet in the middle. "We really need a campfire for this, you know."

"Good idea. Soon as it's warm enough, we'll make a fire ring in the back yard. The first business tonight is to consider Grandma's proposals. Second will be the usual stuff. Any comment?"

Pete and Sarah both nodded.

The phone rang. No one moved. With three rings the answering machine kicked in. Pause. *Beep.* Grandma's voice came through loud and clear. "Why aren't you answering the phone? I know you're home. Send Sarah over. I need some things from the cupboard." Click.

Sarah watched her mother's face.

Lida smiled. "We have business on the floor. We'll do that first. Grandma wants me to quit work so I can be here at home, and she wants us to put a double swinging door in the living room by the stairs, so we can come and go from her side and she can come over without going outside and down off the porch and around and up. She can't negotiate all those porch steps well. Comments?"

"Which one are we taking first?" Pete asked.

"Let's deal with the door."

"It'd be a lot easier," Sarah offered. "When she wants something, like now, we just run over through the door and do it and come back."

"Yeah, but we don't get any privacy at all then," Pete objected. "She'd want us over there all the time, or she'd be over here all the time. You know how she is."

For five minutes they explored all the pros and cons. Finally Lida asked, "Do the warriors have a consensus on this?"

"I don't think it's a good idea." Pete squirmed. He didn't sit still very long. "I think we'd lose too much. If she insists on it, since it's her house, we oughta put a lock on our side."

"Then she'd always be pounding on the door. I don't like it either, but I don't know what we're going to do." Sarah sighed. "We have a duty to her. She's our grandma, after all. And your mom."

"How much duty?"

"I don't know."

"Speculate."

Sarah thought a while. "To meet the needs she can't. To love her. To do what's best for her."

"I agree." Lida nodded. "So we all three agree it's not a good idea. Remember last week we talked about boundaries? I think it would be doing her more harm than good to let her become too dependent on us. For her sake, I think we should encourage her to get along as much as possible on her own."

Sarah nodded vigorously. "I enjoy being able to help with things she can't do alone. But like tonight. She needs something from the cabinet. Why doesn't she just put it on a lower shelf? I'm always going over there getting things she could reach if she'd put the stuff she uses every day down lower. Or if she'd just stand up. She can stand up fine. It's just for moving around that she needs her wheelchair."

"Mom? What are you going to do about working?" Pete shifted to kneeling. "Gonna quit?"

"What do you suggest?"

"Don't quit. We can use the money, and besides, as you said last week we should all have outside interests so we don't get too wrapped up in each other. I think you'd be lousing that up."

"Again, I agree. Vote?"

Heads nodded gravely. Pete dropped a marble in the middle of the circle. "I vote we don't put the door in."

"Me too." Sarah laid a marble down.

"And me." Lida put her marble there. "My job isn't subject to vote, but I declare my intention: I'm not going to quit." And she laid a marble in the middle.

Pete put a blue aggie beside hers, his agreement. Sarah laid a marble there too. Consensus.

The Family Meeting

When counselors call a family together as a group, we refer to the gatherings as conjoint sessions. With these sessions we try to model the way a family meeting at home might go and endeavor to teach families how to conduct family meetings.

As important as the business conducted is the symbolism of the family drawn together to a common purpose. Just as we sometimes physically position families in healthy configurations, showing them how they might readjust their boundaries, so does a regularly scheduled family meeting give physical voice to a silent concept. The meeting says: *We're committed to sticking together and learning to cope. Life isn't easy, but we can get through it better together.*

A family meeting is a talk time. However, kids seem to hate calling it a family meeting or family council. If you choose to conduct your own family meetings, you might tap the kids for suggestions on what to call it. Lida is one-eighth Cherokee, so she and her two kids took an Indian theme. Pete was the one who came up with "war council."

Ground Rules
Keep It Light

A touch of humor helps. When the Armstrongs decided to pursue the war council motif and adopted sitting in a circle on the floor, the kids came up with all sorts of puns: Business on the floor, speaker on the floor, a motion on the floor as Pete writhed. A little frivolity never hurts. Sarah tended to extreme sobriety, but Pete was a cutup. Lida encouraged both.

Never should someone enter the meeting defensively. Older children may well approach your initial attempts at meetings with a certain suspicion. This is another ploy to shape us up, right? You want something, right? If you keep it light and keep it open, that defensive attitude will fade.

Don't worry about clumsiness. Especially in the beginning a family meeting might go quite badly. People can't say what they think adequately, older kids become impatient with younger ones. Hang in there; it gets better.

Everyone Participates

How young is too young? Many of our clients bring toys to the table to interest the toddlers and preschoolers, whose attention span isn't up to that of older siblings. Even babes in arms can feel a part of it simply by sitting in the high chair or a lap. The family identity, the egomass, is stronger for no other reason than that the family is together. (PS: The little ones now and then will amaze you with some profound contribution you weren't expecting at all. They see very well.)

Lida's divorced husband offered no emotional contact and little financial support. The family meeting provided Lida and her kids a cohesiveness they could have achieved in no other way.

Families who have committed themselves to God will want to invite Him in on the proceedings. He should be a recognized part of a family meeting, as He is in the marriage itself.

Also, everyone should have a vote on some issues, as an aspect of participation, but not everything should be subject to vote. The kids can't, by simple majority, vote in Oreo cookies for supper, for example. You'll note that Lida identified two categories: things subject to vote and declarations of intention.

This family expressed the vote in a graphic, tangible form with marbles. The members all could see, with their own eyes, that they had a say. This is particularly effective for smaller children. It gives physical form to an otherwise abstract concept. Lida declared her intentions and gave form to them with a marble. The children were free to withhold agreement by withholding their marbles. In this case they agreed with her decision. In other cases they did not always agree.

An adjunct of "everyone participates" must be "anyone can disagree without prejudice." Otherwise you won't get full participation.

Someone Is in Charge, a Master of Ceremonies

Someone, probably Dad, must take responsibility for making sure the family meeting runs well. The leader must also make certain everyone submits to and respects everyone else. The parent and child roles are not lost, but this meeting should be as nearly egalitarian as possible. Children are responsible for their own behavior. In the Armstrong war councils, Lida took care to model open give-and-take in a positive way, showing by example how compromise is desirable in some cases, out of order in others.

Schedule Meetings Regularly

Every Sunday evening? Friday after dinner? Midweek, with the weekend coming up soon? What fits best? Whatever your final decision is regarding time, establish a schedule and stick to it. Give the family meeting top priority. Only when Mom and Dad consider it important enough to schedule around it will the children take it seriously.

Topics Are Important If a Family Member Considers Them So

Mom and Dad don't consider the frequency of spinach on the family menu to be of paramount importance. A five year old just might. So you discuss spinach.

Lida read quite a bit about the importance of boundaries. As an official topic of consideration, she passed the essence of what she learned on to the kids. This was a topic important to her and, she knew, to the kids also. She and they together had explored their own boundaries and Grandma's the week before. Note that even bubbling, off-the-wall Pete could pick up on this concept when it affected him and his family personally.

Almost No Topic Is Off-Limits

Almost. Some things are properly discussed in private between two persons. If such topics come up in the joint session, arrange definite appointments between the interested parties to handle them later, privately.

Forbidden topics certainly include anything the parents might bring up that would generate emotional incest. Sometimes the complaint of one individual toward another should be handled privately, brought before the family only if one of the two remains dissatisfied. Jesus in Matthew 18 set up a good working guideline for this: If a man has something against a (spiritual) brother, take it to him privately. If the man cannot receive satisfaction, he brings along a couple of friends and again approaches the brother. If satisfaction still evades one or both parties, they bring it before the full assembly to be adjudicated.

By keeping this subject matter open, you can better hear what exactly concerns your youngsters. Simply knowing what's on their minds can help you assess their degree of dependence/independence, the strength of their identities. Most important, you are showing them you are there with them.

Your Primary Goal Is Communication

This is not an opportunity for the parents to preach. Instruction and reprimand must be handled outside the meeting. Here everyone gets to express what is going on in his or her life. Children may start out shallow, but they'll dig deep if they have the freedom to do so. The trick is to get everyone listening to each other. Listening. That's the key.

Topics to Consider

Lida chose the most important topic, what to do about Grandma, first. If the kids subsequently got restless and petered out, the most pressing topic was already handled. Other topics for possible discussion include the following.

Important Questions and Upcoming Family Events

Other than Grandma, there was nothing else for the war council to consider in this category. So they moved on to other business.

Individual Members' Plans

Pete bubbled over about the junior track meet Friday after school. Could Mom get off work early? She'd see.

"Jerry asked me to go to the fire department skate Saturday, but it doesn't get out 'til midnight," Sarah announced. "I want to move curfew from midnight to 1:00 A.M. Just this time."

"A fire department *skate?*" Lida asked.

"Yeah," Pete butted in. "You should see 'em whizz around the rink in those big canvas reflector coats and the helmets with the visors. And unreeling the hose is a kick."

Sarah scowled at what was obviously a truly obnoxious little brother. "It's a township fire department benefit skating party. Everybody's going."

"And right at midnight," Pete continued, "they torch the lounge and everybody watches 'em put it out. It's a gas."

"We get the idea, Pete." Lida raised her hand, palm out. "Who is everybody?"

"People you approve of. And we'll come right back here after it closes. Please?"

"I don't work Saturday. I suppose so. One A.M. Not 1:01."

Children feel more comfortable in the concrete than in the abstract. They like to talk about things they're going to do, things they've done, pets, friends, possessions. Don't despair if even the teens shy away from abstracts. Again, the goal is communication, both talking and hearing.

Pressure Points

This is not nearly so abstract a topic as it sounds. Pressures are easily felt and seen. Moreover, the children are among the first to feel and see them. Group discussion is an excellent place to check the water regarding pressure. An example we heard in joint counsel recently:

The teen: "Dad, you're real moody lately when you come

home. Short-tempered. You were yelling at me when I wasn't really doing anything. We're worried. Are you under more pressure?"

The dad: "No, not really."

The teen: "You don't have to go into detail; just tell us what's bothering you."

The dad: "You know Sam, the lathe operator? He's been causing some personnel problems. Has nothing to do with the family here. I'll try to leave that at work from now on."

On another occasion a different family reported this exchange:

"Mom, how come I have to make my bed in the morning? I have to get ready for school and eat breakfast and feed the dog, and I think it's too much. I feel real rushed. Pushed."

"You have to make your bed because it's good discipline. You're going to be faced with the job your whole life. We want it to be such a habit that you can do it without thinking. Let's take some of the pressure off by getting you up fifteen minutes earlier."

"Aw, Mom, no! Maybe if I feed the dog at night and Jerry feeds him in the morning."

"Jerry?"

"I got enough to do. I fed him all last year and I survived."

Mom started looking at alternatives. "We can feed the dog dry food in the morning and canned at night. The dog dish in the pantry is right next door to your bathroom. Try scooping his dry food while you're brushing your teeth and report back next week. But you must continue making your bed when you get up, just as the rest of us do."

Assessment of Attention

A host of distractions rob children of the attention they need to satisfy their hunger; when you seek out the reasons children aren't getting sufficient attention, you're looking for causes. Here, you also look for the effects. We strongly suggest you assess each child's attention hunger periodically, whether you hold meetings or not. Is each child receiving appropriate attention? If not, why? Frequently, one child requires more, due to an illness or a special project, for example. Your time is finite; are the other children receiving, or going to receive, similarly adequate attention?

A sixth-grader: "I feel left out. Mom, you're doing all the stuff for the charity bazaar, and Dad's helping them rewire the seniors' center basement. I feel ignored."

Up to now neither Mom nor Dad had noticed how much time their activities were taking.

The mother: "What would you like to do?"

The child: "I don't know. Something."

The mother: "I don't know either. The bazaar is Saturday. Can I hire you as a clerk to help take money? I think we're going to need more people on the sales crew than we have. After the bazaar is over, let's go out for pizza and decide on something nice to do together on Sunday."

Attention hunger has two faces. The council provides opportunity for a family member to remind others of a need for attention. But it also provides opportunity for family members to tell someone, "You're asking for too much attention in the wrong way. We're tired of your tantrums and pouting." This sort of thing works only if the parents are not taking an us-big-guys-versus-you-little-guys attitude. If the children feel threatened or coerced, they'll gang up as a sibling unit.

The family council is also a great way to promote another area of human need, the expression of feelings.

Feelings

So many families we deal with have no idea how to express feelings or, in many cases, what those feelings are. Sadness? Anxiety? They are painful, so we tend to hide them or dismiss them without examining or dealing with them. Our children follow the patterns we set. Therefore we, the parents, must take the lead, sometimes forging new paths of our own. The first step is to find the feelings and talk about them; the next step, to see them in others.

Lida Armstrong never felt very empathetic toward others. In fact, she had trouble getting in touch with her own feelings. Now as a parent she was called upon to help her children learn a skill that had eluded her.

"Pete, what's happening between you and Walter?"

Pete shrugged. "Nothing'."

"I realize that. He hasn't been around for two weeks. No more best friends?"

"Yeah."

"How does it make you feel?"

"He was getting boring anyhow. Always talking about girls. Really dumb, you know?"

"Losing a best friend hurts," Lida commiserated. "I know; I've done it a million times. Want to talk about it after the war council?"

"Nothing to talk about. He's a big fat zero. But yeah, I guess so."

For flippant, bouncing Pete, that was a major expression of need.

We find that women and girls are almost universally better able to identify and express feelings than are men and boys. Women not only verbalize their feelings well, they are good at spotting nonverbal cues too. Men may pick up cues effectively but, lacking oral expression, dismiss them. In time, men cease looking for either verbal or nonverbal cues about feelings. The result: males tend to avoid feelings more than females. Thus, when discussing and exploring feelings, women and girls will probably take the lead.

Celebration and Grieving

Examine the weave in a caned chair. The pattern goes horizontally and vertically and diagonally in two directions. So it is with celebrating and grieving. Two different and distinct aspects interweave themselves to create the fabric of our joys and sorrows.

First, help children identify the causes for celebrating and for grieving in each single event. Discuss them, working out where the balance is between celebration and grief.

One of our young clients in counsel, an eight year old named Holly, told about such an occasion. Grandma had been getting progressively worse for years as arthritis pain in her hips slowed her down. She was limping around with a cane when she tripped over Holly one day and broke her hip. Holly, already insecure, was absolutely devastated.

Doctors fitted the broken bone with an artificial joint. Three months later they did the same with the other, unbroken, side. Grandma walks virtually pain-free now, with no need of cane or assistance.

"So, Holly, what was there to grieve?"

"That she tripped over me. I felt so bad. I felt like I was the fault. I still feel that way a little."

"What else?"

"Well, she was in pain so long when she walked. For years. Somebody told her you can't do much for arthritis, so she put up with it for a long time. And then she had to be in the hospital so long. I felt really bad."

"What else?"

"Well, uh, it cost a lot. Her insurance or Medicare or whatever didn't cover all of it. Mom and Dad had to pay some."

"And what is there about this whole thing that we can celebrate?"

"You mean there's a good side?"

"Sure. Think about it. The good side can be hard to find in a sad situation, just like things you grieve are hard to find in some happy situations."

"Well, uh, Grandma walks real good now. She says she never would have gone and had that done, except they took X rays and said they could fix it. She calls it her lucky break."

"What else can we celebrate?"

"I don't know." Holly thought for a while. "Mom says it used to be that if you were old and broke your hip, that was it. You didn't walk any more and you spent the rest of your life in an old folks' home. She says it's so lucky they can fix that kind of thing now. We should celebrate that."

"I agree."

The balance—wherever there is grief, there is cause for celebration.

While this balance teeters in place, the family needs to also look at another balance: Each family member feels grief and celebration individually, and feels also the collective grief and celebration of the family as a unit—that good old egomass in others.

Mah-Sek Han, age eleven, auditions for first violin with the Regional Youth Symphony and wins first chair. His celebration is obvious. There is also grieving, for his father has been called to urgent business in Boston and cannot be present to join in the celebration.

As both Mah-Sek and Mah-Sek's family join in celebration, they should be aware of the second aspect, the important line separating individual and collective celebration/grief. True, joy and pain are shared as a family. But the family is a collection of individuals with individual boundaries. Family members must not excessively carry each other's pain or vicariously depend upon each other's joy. Mah-Sek's little sister is proud of her brother. But she is not just Mah-Sek's sister, she is Mae-Ying Han. Regardless of Mah-Sek's triumphs and failures, Mae-Ying's identity depends upon her own strengths and weaknesses, not his.

In your family keep an eye on the balances required to handle celebration and grief. Temper the blows of life by recognizing those balances. Also, protect the boundaries and identities of the family's individuals by recognizing the balance between the two aspects of celebration and grief, the shared and the private experiences.

Polarities

Children function primarily in black or white, good or bad, yes or no. Shades of gray tend to escape them. Fortunately, life is made just for them, for life is itself a twisted set of polarities. The *pas de deux* of grief and celebration is only one example.

The family as a group is where children can best learn to handle the ambivalence of these constant opposites. For instance, Joey Trask and his mom oscillated wildly for months between close and distant.

Another example: scary and exciting feelings march hand in hand.

Children bound almost out of control between extremes before finding a comfortable middle ground. Codependent children find it nearly impossible to get the balance right. They need extra help learning how to handle polar opposites. The family unit offers a cushioning effect in this; Mom and Dad provide the fulcrum of the balance beam—the steady spot—and older siblings, if possible, dampen the wild swings with their own more mature attitudes.

We have found in our experience that the one thing moms and dads ought not to attempt is to cushion children from these polarities, the older children in particular.

Polarities exist in Mom and Dad's relationship. They love each other dearly, and sometimes they can't stand each other. That's natural. If some Christian wives were asked if they had ever considered divorce, "No," they might reply. "Murder, at times, but not divorce."

A family committed, not to a certain pretense, but to the simple truth, will spare small children the gory details without trying to mask from them the realities of living. The parents will not discuss secrets the children are unable to handle, but neither will they keep secrets completely. You will remember that in any family there are no secrets anyway.

We suggest that the family as a unit handle the unavoidable polarities of life—birth and death, love and hate—in two distinct steps.

First, identify that it's true. Grandfather did die; he did not go off to visit relatives in Waukegan forever. Mommy is indeed going to have a baby; that's not a watermelon seed and it will change all our lives forever. It's all right to be angry at your brother even as you love him. He hurt you; those things happen. In the course of time you can forgive him.

Second, help the child develop the skills for making the most of the vividness of life. Remember, children aren't interested in mastery; they are content to learn how to cope. The first and best step in helping a child cope is to provide by example the assurance that the family is dedicated to the truth. The child need not put on a front, need not lie to the world, need not deny what his or her eyes see and ears hear inside or outside the family.

Take the classic example that Dad is an alcoholic. The

family will no longer practice the myth that he is not, that everything is actually all right.

Coming Together Apart

Joey Trask entered Dr. Warren's office and with an impish grin flopped into the side chair.

Dr. Warren studied the boy's hair. He craned around for a look at the back; Joey obligingly turned his head.

Dr. Warren smiled, nodding, and sat back in his own over-stuffed chair. "I'm trying to think where I saw a haircut like that. I remember. The Cowboys quarterback, what's-his-name. The channel 5 sports announcer was interviewing him. My wife informs me he's considered quite a hunk by the ladies. That style looks as good on you as it does on him."

"Dad thinks it's too long in the back yet, but he seems to like it a little."

"It'll grow on him."

"Mom's coming. She had to talk to some secretary a minute."

"How's your dad?"

"Fine. Still leaning on me to try out for soccer."

"How do you feel about that now?"

"I've been thinking about soccer a lot. You know? I never liked it, really, all the years I was playing. I did OK, but it wasn't fun, not even when I was winning."

"Any sports that are fun for you?"

"Naw. The school I'll go to next year is putting together a golf team, I hear. That sounds fun. I might try that."

"Have you mentioned it to your father?"

"Sort of. He wasn't impressed. He doesn't think it's a sport if it's not in the Olympics, y'know?"

Beth Trask entered smiling for Joey's final session and sat down. A few moments of chitchat and she dived right into business. "Whalon and I had a long talk last week about Joey. Whalon doesn't believe Joey's behavior with the music and hair and things is the way you were describing it."

"What do you think?"

"I'm confident you're right, because you and Dr. Hemfelt

were right about me. As Dr. Hemfelt and I talked about my deepest feelings, I realized for the first time how I really feel."

"Can you summarize Dr. Hemfelt's comments?"

"Yes. My father was dictatorial just like Whalon. I never made peace with that, never rebelled. That became unfinished business and Joey picked it up."

Dr. Warren nodded. "You and Joey have been talking about this, I take it."

"Yes. And I believe Dr. Hemfelt was right when he suggested I actually enjoyed Joey's acting out, in a way. It's what I wanted to do when I was a kid and never could. I was giving Joey a loud unspoken message: 'I'm glad someone's finally doing it,' and I didn't know it."

"Yeah. When you asked me why I was listening to my music and wearing my shirts and stuff, I said, 'I don't know.' I thought I was just ducking your question. But when I thought about it, I really didn't know."

Dr. Warren addressed them both. "Where there are codependency problems such as control issues, the hidden policy is almost always 'Don't feel, don't talk, don't think.' That doesn't help you a bit when you try to sort out true feelings. You've both made splendid strides."

"It's not really Whalon's fault," said Beth. "His alcoholic father, for instance. All this business being overinvolved and overcontrolling is understandable; 'I'm giving him what I never had,' he keeps saying, 'and Joey doesn't appreciate it.' It really hurts him. He just doesn't understand."

"Yeah," Joey added. "I guess he's just trying to give me too much of what he never had."

"Good insight, well put." Dr. Warren smiled. "So what are your plans from here on?"

Beth laughed. "Whalon thinks a family meeting is nonsense and doesn't want to sit down and talk to Joey until he shapes up and gets back into sports." She raised a finger, her eyes sparkling. "But! There was one place I have always been in control: Sunday dinner. So I sort of adapted dinner after church into a family meeting, but I didn't explain it that way to Whalon. If Whalon starts preaching at Joey, I just say, 'No friction at the table, please,' and change the subject. We're actually talking now. Real talk."

"How do you feel about that, Joey?" Dr. Warren asked.

There was that shrug again. "OK. I wondered for a while if it wasn't lying to Dad or being sneaky, but it's not. I think he knows exactly what's happening. But he has to—how do the Japanese talk about it—save face? You know, that sort of thing. He just has to look like he hasn't changed and he's still on top. It's OK."

"Does this mean your father is starting to change his parenting strategies?"

Joey looked at his mom.

Beth frowned. "I think so, in a way. We were talking about Joey's schoolwork, for example. He said Joey has to work harder and do better. I said, we can't make him do it. We tried that and it's been a flop.

"So I think I've convinced him that the way to go is simply to say, 'Joey, your schoolwork is up to you. If you fail, it won't be because you can't learn but because you don't try. We'll help, but we won't make it our responsibility. It's yours.' We expect him to pass. Anything beyond that is up to him. Whalon thinks we're not pushing him enough, but he's agreed to try it."

"What changes are you yourself making?"

"I think . . ." She shifted on the sofa to better face Dr. Warren. "I think, I can now say from my heart that it's all right for Joey to grow up. I think I've made peace with the fact that I can never have my little boy back."

CHAPTER 17

From Here on Out—Reintegrating

Scene: Friday, the dining-room table following dinner. The Kolbins attempt an informal family meeting to plan the weekend.

Regina: Can I go now?

James: We want to decide what we're doing this week-end. Help us here.

Regina: But my TV show's on. You said I could watch it.

Melanie: Then let's work fast. We were thinking we might go to the zoo tomorrow. Would you enjoy that?

Regina: Yeah. Can I go now?

James: Victor?

Victor: Can I watch TV too?

Gerald: *(Fusses to get down from his high chair.)*

James: *(lifts Gerald to the floor)* Oh, go ahead. All of you. *(Victor and Regina scurry off to the living room. The baby crawls into Melanie's lap. James sits down again.)*

James: It's useless. This family meeting stuff's not cutting it.

Melanie: Look at it from their viewpoint. They've never been to the zoo. Gina read about it in books; that's all. Vic's never even heard of a zoo. This is all pretty new to us. Let's give it a chance.

End scene.

The Kolbins actually were doing a lot better here than James thought. Rather than instantly becoming impatient with their lack of interest, Melanie remembered to think about it from the children's perspective. She's trying to understand them better—"where they're coming from," to quote the hackneyed phrase. James involved everyone in the decision that affected them all. The meeting was actually quite successful because it accomplished what such a family meeting should, however informal: it brought the whole family together to discuss their common interest. And the children participated as much as children that age can be expected to.

Rebuilding the Skyscraper

We mentioned previously that as the skyscraper of a child's life slowly rises, it is not always possible to go back and redo those stories that were not properly built to start with. Sometimes all we can expect to do is shore up the shakiest levels. The Kolbins are beginning to do just that.

Shed the Myths

When working with families, Drs. Warren and Hemfelt both find they must get parents out of the fatal mindset that free time is wasted time. The Kolbins could also have decided simply to hang around the house and goof off. Rake the lawn. Play a game with the kids. Build some birdhouses. Set up the croquet game on the clean lawn. Put the garage in order. Maybe wash the car. Send James and the kids down to the store to choose some hot dogs and pick up charcoal briquets for a lunch cooked *alfresco*.

In this high-tech, run-run age, families find it exceedingly difficult to simply sit back and fool around. And yet that relaxed atmosphere of simply being—that's all, just being—nurtures the children's sense of family beautifully.

Keep It Simple

This particular weekend, the Kolbins planned an activity neither elaborate nor detailed. It was not a thing that required scheduling a week in advance. (As the children grow older, planning will have to get a bit more definite when ticket purchases, reservations, travel arrangements, and such become part of the picture.)

310

Parents who aren't used to unstructured family activity have a tendency to hear "fun with the kids" and think "Disneyland." Big wingding weekends are great once or twice in a lifetime, but they don't have to occur every weekend.

The Kolbins have the right idea, though, with their day at the zoo. Other than admission, there's little expense, particularly since Melanie packed a picnic lunch.

Notice that the Kolbins did not wait until next morning to bring up the idea of a zoo trip. If you're going somewhere with small children, you do well to get cracking in the morning.

The Kolbins were out and rolling by 9:30. They arrived with time to spare and found close parking. James bought the admission tickets, but Victor handled their distribution, meting them out to the family members just before they went through the turnstile.

James rented two strollers. One was for Gerald, the other for Victor and Regina. They took turns riding and pushing each other. Sometimes James dragged the extra stroller around empty, but by noon Regina and Victor were both showing signs of wear, and that stroller came in handy.

They went home not too long after eating their picnic lunch, as everyone enthused over the animals they liked best.

Keep It Personal

"You know?" Rob Newport mused. "You rarely hear the term 'Sunday driver' these days. That was a driver who ambled down the road at less than the speed limit, gawking at the scenery. It was a disparaging label, Sunday driver, and you didn't have to be driving on Sunday to earn it. When I was a real little kid, we'd take a Sunday drive. Just driving around, looking. I guess nobody does that anymore."

Few do. Such a simple thing. And yet, that sort of activity, involving not so much driving around as talking about what is seen, is very rewarding to kids. Sharing opinions, pointing out things to each other, arguing the relative merits of this bridge over that one—such is the stuff that makes children feel a part of the group and helps everyone know each other better.

Going to a movie, as another example, counts far more than does the movie itself. What enhances the parent-child bond is getting there, buying the ticket, picking out the popcorn, and most of all talking about it before and after. In short, *person-to-person interactions build childhood relationships rather than the activities themselves.*

To erect a solid skyscraper and shore up the rickety levels already in place, you need personal, one-on-one contact with your child—"time in the saddle," a laconic cowboy once called it. Nothing else will do.

Getting Started

Start When the Children are Young

It's awfully hard to enjoy laid-back, relaxed activities as a family if parents and kids haven't done it before. It's especially difficult to begin with no background experience.

Beth Trask quickly learned that. "Let's get you and Dad together to do something fun" was met with disdain by both Joey and Whalon. Whalon acted rather embarrassed. Coach and player on the soccer field is one thing. Something "fun" without a specific goal of self-improvement felt downright effeminate. Women went shopping, wandering about without a clear objective; that's what this idea felt like. Joey misinterpreted the suggestion as yet another attempt to get him to knuckle under and be the good little kid again.

Fun. Despite all the activities in which the Trasks engaged together, they had no clear idea of fun. Almost always in the past, Whalon chose the activities, and he chose them for their value. Did this outing make us smarter? Stronger? More coordinated? Better players? Did it improve our spirituality? If not, forget it. Fun took the back seat.

Teach Fun

Children of an earlier generation would blink in amazement. Teach a kid how to have fun? Kids invented fun! But in our practice we come across many children today whose

312

lives are either so organized or else so consumed by TV and videos that they have no idea how to play and have fun. Too often, neither do the parents, for they have forgotten how.

In counsel we work with individuals first, Dr. Hemfelt with adults and Dr. Warren with children, helping them grasp the concept of fun and play. As the family then comes together, reintegrating as a unit, the fun aspect emerges as a secondary effect.

We might start by talking about it.

"What do you like to do?"

"Have you ever tried [going hiking, building with blocks, working a jigzaw puzzle—age-appropriate activities]?"

"If you were to get up on a horse and go for a ride right now, what do you think it would feel like?"

We might thumb through a toy catalogue with the child. "Here's a Lego set. Ever play with them? They have an airplane put together in the picture here. How might we make a boat out of that?"

To adults, we might suggest attending a hobby fair. The weekend newspaper lists meetings of various hobby enthusiasts; miniatures, gardening, needlework, woodworking, and solo sports activities all have their societies and practitioners, and they love to talk about their interests. County and regional fairs frequently hold demonstrations in their hobby halls. Go exploring.

As we counsel patients we often model play, particularly for children. A two year old is probably pretty good at play. But that's about the age when kids start taking television in heavy doses. By three, the skill may be lost, atrophied through lack of use. Two, three, six, or twelve, we simply sit down on the floor and have at it with them.

Dr. Warren got into some serious Tinkertoy building with Jennifer Newport. "The two different knobs here have different-size holes, see? These, the dowels, fit tightly. This one is oversized enough to spin on the dowel. It's good for wheels; anything from ferris wheels to cars and wagons. Let's make something with wheels. What do you suggest?"

"A sports car. The wheels turn, huh? Can it roll across the floor?"

"We'll see."

"Brian has some of these at home. He says they're for little kids."

"I'm not very little." Dr. Warren chuckled. He assembled two knobs and a stick. "We need three more of these whatsits. Will you make them, please? I wonder what it would be like to drive one of those minicars: you know that track out by Garland, with all the old tires stacked up to protect you on the turns?"

"Oh, those things! Go-carts. Yeah. They sure make noise. And driving them around those corners . . ."

By the time Jennifer copied Dr. Warren's sample whatsit and built three more, he had another prototype made. "And three more of these." They assembled the parts and indeed it rolled across the floor—after Jennifer replaced a wheel that kept sticking.

The next week they built a bakery out of plastic bricks and stocked it with bread loaves, rolls, and doughnuts made from clay. Dr. Warren deliberately pursued two simultaneous ends with these sessions; he modeled play and talked about prospective fun things and he also talked to Jennifer about weighty matters. As she got wrapped up in play, she became quite open in her conversation. Your child will as well, probably. It's a wonderful way to learn about your youngster's depths and inner fears.

Try Things Together

Both in counsel and in this book, we hesitate to suggest rote lists of things, lest the client or the reader try to plug in cookbook "surefire" activities without thinking about the underlying concepts. It's not what you do as a family, you see, but the process of doing it, of being together in something. In other words, don't do something a book tells you to do, but rather make a decision to engage in the process.

If you've not done anything relaxed, unstructured, and fun together before, we recommend you start with little things that require an hour or two. Put up the Christmas tree together. Walk across a nearby college campus and try to identify the trees. Save the massive all-day projects for when your family works comfortably together as a unit.

Like the Kolbins, let the family as a group decide what to do at least some of the time. Other times, the parents might declare an activity by divine fiat. At all times the parents set the guidelines—nothing illegal or dangerous.

Fitting Reward

"Joey, I'll pay you ten bucks if you'll let me burn that T-shirt." Whalon wasn't jesting when he made the offer.

"Nothing doing, Dad! It cost me twelve."

"Yeah, but it's used. OK, twenty."

"No sale."

A few months after Joey's twelfth birthday, as his rebellion began to mushroom, his father tried this and other bribes to shape his kid up. "Ten dollars plus the price of the haircut to trim your hair up to where it should be." "Get rid of those rock tapes and I'll restore your allowance." Joey could have retired wealthy, had he played his cards differently. But principles are important to an emerging teen.

Rob Newport tried a similar reward system with Jennifer. "You go all day without Mom yelling at you, and you can stay up an extra hour to watch TV." It didn't work any better than the Trask bribery.

Rewarding a child with money or things does nothing toward building a solid family or a healthy child. Reward the child with positive social interactions.

Bribery of the sort Whalon Trask attempted does not foster strong family ties. Person-to-person contact is part of reintegrating the family. Relationships are the core of the child's existence and should always be valued above material reward.

When we recommended that to Alice Newport, she took it to heart and told Jennifer, "If you make your bed quick like a bunny and hang your stuff up, we'll have time for a game of Old Maid before you go to school. But the work has to be done first."

As children enter adolescence, they interact socially less with parents and more with peers.

Beth Trask was finally willing to accept that. On one occasion, for instance, she told Joey, "If you and Barry want, I'll drive you over to the mall. But you have to have your book report done first."

Making a Difference

All play and no work makes Jack a drone.

Not only do we want our children to grow up with a chance at happiness, we want to instill in them an idealism, a godly perspective towards others.

Fueling the Family Egomass

Lida Armstrong grew up on a dairy farm. "Nothing," says she, "absolutely nothing ties you down like those miserable cows." Every day twice a day, milking consumed hours. Then you flushed the milking machine; every surface of all the pipes and equipment had to be sterilized. Then you hosed down the milking parlor, shoveling out what had to be shoveled. And then here came the cows again to start it all over.

Lida grew up in the barns. At eight she was washing off the cows' udders just before they were milked. At ten she was shoveling. At twelve she operated the milking machines. Her family's dairy was not the biggest or its equipment the latest, so at fifteen Lida was stripping the cows—taking the last of the milk by hand after removing the milking machine.

"You can't imagine how much drudgery goes into a carton of milk," she mused. "And yet, we didn't notice it. I mean, we kids complained about the work all the time, but we didn't think about it. We didn't dwell on it and think we were being abused or anything. It was a part of life, a part of being that family. And we really cared about the cows."

"Did you get a lot of teasing at school?" Dr. Warren asked.

"Not a whole lot. You know, though, my town friends didn't have the foggiest idea what work was all about. Jackie came closest; she had a paper route. But when she was done, she was done. And her family wasn't involved; it was just her. Our dairy was the whole family's operation."

Lida Armstrong learned important lessons that her friends from town missed, concepts ingrained into her. She learned as a child the importance of taking good care of something that depends upon you. She learned about investing her energy in another. She also experienced family. A family-centered project such as her parents' dairy farm fuels that communal identity, the family egomass. She belonged, and that belonging is what a child needs most of all.

We feel safe in assuming that you are in no position just now to run out and buy a dairy farm. Fortunately, part of the process of family reintegration, which could conceivably be served by a dairy farm, can be served in many other ways more easily. Keep in mind the end: to make the family identity solid and to make the children an integral part of that family, for they will draw a large and necessary amount of their identity from the family.

We have found that families who work together in charitable enterprises benefit immensely. We recommend community activity for any family.

Charity Begins at Home

A small town in east Texas turned out at 2:00 A.M. one morning to watch a spectacular fire on High Street. A one-family dwelling went up in a blaze stretching halfway to heaven. The family of six escaped safely, though their home and belongings were a total loss. The local Kiwanis held a benefit barbecue for them, but the clothing drive was handled by a ten year old, Mark Fry.

Mark was one of the citizens, awakened by the sirens, who got up to watch the excitement. The next evening at supper he announced to his family that he wanted to gather donated clothing and household items. He even had a fairly complex plan for rounding up neighbors' gifts. His father could have turned the idea over to a service organization better equipped to handle the job, but he knew his son well (and that is an important key). He said, "If you start it, you'll have to see it through. I'll be behind you, but I won't do it for you. If you still want to, go for it!"

Mark figured out a collection route. He called the neighbors, asked for donations, and promised when he would come by to collect them. From a local contractor he arranged a driver and one-ton stake-side truck. He enlisted the rest of his family as helpers, but Mom and Dad did not take over. It was Mark's show, start to end.

As the burnt-out family moved from their motel room to a vacant rental, the truck pulled up to the door, nearly filled with clothing and used furniture.

Not many ten year olds could handle a project that extensive, but the keys to its success will help any family project.

- Mark's father promised, "I'll be behind you." That's what kids need, regardless of the scope of their endeavors. Mark wasn't hung out in the wind and rain alone, like the only shirt on a clothesline. Had he run into serious problems, he would have had backup. Your family similarly can act either as prime mover or backup in various family enterprises.
- It was local and doable. Had Mark set out to end world hunger, his father would quite properly have discouraged him. Make certain a project in which the family is involved fits the family's resources.
- The family could see results. Children function best when working with tangibles. Don't we all?
- The commitment to others became the bottom line. Mark didn't do it to look good. He didn't do it to benefit his own family. He watched the blaze and thought about these people's terrible loss. He could help! And so he did. But he could not have done it without the support of that all-important family united behind him.

Working Together

We find that, universally, families benefit when they involve themselves in the welfare of others. Some save money to give to the poor. Some prepare dinners for shut-ins. They make toys for local children's hospitals or Christmas toy campaigns. The Kolbins decided to adopt an animal at the zoo; they read the list of animals from the zoo's adoption program and the kids chose. A few pick a cause to support as a family. Although we do not normally make specific suggestions, we offer some guidelines.

It Should Truly Involve the Family

Suppose, for instance, that the whole Krentz family is out demonstrating against euthanasia. There is their six-year-old girl waving a picket sign. Ask the child what *euthanasia* means. She frowns. "I don't know." The whole Krentz family in this case is not involved. Rather, the parents feel strongly about a purpose and have enlisted the kids. Good modeling but not good togetherness.

When the Parsonses worked together as a family to support the local animal shelter, it was truly a family enterprise—all the family members understood and cared about what they were doing.

Don't Make It Overtaxing

The Parsons family got so wrapped up in the animal shelter that they found themselves down there every weekend, doing something or other. When Papa Parsons realized what was happening, he had to say, "Whoa! We're getting so involved here we're neglecting everything else, including each other. This weekend we take a picnic to the county park and spend the time relaxing."

Avoid Possible Codependent Attachments

The hardest thing in the world for a servant to do is to maintain a firm personal boundary. The same is true of families. If you, the parents, see a growing dependence on your family by the people you are serving, particularly when your family is engaged in face-to-face service toward others, it's time to examine boundaries.

Take-Away Value

Dr. Warren played his next-to-last domino. "Brian and I have been talking a lot about his need to fix everything, and especially to be a daddy to you. I think he's showing improvement. What do you think?"

"I don't know." Jennifer went to the bone pile. "He doesn't

act so tense anymore, and he doesn't yell at me and tell me what to do all the time. Do you have a six?"

"I'm sure not going to tell *you* if I do! Do you think I'm that silly?"

She giggled, "Worth a try," and played a five-seven.

Dr. Warren went to the bone pile. "How do you think Brian feels about all this?"

"I don't know."

"Think about it. He must have very strong feelings, right? What would your feelings be if you two were reversed?"

She lost interest momentarily in the game, an unusual situation. "I suppose first I'd feel kind of left out. You know, I couldn't boss my sister around. Then I'd feel relieved because everyone tells me it's not my fault when she messes up."

Dr. Warren laughed. "Your answer really pleases me! I remember when you weren't sure how to explain your own feelings. And now here you are putting yourself in someone else's shoes. It's an important step toward being grown up, the ability to understand that other people have feelings."

"Yeah, but did I guess right?"

"I'm not going to say. Brian's conversations are private and I don't talk about them with others, the same as I don't talk about conversations with you to anyone else."

"That's good. Yeah." And she played her double six.

Feelings

The family stitches itself together anew. Its members learn to understand each other and themselves. The children thrive in a healthy home climate that aids the growth tasks facing them. All easy to say, but so hard to do. Here are some principles to keep in mind as healing takes hold in your family.

First, we as adults must help our children understand that other people have feelings. Second, we must help them understand the reasons for personal boundaries. *My feelings are mine and yours are yours. I keep mine inside me and I'm not going to let you damage them. You might hurt them, but I am the one in control of them.* Third, we must respect

kids' feelings. For instance, you'll want to avoid statements such as these:
- "Oh, come on! You don't really feel that way."
- "Nonsense! That's nothing to be afraid of."
- "Shame on you for thinking that's funny!"
- "Don't you dare get angry over such a silly little thing."
- "The divorce is final and we're just going to put it behind us."
- "I can't see why your feelings should be hurt. I didn't mean it."

It's so easy to dismiss children's feelings. It's so easy to forget that a child's feelings are just as intense as yours and mine.

Autonomy

How do you instill a sense of autonomy in a child, who is nowhere near ready to shoulder any? Dr. Warren tackled that task while talking to Pete Armstrong one day.

Pete perched on the outside bench by the frozen yogurt parlor. He licked a big slurp off his vanilla cone. "Dad scares me. Not when he's high, because then he's the neatest dad in the world, you know? When he comes down."

"Explain." Dr. Warren licked around the edges of his Integration cone—equal parts licorice and vanilla.

"He gets grouchy and yells a lot and throws stuff around. He says I lie about him to Mom. Says all sorts of things that aren't true."

"Is that good?"

"No. At least I don't think so. But he doesn't do it all the time. So he's not really bad, you know?"

Dr. Warren took another lick. He asked, "What do you do when he frightens you?"

"Crunch up and make myself look small until he snorts another line. Then he's OK."

"He's OK when he's high, is that what you're saying?"

"Yeah." Pete's cone was nearly gone already.

"You know I'm a doctor, right? I see a part of it you don't. Medically, Pete, he's not OK. He's really messing up his body with that junk. He's snorting more now because it takes more to get the high. And the high isn't as high as it used to be, but the lows are lower."

"Yeah. That's right, now that you mention it. The downs are really bad, and he's not as fun when he's up. It's different than it used to be."

Dr. Warren nodded, then asked Pete, "Is it OK to do something illegal?"

"I guess not, but everybody does."

"No, Pete, that's not true. Ask a drug addict if everyone does and he'll say yes because that's what he wants to believe. The truth is, most people obey the law because they know that's how society works best."

"Dad says he's an adult and he can do what he wants. He says what he does in the privacy of his own home is nobody else's business."

"It's a good point. But consider the other side of the coin. When you destroy your own health with illegal activity you might get busted for, you're not doing much for the rest of your family, or society, either. Then there's the public cost of helping you get well, of prosecuting you on drug charges. That's not being very good, I don't think."

"Yeah, I suppose."

"Ever hear the word *autonomy?*"

"*Automoton.* That's a robot. A droid. Robots aren't the same thing, huh?" The vanilla cone was gone.

"They're the exact opposite." Dr. Warren finally finished enough of his frozen yogurt to hit cone on the next bite. "*Autonomy* means independence. Totally separate from anyone else."

"That I like! Do your own thing, man."

"Exactly. But when you're completely off on your own, you don't have anyone loving you or anyone to love. You're all alone."

"You do the autonomy thing but keep your family around."

"Doesn't work that way. With complete autonomy it always ends up that you're alone. But there's a better way. I've learned that the best course is serving each other. What you have then is autonomy with attachment. That means mixing dependent and independent into interdependent."

"I don't get it."

"Autonomy means you're your own person. Independent. But attachment means you stay close to the people you love. Dependent."

"Yeah. That's what I was saying."

"In a healthy family the members are neither completely dependent or completely autonomous. That means they do what is best for each other. You don't have friends long if you don't return their love."

"What does that have to do with Dad and me? Wait. I see, I think. He's not doing what's best for us, right? And I'm supposed to do what's best for him."

"It's hard being autonomous when you're eleven. Very hard. It will get easier as you get older. It's one of the goals your mother and I both want for you, the healthy way to grow up."

"Yeah, but I can't control what Dad does."

"That's so very true. But you can control what Pete does. Pete can be autonomous and say phooey on the world, or he can work on being autonomous with attachment—being his own person, yet giving and receiving love. Helping others."

"OK. I want to start now." He sidled in closer on the bench. "Can I help you finish that cone?"

CHAPTER 18

Wrap-up

Beth Trask perched on the edge of her chair as the Texas sun streamed in over her shoulder. "Well. This is like saying goodbye to an old friend. I guess I won't be seeing you anymore; I mean, at least on a regular basis. Funny feeling."

"If you encounter problems you can't handle, I trust you'll call." Dr. Hemfelt smiled. "But there shouldn't be many you can't."

She smiled. The smile faded. "Do you realize how miserable the rest of my life would be if Joey hadn't forced us into this?"

"That's the whole purpose of coming to terms with yourself inside, as we've done here. Paul—Dr. Warren—and I agree on this: The key to healing, or perhaps call it the ultimate goal, is to see yourself as God sees you and ultimately to become all He has in mind for you. There is lasting happiness."

"I agree. I spent years trying to be the perfect little wife and it was a sham. I wasn't being submissive in a true sense, just in surface things. And boiling underneath. It's different now. I've made peace with who I am and what I ought to do—and ought not. I understand Whalon well enough now also that I can work with him instead of just backing off and shutting up when I disagree."

"Do you think he'll consider therapy? Either with a counselor or through reading?"

"Probably not. But he's made changes for the better. And I think he'll continue doing so. He doesn't admit it, of course, and Joey and I don't mention it. Understand, it's still not good. He hasn't dealt at all with all the pain of his past; an alcoholic father who abandoned his family, and all Whalon says is, 'It happens.' At least now Joey and I understand better why he's the way he is. We can tell when it's his past talking and forgive it."

"Well put. God bless you and your family, Beth." Dr. Hemfelt rose and offered a hand.

He got a grateful hug.

James Kolbin stretched out on the warm tile. "Vacation. Never thought it would happen."

"A three-day vacation, but it's heaven. No two year old attached to me, no four year old whining, no seven year old brewing up trouble." Melanie leaned over enough to kiss him. "Thank you."

"We'll do this a couple of times a year at least. We need it. I didn't realize how badly our marriage had deteriorated into a baby-sitting pit." He felt the sun on his face and thought about how much he missed the sun in that cavernous office building every day. "I signed up for a night course at the college."

"Learning what?"

"Decision-making techniques. It's offered over winter quarter too. If it seems good, maybe you can take it then. Dr. Hemfelt says not just one person but both should be able to act decisively."

"We'll see. Did you talk to Grandpa before we left?"

"Yeah. He was not a happy camper. I explained that we learned about a family that had been flooded out; he said he read it in the paper too. Tragic, he said. Then I told him we were giving them our living-room furniture. He blew up. And when I told him we'd been storing our modern pieces in the attic and that's what we were going to use, he really hit the roof."

"He'll change his will again."

"So be it. I'm not going to walk on eggs when it's our kids who are paying for it. The children come first. If that's the only way we can get rid of the stress, that's what we do."

Melanie watched blue sky a moment. "Remember what Dr. Hemfelt said in one of our sessions? It comes from a recovery group slogan, I think. 'If you don't pass it back, you pass it on.' If we don't pass our anger back to Joseph, it will plague our kids. That really stuck with me."

James nodded. "The intergenerational thing. Well, we're dealing with anger when it happens now. No more passing it on."

She rolled toward him and lifted her head. "I'm very proud of you." She sat up suddenly. "I just now made a decision. Buffet dinner at Louie's and back to the hotel room."

"I thought you wanted Italian food."

"But you wanted beef and potatoes. Louie's has both. Let's go."

He took her hand for the walk back to the room, but somehow that didn't seem enough. They left poolside arm in arm.

Dr. Warren frowned. "Are you sure this is the place to eat?"

Joey led the way through the door. "Trust me. You want to see who's who on the scene—here's the place."

"I think I'd put the quality of the food above the scene, personally." Dr. Warren took his place behind Joey in an eight-person line awaiting service. This was a fast food place like so many others, but it offered everything from fajitas to pizza. People in their early teens bounced from booth to booth laughing and talking, this group conversing with that one, yet separate from them. To the untrained eye, "the scene" equalled "chaos."

"Come on, Dr. Warren! That's what an old fogey would say. You wouldn't want to look like an old fogey."

"I am what I am!" Dr. Warren said as he gestured palms up in mock desperation.

Joey turned suddenly and held Dr. Warren eye to eye. Dr. Warren thought briefly of the sullen boy with downcast eyes who sat in his office not that many months ago. This wasn't the same kid. Joey breathed, "Yeah! That's it! That's exactly what you've been saying, isn't it! Decide who you are and what you want, and make your own choices."

"You've been doing that. You understand the principle now; I know you do."

"Yeah, I guess so." He frowned thoughtfully and stared

out the window at nothing. "Sometimes I wonder if I'm being two-faced when I wear some of my shirts when I'm with other people but not when I'm home. Guess I'm not into shaking my parents up as much as I used to be."

"It's not two-faced. They know what you're doing and they're accepting it. You've chosen to respect them, to stop offending them, and it's an excellent choice. A godly choice. Scripture written all over it."

"Ephesians 6:1. I won all those memory-verse contests, remember?"

"But now you're not memorizing words from a book; you're applying them where it counts—in your relationships with others. That's true Christianity."

They moved forward to third in line.

"Mom's doing that, too, now, it seems. Being a real Christian instead of putting on this goody front. Know what I mean? And she still yells at me, but it's usually for something she oughta yell about."

"If your only reason for doing something is to do battle with another person, it's not a very good reason. I mentioned that in our visits. She asks herself 'Why am I doing this?' now, the same as you do."

"Hey, listen; the music they're playing on the overhead. Hear it?"

"How could I fail to?"

"Ever listen to the words?"

"Swahili, isn't it? I can't discern them. Can you?"

Joey stepped up and placed his order to the counter and addressed the counter girl. "Two Rocker Specials and two swamp waters." He grinned back at Dr. Warren. "Wait'll you try this."

"Swamp water?"

Half orange drink and half root beer."

"Swamp water!"

"The words in that song talk about how sex is like a devil's kiss. I never noticed it until I really started listening. Used to be my favorite song too. You know, I don't think there's two kids in here right now who really listen to the words. If they did, they'd turn it off. It's weird. Warps your mind."

328

"It's not my mind I'm worried about warping right now."
Swamp water?!

"I can't believe it. Silence." Sarah Armstrong came jogging downstairs. She paused to examine the new door going in between Grandma's side and theirs. The carpenters carried the last of their tools out to the truck. "Maybe this was a pretty good idea of Pete's after all."

Lida nodded. "I'm satisfied with it. This weekend we'll paint it to match the rest of the woodwork."

"This weekend we're supposed to go over to Dad's."

"Oh, that's right. But I told him I'm not going to take you over. If he wants you there he can come get you. He may or may not show up. If he does, we'll work around it. One coat of paint Friday night and the second coat Sunday night maybe."

"Did you warn him about driving under the influence?"

"Yes, and I told him what you two decided to do if he tries to drive when he's high. I wish we'd stopped all that enabling years ago. I didn't realize."

"Lotta stuff we didn't realize, Mom. Now we get Grandma more independent, right?"

"Oh, let's hope so!"

Pete came bounding in the front door. "All right!" He measured the new door with his outspread hands. "Perfect!" He paused. "How does Grandma like it? Has she seen it yet?" He pushed open the both-ways swinging door. It whispered back and forth and settled shut. He pushed it all the way open. It stayed.

"She hasn't tried it yet."

"Here she comes now," Sarah muttered.

Grandma came tooling her wheelchair from her front room toward her staircase. She hesitated, then came ahead. "Took them long enough. Did you pay them, Lida?"

"Yes, Ma. It's all taken care of."

Grandma stopped the chair. "It doesn't fit! Call them back here! The chair won't fit in the doorway. Look at that. They knew what it's for and they made it too narrow. Call them back right now!"

"No, Ma. They made it exactly the way it's supposed to be."

"The chair doesn't fit through the door, Lida!"

"It's not supposed to.'"

"Of course it is. What do you mean?" Grandma glared at Lida. "You did this on purpose, didn't you!"

"Yes, Ma, because we love you. Remember back on the farm, when the calves were born? If they didn't get up on their feet they were lost. Sometimes I thought, 'That poor thing's too weak. It'll never make it.' But with some help and some struggling, they did. We're helping you get back on your feet, Grandma. It's important to your welfare, so it's important to us."

"That's nonsense! Call the carpenters."

Lida stepped through the narrow doorway and kissed her mother's wrinkled brow. "We love you, Ma."

Alice painted the game hens with orange sauce one more time and left the lid off, so that they would brown in the oven. Almost ready. She gave the vegetables a stir and poured tomato juice into two stem glasses. The Westminster chime in the mantel clock announced the half hour, it's "mi" note wheezing instead of bonging. They really ought to take the clock in and get that fixed.

Jenny-Jo appeared in the kitchen doorway. "Dad's home. Can we eat now?"

"Dinner's at six, same as it was five minutes ago. Is your homework done?"

"Aw, Mom."

"Do you want time for a game of checkers after dinner?" Alice didn't wait for an answer. "Go finish up. You'll be done before dinner and the evening's yours. Ride your bike, play a game." She wiggled a hand. "Go." She carried the two glasses into the living room.

Rob was hanging up his jacket and hardhat. "Jenny-Jo left her bike out on the lawn."

"She says she wants to ride a little after supper. Putting it away is on her list of things to get done." Alice handed him the appetizer and settled onto the sofa with her own glass.

He plopped down beside her—carefully, lest he spill to-mato juice on his torn, smudged, paint-splotched coveralls.

"I'm so glad you've been getting home on time. Thank you. It makes planning dinner so much better."

"I said I would, and I will. I remember when you used to plan dinner for five and then get bent out of shape when I wasn't there."

"Six o'clock has worked out fine. Oh, Jenny-Jo got her re-port card today. It's not wonderful, but it's getting better."

"She probably has a lot of catching up to do."

"That's what Miss Hosmer says. I talked to her on the phone this afternoon."

"Where's Brian?"

"I don't know. He's not home yet."

They talked for another twenty minutes before she went back to the kitchen to put dinner on the table. As Alice set out the vegetables and garnished the birds with parsley, she thought of the changes in their life over the last six months.

Jenny-Jo was still obnoxious, but she wasn't constantly clanging around anymore. She had settled considerably and seemed to know her mind better. She didn't cling and whine so much whenever she got into a new situation. Progress.

Brian. Alice had never guessed how pressured Brian's life had been—the pressure to be good, the pressure to fix all the family's problems, the pressure to provide for Alice the af-fection and companionship Rob did not. Dr. Warren seemed to think his attitude was pretty healthy now. Who knows? Progress?

Rob. She had been afraid their sexual relationship would fall apart completely when she got out of the hospital; he was so angry, so disappointed with her. It was the best it had been in years. Was she pleased? She wasn't sure yet. After all those dry seasons, she was uncertain how she felt now. His weight was still up there. He'd probably never lose it. But he was certainly a lot more attentive and considerate. That's progress.

And herself. Sometimes grief still overwhelmed her, when she thought of all the years she had literally missed out on. She had robbed herself of life just as surely as if she had murdered herself for that length of time. She couldn't remember Jenny-Jo's first grade at all. She couldn't remember Brian's state spelling bee championship and she had been there. What a rotten mother. No. She paused as she poured hot bacon dressing over the steamed chard. Negative message again. She *had been* a lousy mother. She was on top of it now, ready to resume her proper role and perhaps even to make some amends. She was actively attending AA meetings to address the emotional and spiritual issues that had caused her chemical dependency. Perfection? No. Progress? Yes.

"Mom?" Jenny-Jo called. "Do we have to wait for Brian?"

She carried the vegetables and potatoes to the table. "No. I told him 'Dinner at six; be here.' He's on his own." She sat down.

"Aw, Mom! You know I hate spinach! Do I have to eat it?"

"Yes. But tomorrow we will have something you like especially, all right? What will we have?"

"Creamed corn! Can I help fix it?"

"If you like, yes. Rob?"

Rob asked a blessing and picked up the carving knife. He didn't comment on the meal; dilled potatoes, chard with the sweet-sour bacon dressing, and orange-glazed cornish hens with mushroom stuffing. But he paused suddenly, studying the dishes. He smiled slightly, a happy, oh-my-look-at-this smile. That would do.

Rob cut the birds in half as Alice passed the serving bowls to Jenny-Jo. She took chard with reluctance, her nose wrinkled. She rattled on about her report card and why it ought to be better and how all those spates of bad luck at school prevented excellence. Her mouth was going but at least her body sat still.

Brian burst in the front door, jogged to the dining room and slammed breathlessly into his chair. "Sorry I'm late." What was this silly grin on his face? Alice knew the look, but she'd never seen it on him.

Rob worked his mouth, savoring some morsel. Then, "So how'd it go at school today?"

"OK. Went over to the library afterward to study." He

piled chard on his plate. Alice happened to know he didn't like it any better than Jenny-Jo did. He plopped his half a bird beside it. "Dad? Can I borrow the car Saturday? I, uh, there's this girl, Wendy, she happened to be at the library this afternoon, and we're, uh . . ."

"Just happened, huh?" Rob looked knowingly at Alice.

"Yeah. We're talking about going to the movies this weekend. Can I?"

"Brian has a date!" Jenny-Jo guffawed. She giggled so hard she choked and sprayed chard all over the table.

Progress, not perfection. Progress can happen in your family too. Why not begin today?

APPENDIX A

How the Church Can
Help Single Parents

Single parents require far more in the way of support than
a singles Bible study on Tuesday nights or a few parenting
courses down at the Y. "Pure and undefiled religion . . . is
this," said James in his letter to Christians, "to visit orphans
and widows in their trouble, and to keep oneself unspotted
from the world" (1:27).

Whether you choose to consider divorced parents in the
same category as the widowed or not, the children remain. It
is the children who need the help, innocents who had nothing to do with their parents' actions. Secular organizations
can help, but it is to the church that James addressed his
concern. There are several ways a church can provide long-
term committed help.

Provide an Active Support System

Singles need all the help many married parents need—day
care, social opportunities and gatherings, financial and edu-
cational advice. In addition, they need financial aid at times,
and most of all, warmth and inclusion in family activities.
This means inviting them on family outings, inviting them
over for the afternoon or for dinner or for whatever. Adults
and children both hunger for a family setting and too often
never get it.

Properly done, this kind of support is a lifetime commitment to the young, not just a fad project. It presents difficulties anywhere, but particularly in the church. Most single
parents are women, although the proportion of custodial
fathers is growing slowly. A widowed or divorced woman is

KIDS WHO CARRY OUR PAIN

perceived as predatory, regardless of reality. Deep in the silent chambers of the married woman's heart, this woman poses a threat. Keep her at arm's length! Married men, too, though their attitude be unvoiced and probably not conscious, see in single women a temptation. The same unfair stigmas plague single fathers.

And yet, a strong system of help for single parents requires the involvement not just of a few older ladies making casseroles but of the men in the church—indeed, of every member.

One further stumbling block hinders the kind of long-term program singles need so desperately—the singles themselves. Deep down, singles fear that the marrieds simply can't understand what it's like. Then there is the unwarranted feeling on both sides of the fence that the married folk have it together and the singles blew it—that somehow the still-marrieds are thus "better." In far too many war-torn homes, nothing could be farther from the truth.

If a program for singles is to succeed, therfore, it must be a commitment by equals to equals. None of this "we up here are ministering to you poor folks down there" nonsense will do. We are all fallen. We have all erred. And we are all supremely and sacrificially loved.

The Kids Need a Support System of Their Own

They need healthy adults, especially healthy males, to become actively involved with boys and girls. This, too, must be maintained on a long-term basis. A role model, an ersatz uncle, a substitute parent to replace the one missing or absent. This is the best defense against the hazard that the single parent and child will become overly enmeshed. For the unspoken message in the single-parent home is, "I need you and you need me. You can never grow up and separate, or we will both suffer too much." The secondary adult, the fill-in substitute, can indeed meet some of the growth needs of children in single-parent families.

336

Almost every year, a little high school in rural Washington state would see at least one senior die in a drunk-driving accident related to graduation activities, particularly the keggers that had become a graduation tradition. Concerned locals put together a Senior Surprise and invited any senior who would sign a no-drinking-during-graduation-week pledge. At 8:30 A.M. the day before graduation, students gathered for an adventure about which they knew absolutely nothing in advance, not even the direction they would go. For the next twenty-four hours they traveled nonstop from one rousing event to another—white-water rafting or skiing, dinner in a castle or at a ranch, the events often separated by a hundred miles. Home the next morning, they slept most of the day and graduated that evening. Within three years, the Senior Surprise enjoyed 100 percent participation and there have been no alcohol-related graduation-week deaths since.

Chaperones for the Surprise are always comfortably married couples. A secondary purpose is to model marriage itself for the students, for half of them come from broken homes. Local churches and businesses work together to pull off this singular Surprise. Ultimately, they all benefit, both up front and down the road. The elaborate Surprise shows that cooperation between groups can make a powerful difference. Just this sort of joint support from concerned leaders in the churches and in the businesses is necessary if children of single parents are to grow up into productive, happy citizens and customers.

Think!

Review the developmental tasks and growth steps we outlined in part 1. Use this book to acquaint yourself with what the single parent lacks in each step. Do this whether you yourself are a single parent or not. Even if it does not directly relate, you profit from being aware, by understanding better the problems singles face. Now apply what you see to the exact situation in your church. Who needs what? Only you can determine that. Then, shape a long-range program to meet those needs.

APPENDIX B

Support Groups and Other Sources of Help

These recovery resources for codependent parents can serve you well in two ways. They are, of themselves, an important source of help. Also, the volunteers or employees know about other related resources in your area. Use them and their advice to tailor a program of help to your specific needs.

The support groups welcome you without prejudice. However, groups addressing sexual addictions must necessarily be very careful about who is sitting there listening. They will screen you thoroughly. If your need is real they want nothing more than to help you. You will appreciate the security their screening provides.

You can reach these groups, some of them recently formed, by consulting the white pages of your phone directory. If what you need doesn't seem to be there, call a related organization; they will be able to help you contact the group. Or, search through the phone directory of a larger city for a reference number, often an 800 number. Reference major cities. Most county and many city library systems have a reference number, often an 800 number. Reference specialists at those numbers probably have just the information you need literally at their fingertips.

Alcoholics Anonymous
P.O. Box 459, Grand Central
  Station
New York, NY 10163
(212) 686-1100

National Association for
  Children of Alcoholics
31582 Coast Highway
  Suite B
South Laguna, CA 92677
(714) 499-3889

Al-Anon/Alateen Family
Group Headquarters Inc.
P.O. Box 182, Madison
Square Station
New York, NY 10159
1-800-356-9996
(212) 302-7240

Debtors Anonymous
314 W. 53rd St.
New York, NY 10019
(212) 969-0710

Emotions Anonymous
P.O. Box 4245
St. Paul, MN 55104
(612) 647-9712
(international)
(612) 738-9099 (Twin Cities)

Gamblers Anonymous
P.O. Box 17173
Los Angeles, CA 90017
(213) 386-8789

Narcotics Anonymous,
World Service Office
16155 Wyandotte St.
Van Nuys, CA 91406
(818) 780-3951

Overcomers Outreach
2290 W. Whittier Blvd.
Suite D
La Habra, CA 90631
(213) 697-3994
(Alcoholics and Adult
Children Claiming Christ's
Promises and Accepting
His Healing)

Overeaters Anonymous,
World Service Office
2190 190th St.
Torrance, CA 90504
(213) 542-8363

National Clearinghouse for
Alcohol Information
P.O. Box 1908
Rockville, MD 20850

Adult Children of Alcoholics,
Central Service Board
P.O. Box 35623
Los Angeles, CA 90035
(213) 464-4423

Incest Survivors Anonymous
P.O. Box 5613
Long Beach, CA 90800

Be advised these organizations exist also. Seek them out
locally.

Adult Children Anonymous
Al-Atot

Alcoholics Victorious
(Christian recovery
support group)
Bulimics/Anorexics
Anonymous
Child Abusers Anonymous
Cocaine Anonymous
Codependents of Sex
Addicts
Fundamentalists Anonymous
Parents Anonymous
Pills Anonymous
Sex Addicts Anonymous
Sexaholics Anonymous
Sex and Love Addicts
Anonymous
Shoplifters Anonymous
Smokers Anonymous
Spenders Anonymous
Victims of Incest Can
Emerge
Workaholics Anonymous

RECOMMENDED READING

The following are books we recommend to anyone, parent or not, who is dealing with the issues of codependency and a painful or abusive childhood.

Buhler, Rich. *Love: No Strings Attached* (Nashville, TN: Thomas Nelson, 1988). Popular radio talk-show host Rich Buhler addresses and offers help in solving a problem consistently voiced by his listeners as well as those he counsels: the confusion between approval and unconditional love.

———. *Pain and Pretending* (Nashville, TN: Thomas Nelson, 1989). Buhler helps those scarred by the pain of divorce, chemical dependency, and abuse to reach into their past and uncover the roots of their problems. Buhler's five "seasons of destruction" illustrate how the childhood pain developed and from there leads the reader into a needed and welcomed "season of recovery."

Ells, Alfred. *One-Way Relationships* (Nashville, TN: Thomas Nelson, 1990). By examining the root causes of codependency, Ells offers helpful tools for those struggling with unhealthy relationships. Incorporates the spiritual, emotional, and mental aspects of recovery in a comprehensive approach to healing.

Hemfelt, Robert, Ed.D.; Sharon Sneed, Ph.D.; Frank Minirth, M.D.; and Paul Meier, M.D. *Love Hunger: Recovery for Food Addiction* (Nashville: Thomas Nelson, 1990). The successful ten-stage recovery process used by the Minirth-Meier Clinic in helping patients modify their compulsive eating, by identifying root causes and seeing God's unconditional love as the basis for healing. Includes 150 recipes, meal plans, and suggested exercises.

Hemfelt, Robert, Ed.D.; Frank Minirth, M.D.; and Paul Meier, M.D. *Love Is a Choice: Recovery for Codependent Relationships* (Nashville, TN: Thomas Nelson, 1989). The successful ten-stage recovery process from codependency—a condition in which a person's happiness depends on people, things, or behaviors—used by the Minirth-Meier Clinic.

Smalley, Gary and John Trent, Ph.D. *The Blessing* (Nashville, TN: Thomas Nelson, 1986). Our emotional and psychological makeup is such that we all need what the Bible calls "the blessing"—the knowledge that someone in this world loves and accepts us unconditionally. We especially need this affirmation from our parents. Smalley and Trent outline the specific elements of the blessing and teach readers to integrate these actions into their relationships with spouses, children, friends, and themselves.

Stanley, Charles. *Forgiveness* (Nashville, TN: Oliver-Nelson, 1988). If we do not know we are forgiven, how can we forgive? Men and women who do not know God's forgiveness carry their moral void with them into their daily contacts, but men and women who know the release of forgiveness manifest spiritual health in all aspects of their lives. Stanley examines the relationship between experiencing Christ's forgiveness and loving our neighbor.

Thurman, Dr. Chris. *The Lies We Believe* (Nashville: Thomas Nelson, 1980). The lies we grew up believing—such as "I must be perfect," "I must earn God's love," "I have a right to a trouble-free life," and so on—can destroy our peace of mind. Dr. Thurman gives nine techniques to help Christians to successfully overcome these lies with the truth.

Additional parenting books that we recommend include:

Campbell, D. Ross. *How to Really Love Your Child* (Wheaton, IL: Victor Books, 1977).

Dobson, James, Ph.D. *Dare to Discipline* (Wheaton, IL: Tyndale House, 1970).

_____. *Hide and Seek* (Old Tappan, NJ: Fleming H. Revell, 1979).

_____. *Parenting Isn't for Cowards* (Waco, TX: Word, 1987).

_____. *Preparing for Adolescence* (Ventura, CA: Vision House, 1978).

_____. *The Strong-Willed Child* (Wheaton, IL: Tyndale House, 1988).

Stanley, Charles. *How to Keep Your Kids on Your Team* (Nashville, TN: Oliver-Nelson, 1986).

Elkind, David. *The Hurried Child* (Reading, MA: Addison-Wesley, 1981).

Faber, Adele and Elaine Mazlish. *How to Talk So Kids Will Listen and Listen So Kids Will Talk* (Avon Books, 1980).

_____. *Liberated Parents, Liberated Children* (Avon Books, 1974).

Kimmel, Tim. *Little House on the Freeway* (Portland, OR: Multnomah Press, 1987).

Meier, Paul, M.D. *Christian Child-Rearing and Personality Development* (Grand Rapids, MI: Baker Book House, 1985).

Scott, R. A. "Buddy." *Relief for Hurting Parents* (Nashville, TN: Oliver-Nelson, 1989).

Swindoll, Charles. *You and Your Child* (Nashville, TN: Thomas Nelson, 1990).

Ziglar, Zig. *Raising Positive Kids in a Negative World* (Nashville, TN: Oliver-Nelson, 1988).

INDEX

ABOUT THE AUTHORS

Robert Hemfelt, Ed.D., is a psychologist who specializes in the treatment of chemical dependencies, codependency, and compulsivity disorders. Before joining the Minirth-Meier Clinic, he was an addictions specialist with a Fortune 500 corporation and, before that, the supervisor of therapeutic services for the Substance Abuse Study Clinic of the Texas Research Institute of Mental Sciences.

Paul A. Warren, M.D., is a behavioral pediatrician and adolescent specialist, as well as the medical director for the Child and Adolescent Division of the Minirth-Meier Clinic in Richardson, Texas. He received his M.D. from the University of Oklahoma and completed his internship and residency at Children's Medical Center in Dallas, Texas, where he also served as chief resident. A popular seminar speaker, Warren appears regularly on the "Minirth-Meier Clinic" radio program.